EARLY MORMON MISSIONARY ACTIVITIES IN JAPAN, 1901–1924

T0308870

Early Mormon Missionary Activities in Japan, 1901–1924

REID L. NEILSON

THE UNIVERSITY OF UTAH PRESS
Salt Lake City

The Defiance House Man colophon is a registered trademark
of the University of Utah Press. It is based upon a four-foot-tall,
Ancient Puebloan pictograph (late PIII) near Glen Canyon, Utah.

14 13 12 11 10   1 2 3 4 5

LIBRARY OF CONGRESS CATALOGING-IN-PUBLICATION DATA
NEILSON, REID LARKIN.
EARLY MORMON MISSIONARY ACTIVITIES IN JAPAN, 1901-1924:
STRANGERS IN A STRANGE LAND / REID L. NEILSON.
P. CM.
INCLUDES BIBLIOGRAPHICAL REFERENCES AND INDEX.
ISBN 978-0-87480-989-3 (PBK. : ALK. PAPER)
1. CHURCH OF JESUS CHRIST OF LATTER-DAY SAINTS—MISSIONS—JAPAN—HISTORY.
2. MORMON CHURCH—MISSIONS—JAPAN—HISTORY.
3. JAPAN—CHURCH HISTORY. I. TITLE.
BX8661.N45   2009   266'.935209041—DC22
2009046511

COVER PHOTO COURTESY CHURCH HISTORY LIBRARY

To my mother, Katherine Larkin Neilson,
who encouraged me to be a historian

We are strangers in a strange land
where darkness covers the earth and gross darkness the people.
Here we find a people situated differently from others we have seen
and less likely to receive the gospel.

—Hosea Stout, China, 1853

As I sat upon the veranda of the Hotel, which looks out over the bay
and saw the Japanese men almost stark neacked [sic] *who were working on the*
shore and also those on their boats I could not help but admire their large and
powerful limbs which were developed almost beyond their limits. Seeing also the
apparel and manners of the people, I indeed felt "a Stranger in a strange land."

—Alma O. Taylor, Japan, 1901

It seemed to us when we arrived
that we were indeed strangers in a strange land,
for everything was strange unto us. The people, their customs,
their habits, their food—all were strange.
We could not speak to the people, only through interpreters,
except to those who were able to understand the English language.

—Louis A. Kelsch, Japan, 1902

Contents

Illustrations

Preface

On June 26, 1924, Hilton A. Robertson, leader of the Japan Mission of The Church of Jesus Christ of Latter-day Saints (hereafter Mormon or LDS Church), received a terse cablegram from church president Heber J. Grant: "Have decided to withdraw all missionaries from Japan temporarily. Cabling you twelve thousand yen for that purpose. If more needed cable us. Arrange return immediately."[1] Obedient to the missive, Robertson and his missionary band wrapped up their evangelistic efforts, shuttered the leased mission headquarters, and bade farewell to their hard-won Japanese converts. After twenty-three years of struggle, the Latter-day Saints retreated from their church's missionary errand to Asia for a season. It is important to note that, unlike many liberal and mainline Protestants during the same era, LDS Church officials did not close down Japanese evangelizing operations in 1924 because of any theological or philosophical shift.[2] Rather, LDS leaders hoped to reallocate their finite missionary resources to more promising fields, believing that all nations needed to be warned before the impending millennium. The Japanese had forfeited their chance for a time, they reasoned. The Japan Mission remained closed until after Grant's death and the post-World War II Allied occupation of Japan.

Nine decades after the first Mormon missionaries arrived in Japan (1901), between my freshman and sophomore years of college (1991–1993), I accepted a call to the LDS Japan Sapporo Mission as a full-time volunteer missionary. While evangelizing in Japan I was introduced to the history of Mormonism among the Japanese. After my mission I returned to Brigham Young University (BYU), completed my undergraduate studies, and began working as a business consultant. Years later I again went back to BYU, this time to begin my graduate training in business administration and eventually history. It was during this period that I began to seriously study Mormonism in Japan, relying on the university's rich archival collection of missionary papers.[3] As I read the holograph journals of Alma O. Taylor, who evangelized in Japan from 1901 until 1910, I was struck by the similarities of our missionary experiences.[4] Like Taylor and his companions, I felt like "a stranger in a strange land" as a young evangelist in Japan.[5] At the University of North Carolina at Chapel Hill my doctoral study of American religious history and Mormonism in Asia necessarily expanded into Christian missionary work.

Today, young male and female LDS representatives—dressed in white shirts and dark suits or conservative dresses—are the public face of Mormonism. More than *one million* Latter-day Saints have served as full-time missionaries since 1830. In 2008, there were over 50,000 full-time LDS volunteer representatives evangelizing around the world in nearly 350 missions. These missionaries receive intensive mission and language training (fifty languages taught) at one of the LDS Church's seventeen Missionary Training Centers located around the globe. "There is no other religious denomination in the world—Catholic, Protestant, or non-Christian—whose full-time evangelizing force is even close in size to that recruited, trained, and supported by the LDS Church," two scholars suggest.[6] One could argue that Mormon mission history *is* American mission history.

Mission history is enjoying a renaissance of popularity among historians and religious studies scholars.[7] As such, one would expect the historical and contemporary Mormon missionary experience to be well researched and documented. By virtue of its size alone, LDS mission history should be one of the most important fields within mission studies. Despite the growing body of literature on Christian missionary work, however, scholars have made almost no effort to integrate the Mormon missionary experience into the larger field of mission studies.[8] This is especially true in the case of historical missionary expansion in East Asia. In the hundreds of pages of mission studies I have reviewed, I have found only passing reference of contemporaneous LDS evangelizing.[9] In other words, missiologists have ignored the Mormon contributions to the spread of Christianity in Asia, including Japan, as well as the rest of the globe. LDS missionary work is the elephant in the mission studies room that is apparent to all but discussed by few.

In turn, most LDS scholars have written their mission studies in a scholarly vacuum.[10] "Seldom has the study of Latter-day Saint missionary work been put into a broader historical or cultural context. Mormons themselves could learn from the experiences of other Christian missions as could students of Mormon missionary work," historian David J. Whittaker laments in his historiographical survey of LDS evangelism.[11] Although hagiographic missionary chronicles abound, they usually lack historical perspective and a relationship with the larger Christian missionary community. More specifically, few American scholars have ever published articles, chapters, or books on Mormonism in Japan outside of a Mormon-focused journal or press.[12] I am unaware of a single attempt to compare the Mormon missionary system with that of other Christian organizations in any region, nation, or time period. As a result, the existing histories of the LDS experience in Asia continue to float outside of the larger historical and academic world. The study of LDS missions need not (and should not) continue to fall between the cracks of Protestant, Catholic, and Orthodox evangelism. This book will hopefully lay down a few planks to begin bridging this historiographical chasm by providing non-Mormon scholars with a better understanding of the Mormon missionary experience. Readers will learn about the foundations of the Mormon missionary enterprise. Therefore, this study also fills a gap in the fields of American religious history and missiology.

The Mormon experience in Meiji and Taishō Japan, during the first quarter of the twentieth century, sheds light on the larger issues of mission leadership, missionary practices, and evangelistic trajectories. More specifically, this case study helps scholars learn why LDS leaders first sent missionaries to Japan in 1901, how these representatives functioned as "strangers in a strange land," and what led to the temporary Mormon retreat from evangelizing in Asia in 1924. In this book I argue that the same nineteenth-century LDS theology, practices, and traditions that gave rise to the early LDS Japan Mission in 1901, were paradoxically also responsible for its eventual demise in 1924. I contextualize this larger story of early Mormonism in Japan by looking back to the ill-fated 1854 LDS mission to China, which acts as an excellent case study to better appreciate why the normative LDS missionary approach was so poorly suited to evangelize non-Christian, non-Western peoples.

Moreover, a preliminary analysis of the failure of the LDS China Mission helps historians understand why the later Japan Mission likewise faltered. An unvaried sense of evangelism propriety and practices hindered Mormon missionaries from adapting their message to new cultures, particularly in Asia where the cultural needs were so different. LDS leaders and laity floundered in Japan during the first quarter of the twentieth century as they tried to employ what I call the Euro-American Mormon missionary model (including proselyting practices) while evangelizing the Japanese, a non-Christian, non-Western people. "The Elders have not only had to learn a very difficult language, but also come to an understanding of a people whose ideas, ideals, manners, customs and mode of worship are entirely foreign to their own. How to approach the Japanese has been a problem in missionary work, as they do not believe in God, in Jesus Christ, or the Bible," one missionary summarized.[13] Consequently, the Japan Mission had fewer conversions than other contemporary LDS mission fields and it struggled in comparison with intra-country Protestant efforts among the Japanese.

Acknowledgments

Studying in Chapel Hill, North Carolina, and living in neighboring Carrboro, was one of the most significant and happiest times of my life. I could not have asked for a more wonderful graduate committee at the University of North Carolina. My chair, Laurie F. Maffly-Kipp, went above and beyond the call of duty to help me meet deadlines, shape chapter arguments, and improve organization, as well as being a true friend and mentor. My committee members, Thomas A. Tweed, Grant Wacker, Richard Jaffe, and Terryl L. Givens, likewise provided much needed scholarly perspective and critiques of my original proposal and chapter drafts. Other supportive UNC faculty and staff members include Yaakov S. Ariel, Cathy Ashworth, Myra Quick, Randall G. Styers, and Hope Toscher. I thank the UNC Graduate School for providing me with funding during my sojourn in North Carolina, especially the International Studies Scholar for Tomorrow Fellowship and the Off-Campus Dissertation Research Fellowship.

I was fortunate to research and teach at Brigham Young University during the final year and a half of my doctoral program. The department of Church History and Doctrine provided me with an office in the Heber J. Grant Building, an edifice ironically named for the church leader who both opened and closed the early Japan Mission, where I wrote most of this book. Alexander L. Baugh, Susan Easton Black, Spencer J. Fluhman, Arnold K. Garr, Alonzo L. Gaskill, Steven C. Harper, Richard N. Holzapfel, Devan Jensen, Dennis L. Largey, Paul H. Peterson, Heather Seferovich, Ronald W. Walker, and Dennis A. Wright were especially welcoming and helpful to me on campus. Historians R. Lanier Britsch, Ronald W. Walker, and John W. Welch helped jump-start my writing on Mormonism in Asia years ago. I am grateful to Peter DeLafosse, my acquisitions editor and friend at the University of Utah Press, who has breathed new life into Utah's Mormon Studies booklist and championed works that go beyond traditional LDS narratives, including the international expansion of Mormonism. The editorial and production staff at the University of Utah Press is likewise to be thanked for their skillful handling and polishing of this manuscript. Scholars Van C. Gessel, Greg Gubler, and Sandra C. Taylor kindly reviewed the entire book draft and made a number of helpful suggestions, but I alone am responsible for any errors.

I also wish to express gratitude to the librarians and staff of the following repositories: the Walter Royal Davis Library, the Joseph Curtis Sloane Art Library, and the R. B. House Undergraduate Library at the University of North Carolina at Chapel Hill; the Perkins Library, Rare Book, Manuscript, and Special Collections Library, the Ford Library, and the Divinity School Library at Duke University; the L. Tom Perry Special Collections, the Utah Valley Regional Family History Center, and the Harold B. Lee Library at Brigham Young University; the Church Archives, the Church History Library, and the Family History Library at the Church of Jesus Christ of Latter-day Saints; the Special Collections and the J. Willard Marriott Library at the University of Utah; the Special Collections and Archives at Utah State University; the Research Library and Collections at the Utah State Historical Society; and the Baker-Berry Library at Dartmouth College. All of these libraries and archives provided me with clues to better understand the early LDS missionary forays into—and retreats from—Asia.

Last, but not least, my parents Ralph R. and Katherine L. Neilson provided a great deal of emotional and financial support throughout my graduate training. And my wife Shelly and son John, and now my daughters Kate and Allyson, made the journey worthwhile. I will never forget planning our future at Fearrington Village, Autumn Woods, Duke Trail, and Southern Village.

REID L. NEILSON
Provo, Utah

I

Nineteenth-Century Explorations in Asia

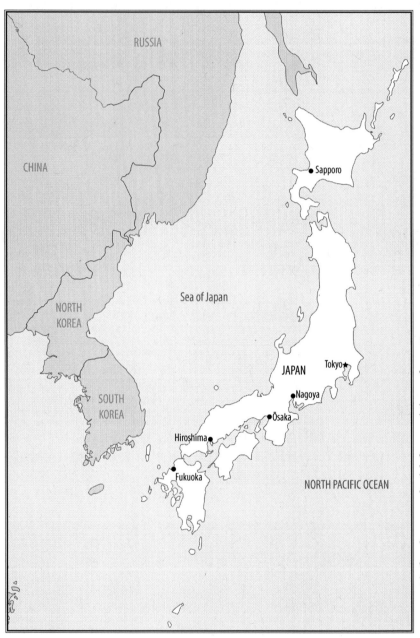

MAP OF JAPAN

1

Mormon Mappings of Asian Religions

I do not believe for one moment that there has been a man or woman upon the face of the earth, from the days of Adam to this day, who has not been enlightened, instructed, and taught by the revelations of Jesus Christ. "What! the ignorant heathen?" Yes, every human being who has possessed a sane mind.

—BRIGHAM YOUNG, 1854

It is unlikely that Joseph Smith, founder of the LDS Church, ever meaningfully encountered a Buddhist, Hindu, Sikh, or a practitioner of Confucianism, Taoism, or Shinto during his life. Born in 1805, Smith, like many Americans of his day, spent his childhood and youth on farms in Vermont, New Hampshire, and New York, isolated from the larger world of Pacific Rim commerce and travel. It is possible, however, that he passed by Chinese sailors working along the seaport docks of Salem, Massachusetts. Smith's parents sent him there when he was eight years old to convalesce with his uncle Jesse after a leg operation. By the early nineteenth century, Salem was a major hub of Chinese trade with North America.

Six years before Smith's birth, Salem's residents established the East India Marine Society in 1799 and began collecting Asian artifacts and curiosities, which they housed in a renovated bank building, the forerunner of today's celebrated Peabody Essex Museum.[1] As a curious young boy, Smith likely visited the burgeoning museum, by that time one of Salem's leading attractions, to pass the time while his leg healed. If so, he was gently exposed to Asian culture through its treasures and relics. Smith's only other youthful encounter with the Pacific Rim would have been through his father, who disastrously attempted to sell Vermont ginseng to a Chinese trading company, whose customers prized it for its medicinal properties.[2]

Even as a grown man in rural antebellum America, Smith would have
had extremely limited, if any, opportunities to learn about the East. The
Mormon prophet spent his life in the interior of New England, in the
Western Reserve, and on the western American frontier in Missouri and
Illinois. He never traveled across the Atlantic or Pacific oceans. An 1833
missionary journey to Toronto, Canada, proved to be the extent of his
international experience. Nevertheless, twenty-five years after first visiting
Salem as a boy on crutches, Smith returned to the maritime town in 1836.
This time he was accompanied by a number of ecclesiastical associates
with whom he hoped to discover buried treasure to help pay off church
debts (Doctrine and Covenants 111).

Smith and his associates tarried in Salem for about three weeks that summer. They visited the newly constructed East India Marine Hall, an imposing columned edifice, which by then housed several thousand objects from
the Orient, as the region was then called. "The objects that were collected
and exhibited by this society helped define the early American vision of
Eastern cultures," one historian suggests.[3] Latter-day Saints Sidney Rigdon
and Oliver Cowdery signed the museum's guest ledger on August 6, 1836,
and Smith left his signature two days later.[4] But early Mormon interests
clearly centered not on Asia but on the past, present, and future of the
Americas (which they believed to be the ancient site of the Book of Mormon, the gathering place for Latter-day Saints, and the building location of
the New Jerusalem). Nevertheless, Smith and his nineteenth-century successors, along with various American Protestants, participated in the mapping of Asians and their religions during the nineteenth century.

Religious studies scholars Thomas A. Tweed and Stephen Prothero
suggest a number of themes to interpret the ongoing religious and social
encounter of Americans and Asians, including *mapping*. "In one sense,"
they claim, "religion itself is a spatial practice, a cultural process whereby
individuals and groups map, construct, and inhabit worlds of meaning."
Mapping can refer "to the ways that individuals and groups orient themselves in the natural landscape and social terrain." Like other nationalities,
Americans have constructed mental maps of the world. They have sought
to "orient themselves in relation to Asia" as well as understand Asians who
have come to the United States.[5]

Nineteenth-century trans-Pacific contacts and exchanges resulted in
divergent American attitudes toward the Chinese and Japanese, as well
as their religions. Like other evangelical Americans, the Latter-day Saints
encountered East Asians and their traditions both at home and abroad. But
I believe that the nineteenth-century LDS theological mapping of Asian

religions was both similar to and different from that of American Protestants. This variance, along with the evolution of their religious thought, is illuminated when one documents how Mormon and Protestant leaders variously imagined their religious traditions in relation to those from Asia through the employ of various typologies. I conclude this chapter by highlighting major trajectories of Mormon thought regarding Eastern traditions and how this factored into the eventual evangelization of Asians.

PROTESTANTISM MAPS THE RELIGIONS OF THE EAST

Before American Protestants personally encountered the peoples and traditions of Asia, they mapped them from afar.[6] Hannah Adams, a New England Protestant dissatisfied with existing eighteenth-century surveys of world religions, lived a full generation before Joseph Smith and the advent of Mormonism. Frustrated by existing accounts of non-Christian religions, she began compiling her own survey in 1778, which she published in 1784 as *Alphabetical Compendium of the Various Sects which Have Appeared from the Beginning of the Christian Era to the Present Day*. Over the next three and a half decades, Adams expanded and nuanced her study as new materials became available. In 1817, three years before Smith reported his First Vision, she published an updated edition, *A Dictionary of All Religions and Religious Denominations: Jewish, Heathen, Mahometan, Christian, Ancient and Modern*.[7] Although "some residue of incredulity, condescension, even hostility, can be found in Adams' accounts of Asian peoples and religions," it was the most complete one-volume treatment of Asian religions to date, Tweed argues. She offered an evenhanded treatment of Asians and their religions to a public who knew little about the subject.[8]

Although Adams's study of the world's religions was a milestone in religious scholarship, it "did not alter significantly the basic map of the religious world that she inherited," Tweed concludes. "In fact, the most basic contours of that map had changed little since the voyages of discovery. New peoples and religions were added here. New boundaries were drawn there." Westerners, including Adams, still envisioned a world easily divided into religious categories of Christians, Jews, Muslims, and Pagans (much like the hegemonic West divided the twentieth-century nations into first-, second-, and third-world countries). Not surprisingly, mainline Protestants both constructed and occupied the highest rung of the resulting ladder of hierarchy. Jews stood on the second step and Muslims, also monotheists, crouched on the third tread. Finally, most antebellum

Protestants, including Adams, grouped the pagans, or those traditions that did not affirm Western monotheism, and placed them on the lowest rung.[9]

Adams's spiritual cartography remained the standard American Protestant view of non-Christian, non-Western religions during the antebellum era.[10] By the second half of the nineteenth century, however, religious scholarship was flourishing, resulting in a flood of knowledge about non-Christian religions. Emerging academic disciplines such as cultural anthropology and comparative religion seemed to reduce Christian teachings and ordinances until they "began to bear an uncanny resemblance to the forms of other major religions." While Christians could contextualize other faiths, the opposite was also true. Biblical higher criticism further eroded Christian faith.[11] Granted, a small number of Euro-American scholars, writers, and theologians sympathized with and adhered to Asian religions like Buddhism beginning in 1844. That year Elizabeth Peabody translated a Buddhist text for *The Dial*, an American Transcendentalist periodical, and Edward Salisbury lectured on Buddhism to the American Oriental Society.[12] Nevertheless, most Americans who dabbled in Eastern traditions were intellectuals, not average Protestants. The vast majority of North American Christians did not have meaningful exposure to non-Christian religions, with the exception of Judaism, until the World's Parliament of Religions in 1893. As such, Asian religions were theologically unthreatening to the West until the late nineteenth century.[13]

This theological encounter, however, along with a number of social, economic, and cultural forces, soon undermined what historian Grant Wacker calls the "Christian fortress" in America after the Civil War. Modernization, urbanization, and industrialization resulted in "smokestacks elbow[ing] out steeples" and the diminuendo of the divine in daily life. Scientific progress, especially the development of evolution and geology, directly challenged Judeo-Christian creationism. Scientists and laboratories began replacing clergy and churches as the ultimate authorities of knowledge. Technological progress in travel and communication multiplied intercultural and interreligious contacts. Cultural and geographical boundaries no longer circumscribed religions. The accelerating encounters with Asian religions demanded that Protestants grapple with a number of theological issues that Hannah Adams never considered. Some questioned if the "theological difference between Christianity and other religions [was] absolute or ... one of degree?" Was Christianity truly superior and the only way to salvation? they wondered.[14] Or, as one theologian probes: "Is the presence of God to be found only within one community of faith? Or is he more chameleon-like than that, dancing through history, enticing men and women into faith irrespective of the cultural shape of their response?"[15] Many nineteenth-century Protestants also struggled to explain the fate of the "heathen" nations and to account for Christian truths in religions predating Christianity. In short, the challenge of pluralism rattled Christian belief. American Protestants were no longer culturally or religiously isolated. Pacific Rim faiths had roused them from their insulated sleep of absolutism.[16]

Not all American Protestants reacted the same way theologically to the peoples and religions of Asia. Religious studies scholars have constructed a three-planked intellectual scaffolding—exclusivism, pluralism, and inclusivism—that helps us nuance the nineteenth-century Protestant reaction. The *exclusivist position* maintains that non-Christian "religions are marked by humankind's fundamental sinfulness and are therefore erroneous, and that Christ (or Christianity) offers the only valid path to salvation."[17] William C. Wilkinson, a leading proponent of the Chautauqua movement and the consummate exclusivist, argued: "The attitude, therefore, of Christianity towards religions other than itself is an attitude of universal, absolute, eternal, unappeasable hostility." Consequently, the "erring religions of mankind" do not even represent "pathetic and partially successful, gropings after God."[18] Non-Christian religions do not help; they only hinder the future of Christianity, according to exclusivists. On the other hand, the *pluralist position*, asserts that all religions are "equally salvific paths to the one God, and Christianity's claim that it is the only path (exclusivism), or the fulfillment of other paths (inclusivism), should be rejected for good theological and phenomenological reasons." Diametrically opposed to Wilkinson, literary critic and abolitionist Thomas Wentworth Higginson advocated religious toleration and suggested that all men and women can find God, but only as they "pass through their own doors," and not just Christianity, until "all will come at last upon the broad ground of God's providing, which bears no man's name."[19]

Most American Protestants choose to stand somewhere between the exclusivist and pluralist rafters. The *inclusivist position* confirms "the salvific presence of God in non-Christian religions while still maintaining that Christ is the definitive and authoritative revelation of God."[20] John Henry Barrows, a noted Congregational clergyman, exemplified inclusivism as he advocated the supremacy of Christianity while allowing for heavenly light and truth in non-Christian religions. "Cherishing the light which God has given us and eager to send this light everywhither, we do not believe that God, the eternal Spirit, has left himself without witness in non-Christian nations. There is a divine light enlightening every man." He further asked, "Why should not Christians be glad to learn what God has wrought through Buddha and Zoroaster—though the sage of China, and the prophets of India and the prophets of Islam?"[21] Some scholars have further delineated the inclusivist position. Diana Eck explains that the "fulfillment inclusivist position" accepts that "non-Christians are genuine seekers of truth found fully in Christ." Other religions are more incomplete than evil or misguided, "needing the fulfillment of Christ." Advocates of this position acknowledge that God and Christ are active in the lives and beliefs of non-Christian believers. This was, and still is, the most popular Christian response to an increasingly pluralistic world.[22]

MORMONISM MAPS THE EASTERN RELIGIOUS WORLD

Eventually isolated in America's Great Basin, the LDS theological response to Asian religions, like those of their Protestant counterparts, changed over time. While the exclusivist, pluralist, and inclusivist typology works well to describe the American Protestant response to non-Christian, non-Western traditions, scholars need to expand and revise their interpretive categories to judiciously explicate the Mormon response to Eastern faiths. At first glance, one might erroneously categorize nineteenth-century Latter-day Saints as fulfillment inclusivists, given the similarity of their descriptions of non-Christian faiths. A more careful observer, however, would conclude the opposite: Mormons believed that their gospel was as old as eternity, a unique Christian theology.[23] Therefore, the construction and fastening of an additional theoretical plank, the *restoration inclusivist position,* is needed. World religions scholar Spencer J. Palmer proposes several ways Latter-day Saints have accounted for Christian parallels in non-Christian religions. Two of his theories, *the light and spirit of Christ* and *diffusion,* seem to be nineteenth-century Mormon responses while the remaining three appear to be twentieth-century reactions to the same theological dilemma.[24]

From Mormonism's 1830 founding, Joseph Smith and subsequent LDS leaders generally employed the light and spirit of Christ theory to account for Christian parallels in non-Christian religions. According to this early explanation, "the spiritual influence which emanates from God is not confined to selected nations, races, or groups. All men share an inheritance of divine light. Christ himself is the light of the world. Even those who have never heard of Christ are granted the spirit and light of Christ." As such, God inspired the founders of Buddhism, Islam, Hinduism, Taoism, Confucianism, Shinto, Jainism, Sikhism, Zoroastrianism, and other Asian faiths, in order to bless all of his earthly children.[25]

While Joseph Smith was almost certainly ignorant of Asians and their religions, as described above, the Mormon prophet did bring forth a number of new scriptures that provided a theological framework for mapping non-Christian, non-Western religions, such as Buddhism and Shinto. According to the Book of Mormon, "the Lord doth grant unto all nations, of their own nation and tongue, to teach his word, yea, in wisdom, all that he seeth fit that they should have" (Alma 29:8); and "the Spirit of Christ is given to every man, that he may know good from evil" (Moroni 7:16; see also Doctrine and Covenants 93:2; John 1:9). In 1832, Smith further revealed that "the Spirit enlighteneth every man through the world, that hearkeneth to the voice of the Spirit. And every one that hearkeneth to the voice of the Spirit cometh unto God, even the Father," in the Doctrine and Covenants (D&C 84:45–47).

As one who experienced the wrath of religious intolerance, Joseph Smith lamented that the "great designs of God in relation to the salvation of the human family are very little understood" by mankind. Muslims condemn the heathens, Jews, and Christians as infidels; the Jews view the uncircumcised as damned "gentile dogs"; the heathens "are equally as tenacious about their principles"; and Christians relegate all others to perdition. "But while one portion of the human race are judging and condemning the other without mercy," the Mormon prophet continued, "the great parent of the universe looks upon the whole of the human family with a fatherly care, and paternal regard; he views them as his offspring." He taught that all of mankind would be given the opportunity to embrace Mormonism in this life or the next.[26]

Other Mormon leaders reiterated Joseph Smith's teachings in succeeding years. Apostle Parley P. Pratt authored *Proclamation! To the People of the Coasts and Islands of the Pacific; of Every Nation, Kindred and Tongue* while presiding over the LDS Pacific Mission in the early 1850s. Printed in 1851 by Mormon missionaries in Australia, his tract announced the beginning of systematic Mormon evangelism in the Pacific basin frontier.[27] Pratt declared the advent of a new Christian gospel dispensation. Despite the universality of the gospel message, Pratt, like Smith, mapped the peoples of the Pacific world into four groups: (1) non-Mormon Christians, (2) non-Christian "pagans," (3) Jews, and (4) "Red Men of America." Pagans (or heathens), according to Pratt, were "those who are not Christians, but who worship the various Gods of India, China, Japan, or the Islands of the Pacific or Indian Oceans."[28] Pratt was not alone in mapping the religions of the Pacific world as one pagan category.

Most nineteenth-century American Protestants likewise plotted the contours of world religions according to traditional guidelines: they were Christians (and therefore saved) while everyone else was a Jew, Muslim, or Pagan (and therefore damned). This order also suggests the level of descending theological esteem most Protestants had for different types of non-Christians. Coming out of the American Christian tradition, Latter-day Saints also parsed the Jews and Muslims into traditional Protestant categories but viewed the heathen nations through a different theological lens: the "prophetic telescope" of the Book of Mormon. According to Pratt, the Mormon scripture, together with the Bible, helped explain: "[t]he fate of nations; the restoration of Judah and Israel; the downfall of corrupt churches and religious institutions; the end of Gentile superstition and misrule; the universal prevalence of peace, and truth, and light, and knowledge; the awful wars and troubles which precede those happy times; the glorious coming of Jesus Christ as king over all the earth."[29] By the end of the nineteenth century, Mormons viewed so-called pagan Asian religions as equal to, if not superior to, post-third-century Christianity.

Joseph Smith was assassinated by a mob in 1844, just as Americans were beginning to meet Asians and their religions. Nevertheless, subsequent church leaders echoed his claim: God had enlightened all mankind, in every land and in every age, through the light and spirit of Christ. John Taylor, a member of the Quorum of the Twelve Apostles, acknowledged in 1853 that "[t]he Catholics have many pieces of truth; so have the Protestants, the Mahometans, and Heathens."[30] And Brigham Young, Mormonism's second president, declared: "I do not believe for one moment that there has been a man or woman upon the face of the earth, from the days of Adam to this day, who has not been enlightened, instructed, and taught by the revelations of Jesus Christ." Even the "ignorant heathen," "Hindoos," "Hottentots," and "cannibals" have benefited from divine inspiration to "teach them right from wrong." Like Smith, Young believed that "[n]o matter what the traditions of their fathers were, those who were honest before the Lord, and acted uprightly, according to the best knowledge they had, will have an opportunity to go into the kingdom of God."[31]

LDS leaders were still employing Smith's views during America's Gilded Age to contextualize Asian religions. Moses Thatcher, another member of the Quorum of the Twelve Apostles, admitted he was "struck by the profound philosophy, pure morality, and the comprehensiveness exhibited in the writings of Confucius and Mencius and the Chinese sages" and considered them "divinely inspired, far-reaching and heavenly doctrines."[32] In 1888, Orson F. Whitney, the presiding bishop of the LDS Church, declared the Latter-day Saints "a people who are not ashamed to pick truth from the dust, to acknowledge truth wherever found, in the religions of all men…. The doctrines of Buddha? Yes, they have truth." As a result, the heathen nations, "who have not the fullness [of truth], but only retain it in a measure, knowing no better, and live up to the light they have, are justified in the sight of God and will stand guiltless before him." But once exposed to Mormonism or "the fullness of truth" all were accountable.[33] Thus, the light and spirit of Christ theory became the leading LDS explanation for the existence and value of Asian religions during the nineteenth century.

While LDS leaders spoke in revelatory terms regarding Eastern traditions, no other nineteenth-century leader spoke on the subject as often as George Q. Cannon. Cannon, first a member of the Quorum of the Twelve Apostles (1860–1873) and later a councilor in the First Presidency (1873–1901), consistently advocated the light and spirit of Christ theory *until* attending the 1893 Parliament of Religions. "We believe that God is the same yesterday, to-day and for ever," Cannon taught in 1869, and "he is a God of revelation." Although God had largely closed the heavens for centuries, he had "bestowed his Holy Spirit" on "millions" of his children, "although not in its fulness."[34]

During the 1870s and 1880s, Cannon continued to teach that "faithful men in all nations" were endowed with great light, including Eastern teachers such as Confucius. Even Muslims, "fire-worshipers," and "idolaters" had "lived up to the best knowledge they had." But they "had not the keys of the Holy Priesthood nor the power and authority thereof to guide them in their teachings; hence, they ran into errors, and this gave rise to a great variety of views and doctrines and to schools of divinity that have existed and that still exist among the children of men." He later asserted that the Latter-day Saints were not "so cramped in their feelings" to believe they are the only children of God who receive His revelations and blessings. Echoing Brigham Young, Cannon taught that "there is no son or daughter of Adam that has ever lived upon the face of the earth who has not the right and who has not obtained at some time or other in his or her life, revelations from God, but who may not have understood what those revelations were." Even "the heathen philosophers" who were ignorant of Christianity still received truth from God.[35]

When his Latter-day Saints were feeling the weight of the American Protestant campaign against plural marriage in the 1880s, Cannon lashed out. He declared that modern Christianity "is but little, if any, better than many forms of paganism." "There have been millions of people, probably, whom the Christians call pagans, whose lives have been as acceptable to the true God as the lives of the same number of so-called Christians," he exclaimed. Until the late nineteenth century, LDS leaders consistently used the light and spirit of Christ theory to theologically map Asian religions, despite formal encounters of their own.[36] This changed almost overnight.

THE WORLD'S PARLIAMENT OF RELIGIONS

In the late summer of 1893, the LDS First Presidency—Wilford Woodruff, George Q. Cannon, and Joseph F. Smith—traveled with Brigham H. Roberts to Chicago to participate in the Columbian Exposition. They also attended several sessions of the auxiliary World's Parliament of Religions.[37] More than any other encounter between Latter-day Saints and Asians, this experience radically altered the Mormon mental map of Asian religions. Like other Christian attendees, the Mormon leaders were awed by the Exposition's international spectacle and astonished by the richness of the Asian religions they encountered.[38]

Upon his return to Utah, Cannon observed that "some things ... are going to puzzle this parliament," at least the Christian contingent, who believed that Jesus Christ had taught novel doctrines during his mortal ministry. "But here come the Buddhists and the followers of Confucius," he mocked, "and they prove that long before the Savior was born many of the truths which He proclaimed were taught by their leading men." Cannon correctly surmised that this anachronistic Christian worldview was "likely to furnish good ground for infidelity and for men thinking that after all there is not so much in this Christian religion as those who advocate it assume; because if Buddha and Confucius knew these truths, where are the claims of the Christians that the Savior was the first to introduce them in His sermon on the Mount?" But Christian parallels in the religions of Asia would not shake the Latter-day Saints, he argued, for they believed that the restored gospel had its roots in the beginning of time.[39]

Like other Christians formally introduced to non-Christian traditions at the Parliament, Mormon leaders reformulated their theological response to Eastern religions. Previously they only had to explain how truths existed in other religions. Now they had to account for striking Christian parallels in those same faiths. In other words, the Parliament prompted an LDS rhetorical shift from the light and spirit of Christ theory to a diffusionary hypothesis: a theology better suited to account for Christian parallels in non-Christian religions.

The diffusion theory proposes that all religions can trace their beginnings to the Christian gospel as originally taught to Adam and Eve by

God. Rather than advocating an evolutionary "fulfillment" model, which was quite in vogue in the late nineteenth century, Latter-day Saints viewed the gospel of Jesus Christ in an antievolutionary framework. They rejected the developmental claims characteristic of fulfillment inclusivists that suggested that Christianity was the pinnacle of human religious progress. Instead, they advanced a declension model, asserting that God had revealed the saving mission of Jesus Christ to Adam and Eve who had taught it to their children and children's children. But their descendants had apostatized, resulting in spiritual darkness until God had seen fit to restore that spiritual light. Thus, humanity experienced a number of dispensations of gospel truth followed by apostasy and hopes for future renewal. In short, Mormons dated Christianity at least four thousand years earlier than other Christians and thereby believed they had cut the Gordian knot of American Protestantism. By moving back the origins of the gospel of Jesus Christ to the time of Adam and Eve, they were able to avoid the timing issue of Christian parallels found in non-Christian religions.[40]

Having just experienced religious pluralism firsthand, Cannon adjusted his earlier rhetoric to match his post-Chicago realities. "The Buddhists and the Shintovists [sic] and the believers in Confucius have a great many truths among them, and they are not so imperfect and heathenish as we have been in the habit in this country of believing them to be." More important, when Cannon explained non-Christian religions, he no longer employed the light and spirit of Christ theory. Rather, he taught that "God has revealed unto us that Adam himself was taught the Gospel in the same purity and with the same power and gifts that it was taught to the Twelve apostles whom the Lord chose as His disciples." In brief, the 1893 Parliament prompted Cannon to shift rhetorically from the light and spirit of Christ theory to the diffusion theory.[41]

Although Cannon, a restoration inclusivist, highlighted the positive aspects of various systems of belief, he became concerned with the growing popularity of Asian religions in America. In November 1893, just months after the Parliament ended, he published an editorial in a Church periodical and denounced the Eastern doctrine of reincarnation as "strange" and "utterly foreign to every principle which God has revealed in the last days to His Church." Every man and woman is given but one "grand opportunity" to appear in the flesh and experience this probationary state of existence in preparation for their future estate. Cannon also commented that since the 1830 restoration of the gospel, "there has been a great disposition manifested by many people to investigate the oriental religions

and to appropriate from them strange ideas entirely foreign to those that
have been believed in by the people of Christendom." He thought it was
an "itching for something new" that prompted some "to adopt strange
views and to announce beliefs that are antagonistic to Christianity," such
as Buddhism.[42]

Brigham H. Roberts also advocated diffusion theory after attending
the Parliament. In 1896 he argued that Mormonism, like mining quick-
silver, is the force that can unite and blend all truth. The blacksmith ora-
tor recalled his own experience in Chicago where he had the "opportunity of listening to an explanation of the religion of Brahma, of the
Buddhist religion, of the Philosophy of Confucius and Zoroaster, and
of the Mohammedan religion, and in short, of nearly all the religions."
Like Cannon, Roberts admitted to being "very much astonished at the
amount of truth to be found in all these systems of religion." He related
how writers including Robert Ingersoll, David Hume, and Voltaire "have
undertaken to prove that Christianity was not an original religion with
Jesus Christ, that is, they insist that Jesus Christ copied his precepts, his
ordinances, and the religious and fundamental truths of his religion from
the religions of the orient."

At the Parliament the similarities between Christianity and Asian religions puzzled many Protestant theologians, according to Roberts. Like
Cannon, Roberts employed diffusion theory to account for these Christian parallels. The Mormon leader contended that LDS scriptures, including the Bible, Book of Mormon, and Pearl of Great Price, "teach the antiq-
uity of the Gospel" and explain the "fragments of Gospel truth held by
the religions of the Orient, of India, Persia, Egypt and some portions of
Japan and of China."[43] Neither Cannon nor Roberts again used the light
of Christ theory to map Asian religions after their close encounter in Chicago in 1893. In brief, the post-Parliament rhetoric of Cannon and Roberts
evidences the LDS rhetorical shift from the light and spirit of Christ rationalization to a diffusionary explanation.

MORMON MAPPINGS

The nineteenth-century Mormon encounter with Asian religions was
significant, perhaps not in scope, but certainly in results. The LDS theological mapping of the East was somewhat reminiscent of American Protestantism's spiritual cartography. Both Joseph Smith and his associates
plotted all Asians as "heathens" and their traditions as "pagan," like other
Americans. But the Latter-day Saints viewed the Asian nations through

the prophetic telescope of the Book of Mormon and modern-day revelation, which rendered non-Christians as capable of salvation and partakers of divine light. Mormon leaders employed a "light and spirit of Christ" theory to account for truth in Asian religions until the 1893 Parliament of Religions.

But when the Asian proponents of Buddhism, Confucianism, and Hinduism demonstrated in Chicago that their belief systems predated traditional Christianity, the unfazed Latter-day Saints reformulated their theological response and began to employ a declension model of diffusion. As restoration inclusivists, the Latter-day Saints were theologically driven to eventually evangelize the peoples of Asia, despite the truths they found in the teachings of the Buddha, Confucius, Mencius, and other Eastern founders. Ironically, the Mormons likewise evangelized the Christians of North America and Western Europe under the same worldview, believing that only their unique brand of restoration Christianity enjoyed a fullness of truth.

2

Mormon Encounters with Asians

In a former letter, I have given you some Idea of the Chinese.
Since writing to you on that subject I have had the pleasure of extending
my acquaintance with that people, and the more I learn about them,
the more highly I esteem them, and wish to learn of them.

—Alexander Badlam to LDS leaders, 1855

On the heels of the age of discovery, European powers sought to expand their influence and dominion around the globe. The newly discovered Pacific world became the military, financial, and spiritual battleground of ongoing European feuds and imperialist ambitions. Spanish Catholics, emboldened by papal decree, determined to transform the Pacific basin frontier into Catholic territory. They were successful in their evangelistic ambitions in Guam, the Philippines, and throughout much of California and the American West, where they constructed a string of missions that cobbled together Spain, Mexico, and the Pacific Coast. Dutch missionaries also made their way to the Pacific world but often engaged in lucrative trade opportunities at the expense of evangelism. Russian Orthodox missionaries turned their attention to the Eskimos and natives of the Aleutian Islands in modern-day Alaska. British Anglicans appeared in the Pacific Rim by the beginning of the nineteenth century, moving quickly to colonize Australia and New Zealand. Although the Spanish, Portuguese, and Dutch had enjoyed a presence in Asia for hundreds of years, British missionaries did not begin evangelizing in Asia until the start of the nineteenth century. The London Missionary Society, organized in 1795, focused much of its energies on Christianizing the down-under natives. They soon expanded their missionary outreach to the isles of the South

Pacific, including Tahiti, where they enjoyed measurable success among the islanders. The British were followed by French Catholics, who arrived in the region during the 1840s. By 1886 the French had displaced the British from parts of Polynesia yet seemed content to remain there rather than expand.[1]

American Protestants were latecomers to the Asia-Pacific world. During the eighteenth and early nineteenth centuries they were preoccupied with more pressing domestic concerns, including westward expansion and the evangelism of Native Americans and displaced Africans in the United States. The American Protestant missionary encounter with the peoples of the Pacific basin frontier began in 1810 when Congregational leaders in New England met to form the American Board of Commissioners for Foreign Missions (ABCFM), a group that soon became the dominant American missionary organization. Two years later the ABCFM sent missionaries to South Asia but later determined to begin full-scale missionary work in the Sandwich Islands. During the next several decades these missionaries enjoyed tremendous success as they Christianized and Westernized the Hawaiian natives and expanded the political influence of America into the middle of the Pacific. The first American missionaries did not reach China until about 1830. Despite numerous political revolutions and social upheavals in nineteenth-century China, many American groups remained committed to evangelizing the Chinese. They also made evangelical inroads into Japan by the early 1870s.[2]

The American missionary movement in the Pacific basin frontier was unique in several ways. First, a wide variety of American Protestants fanned across the Pacific, mirroring the plethora of Protestant sects and denominations back home. Next, a number of American evangelical groups would make their way to the Pacific at many various points between the 1820s and 1890s. Third, unlike the Europeans, who generally focused on a particular area in the Pacific, the Americans eventually encompassed the entire Pacific Rim. Lastly, American missionaries spread Western culture in the region more than any European nation.[3] By the end of the nineteenth century, the three Ms of American civilization—military, merchants, and missionaries—had spread across the Pacific Rim. But it was missionaries, more than any other group, who moderated the exchange of information and representation between Americans at home and their Asian counterparts abroad.[4] Historian Grant Wacker argues that "[t]he missionaries' perceptions moved from abhorrence to grudging admiration to varying degrees of approval of the ethical and religious ideals of the peoples among whom they worked" during this era.[5]

As Americans and Asians have met each other at various sites around the globe—especially in the Pacific world—religious studies scholars Thomas A. Tweed and Stephen Prothero further suggest that the term *meeting* can also help tell the story of the encounter between the two groups. Historically, these meetings have been literary, artifactual, and interpersonal. *Migration* is another theme they recommend to narrate the trans-Pacific encounter, as the different peoples of Asia have spread across the Pacific and into the Americas through migration.[6] As nineteenth-century Mormonism was essentially an American religious movement, the result of displacement and gathering to the Intermountain West, these themes are well suited to help explore the early Mormon encounter with the East.[7]

LATTER-DAY SAINTS MEET THE PEOPLES OF THE EAST

Nineteenth-century trans-Pacific contacts and exchanges resulted in divergent American attitudes toward East Asians as well as their religions. Like other evangelical Americans, the Latter-day Saints encountered Chinese and Japanese and their faith traditions both at home and abroad. Latter-day Saints enjoyed a number of Asian encounters as missionaries and travelers abroad and as hosts in Utah. These limited meetings were an important basis for the LDS evaluation of East Asians. While the Mormons initially focused their attention on the Chinese, it would be the Japanese who held their greater esteem by the turn of the twentieth century. Although the Protestants actively evangelized Asians in their midst, the Latter-day Saints generally did not, due to racial, theological, and logistical concerns. Taken together, these types of encounters between the Mormons and East Asians acted as a catalyst for the creation of an Asian LDS mission field at the turn of the twentieth century.

During the 1830s and 1840s, Joseph Smith sent missionaries throughout North America and to Europe to spread Mormonism. It would not be until after his murder and the pioneer exodus to the Utah Territory, however, that Mormons would actually meet any Asians at home or abroad. Not surprisingly, many of the earliest meetings between the two groups were the result of missionary work in the Pacific basin frontier.[8] Brigham Young and other church leaders discussed sending missionaries to East Asia soon after gold was discovered in California. In March 1849 the Quorum of the Twelve Apostles sent out a letter to church members at home in America and abroad in Britain. After sharing living conditions in Great Salt Lake City and discussing the prospects for future settlement, the leaders noted that one elder had returned the previous October from evangelizing in the South Pacific. Moreover, they announced that an apostle would soon attempt to establish additional Mormon outposts in the Pacific, including one in the Pacific Rim nations. "Parley P. Pratt may accompany them to the Islands or to Chili [*sic*] with a view to establish the Gospel in South America, Australia, New Zealand, China, Japan, the various groups of the Pacific Islands, or to each or either of these places as the way may open up."[9] While serving as president of the newly formed Pacific Mission, Pratt did travel to Chile and attempted to start missionary work in South America, but he never made it to China or Japan as hoped.[10]

Millenarian fever led to a number of important interpersonal meetings between Latter-day Saints and Asians. LDS leaders and members alike kept busy divining the signs of the times during the middle of the nineteenth century. They were convinced that Christ's Second Coming was at the door. In 1848, months after the first Latter-day Saints entered the Salt Lake Valley, revolutions broke out in Europe, first in Sicily and then in France, Germany, Italy, and the Austrian Empire. Although all of these continental revolutions ended in failure, they intensified the feeling that mankind was living on borrowed time. Alarmed church leaders debated where to send missionaries to raise the warning voice.[11] In light of these apocalyptic conditions, they issued a general epistle in September 1851. Young and his counselors made reference to the revolutions seemingly exploding all across the globe. They also hinted that they might call missionaries to China and Japan, "which for ages have sat in darkness."[12]

In August 1852, hundreds of Latter-day Saints gathered in downtown Salt Lake City for a missionary-themed general conference.[13] Brigham Young, believing the millennium was impending, called over one hundred missionaries to labor in the European nations of Ireland, Wales, France, Germany, Norway, Denmark, and Gibraltar; in Cape of Good Hope, Africa; in North America, specifically Nova Scotia, the West Indies, British Guiana, Texas, New Orleans, St. Louis, Iowa, and Washington, D.C.; and the isles of the Pacific, namely Australia and the Sandwich (Hawaiian) Islands. Young also assigned a number of men to commence missionary work in the Asian nations of Hindustan (India), Siam (Thailand), and China.[14]

That fall nearly forty missionaries called to the Pacific basin frontier departed from Utah for the California coast, where they started out for Asia, Polynesia, and Australia. The handful of Mormons assigned to South and Southeast Asia struggled in their missionary efforts for several years before abandoning their evangelism posts. Their evangelism practices were ill-suited for the Indians and other Asians they encountered who hoped to benefit financially from their association with Westerners. The elders also lacked the necessary language skills to work among the non-English-speaking masses outside of the British cantonments. Unlike their counterparts in North America and Western Europe, who relied on the financial generosity of church members and strangers in their mission fields, the Mormon elders in India, Siam, and Burma found that the Asians were too destitute and philosophically unwilling to underwrite their missionary endeavors. The Mormons also suffered from pitiable living conditions, sickness, inadequate medical care, and lack of transportation. They only converted about seventy people, many of them expatriate Europeans, before returning to Utah.[15]

The missionaries assigned to China, and led by Hosea Stout, were even less fortunate. Three of them arrived in Hong Kong but were unable to generate any interest on the part of the native Chinese or the expatriate Europeans. To make matters worse, the Taiping Rebellion, which lasted from 1850 until 1864, was raging on mainland China.[16] In a letter to Brigham Young, one of the missionaries described their precarious situation. "The foreigners in Shanghai have formed themselves into an armed neutrality to be ready for the worst—not knowing what may happen. There is a great deal of excitement in all the trading posts. The troops here are held in readiness to act as occasion requires." Even though American warships had arrived in the East China Sea, the missionary judged China "in a state of excitement, very unsafe to penetrate to the interior." The same went for other foreign settlement ports dotting the East and South China Sea.[17] Natural conditions such as the heat, humidity, and precipitation of Hong Kong added to the elders' discouragement. Unaccustomed to the sticky humidity, scorching temperatures, and heavy rains, the elders found it difficult to hold outdoor meetings.[18] Soon they determined to temporarily abandon missionary work in China. They returned to America on the *Rose of Sharron* and eventually made their way back to Utah.[19] In 1856, Mormon leaders shuttered missionary work in all other parts of Asia.

Brigham Young did not send missionaries to Japan in 1852, when he sent representatives to other Asian nations, because it was closed to the commercial, diplomatic, and religious overtures of the West until 1854, when Commodore Matthew Perry and his gunboats forced Japan's Tokugawa government to normalize political and trade relations with the United States.[20] To most Americans, Perry's diplomatic opening of Japan was another confirmation of their country's growing power. But the watershed event suggested something different to the millenarian Mormons. In September 1854 the church's *Millennial Star* featured an article on the opening of Japan. It rehearsed the exploits of Perry's naval expedition and suggested what the resulting opening of Japan would mean for the United States from a political, economic, and social perspective. But it also pointed to new missionary opportunities in Asia. "While the gospel is being preached in every quarter of the globe," the author wrote, "there has been but little opportunity to plant it on the eastern coasts of Asia. This treaty with Japan, and the revolution in China, will probably open the way for it to be preached in those two great empires."[21] Church leaders looked forward to the time when they could send missionaries to the Japanese.[22]

The first interpersonal meeting between the Mormons and Japanese likely occurred in 1858 when William Wood, a twenty-one-year-old Latter-day Saint and member of the British Navy, enjoyed shore leave on Japanese soil. "I discerned a remarkable spirit of reform in them; more so than in any people I had met," he recalled of the Japanese. "I felt a desire to preach the Gospel to them."[23] Wood later immigrated to Utah, but he never returned to Japan. "I have thought it possible that I was the first Mormon to visit Japan, and this increased my desire to present the Gospel to them," he reminisced. "Years after, when I had gathered to Zion ... this feeling increased in my mind so much that in my prayers I often mentioned it. However, it was some years before the door for the Gospel was opened by Apostle Grant to the Japanese people, and I had become an old man."[24] Although Wood appears to have been the first Mormon to encounter the Japanese, others would follow.

Another informal meeting of Mormons and Japanese occurred decades later when LDS leaders attempted to rekindle evangelism in South Asia. Church members William Willes, George Booth, Henry F. McCune, and Milson Pratt boarded the *City of New York* in San Francisco bound for Japan en route to India. Willes broke up an argument between a drunken crewmember and an English-speaking Japanese Christian named Ishiye while at sea. Thereafter, Ishiye showed interest in the missionaries and listened to their message.[25] He informed the missionaries about evangelism prospects in Japan and disclosed that all religious teachers were under the protection, and constraints, of the Japanese government. The Japanese Christian also offered to have "a favorable mention made" of Mormonism in Japanese newspapers and invited the missionaries to return to Japan as his guests the following year.[26] When their ship stopped over in Yokohama, the missionaries disembarked and visited with several expatriates living in Japan. They learned that while Japan was open to Christianity it was yet "very much hampered with restrictions that are galling to free Americans." Although Westerners were free to move about the handful of foreign settlement ports, they could only travel throughout the interior of Japan when accompanied by Japanese guides, Willis wrote to George Q. Cannon.[27] The Latter-day Saints left Yokohama days later for India, and did not pass through Japan before returning months later to Utah.

There were also several interpersonal meetings between the Mormons and East Asians in the American West. The Iwakura Mission, a delegation made up of high-level Japanese officials, passed through Utah on its way east to Washington, D.C., in 1872.[28] Fierce snowstorms temporarily blocked the mountain railway passes and stranded the delegation in Salt Lake City for nineteen days. Seeking to make the best of the situation, the Japanese commission visited the newly completed Tabernacle, explored a local museum, and admired the stone foundations of the Salt Lake Temple. They also called on members of the Utah Territorial Legislature, the Utah Supreme Court, and Brigham Young. Moreover, they observed the territorial military, learned about the local educational system, and attended receptions and banquets prepared by their Utah hosts. Several delegates even went to LDS religious services and recorded a short overview of Mormonism in the delegation's official records.[29] The Japanese were not alone as accidental tourists in Utah. Salt Lake City residents made their own observations of their Asian visitors. LDS leaders including Angus M. Cannon, George Q. Cannon, and Lorenzo Snow were particularly impressed by the Japanese.[30]

This meeting had far-reaching effects on the future of Mormonism in East Asia. George Q. Cannon believed that the Iwakura Mission's visit to Utah was providential. "It is perhaps not hazarding too much to say that the visit of the Japanese Embassy to Salt Lake, and the principal cities of the United States, is the fore-runner of measures which may, at some future day, be the cause of some of the youth who read this article being sent as missionaries to Japan," he editorialized.[31] Lorenzo Snow acknowledged that the Japanese delegation had left a lasting impression on his mind that acted as a catalyst for the eventual opening of the Japan Mission in 1901. "This is how the thought [of the Japan Mission] originated with me," he later explained to reporters. "When I was president of the Legislative council," he said, "a party of distinguished officials of the Japanese government visited Salt Lake enroute [sic] to Washington.... They expressed a great deal of interest in Utah and the manner in which it has been settled by the Mormons. Our talk was altogether very pleasant and they expressed considerable wonderment as to why we had not sent missionaries to Japan."[32] Nevertheless, Mormon leaders waited three decades before sending missionaries to Japan in 1901.

Two years after the Japanese delegation met the Mormons in Salt Lake City, Niijima Jō, an influential Japanese Protestant convert, passed through Utah on his way back to Japan from Massachusetts in the fall of 1874. As Brigham Young was ill, Niijima was instead introduced to Apostle Orson Pratt, one of Mormonism's leading intellectuals and theologians. "He was very gentlemanly, and answered very patiently all my questions about Mormonism. He desired me to preach the gospel which he preaches, but I thanked him and answered him I should preach the gospel which I find in the New Testament and nothing else," Niijima related in a letter to Alphaeus Hardy, his financial patron affiliated with the American Board of Commissioners for Foreign Missions.[33] Taking no offense, Pratt then escorted his Japanese acquaintance through Salt Lake City, stopping at the Tabernacle, City Hall, and the University of Utah. Given the "widespread controversy concerning Mormonism in nineteenth-century America, and given Niijima's propensity to criticize those with different religious beliefs, his admiration for Pratt and tame criticism of Mormonism is rather surprising," one historian concludes of the encounter.[34]

That same decade Chen Lanbin, China's first minister to Washington, D.C., also passed through Utah and recorded meeting the Mormons. "The religion here is different from that practiced in other states of the Flowery Flag country. According to Western custom, a man cannot marry two women, but this religion permits the taking of concubines," he noted in his diary. The remainder of Chen's account focuses on the history of Utah and the Mormon conflicts with the federal government.[35] Contacts like these demonstrate that Asians were also curious about the Mormons, not just the other way around.

Another high-level contact between the Mormons and East Asians occurred in 1895 when Apostle Abraham H. Cannon and his fellow leaders determined to exploit Utah coal and iron deposits by constructing a railroad from Salt Lake City to Los Angeles.[36] Robert Brewster Stanton, a California mining promoter, confided to Cannon that the Japanese government was in the process of selecting a North American seaport for its national shipping line and claimed they favored San Diego, California. Stanton suggested that he and Mormon leaders join forces and construct a railroad linking the Pacific Ocean and Utah's lucrative coal deposits.[37] In addition to jumpstarting Utah's depressed economy, the proposed joint venture with the Japanese government seemed likely to lead to the creation of a mission in Japan.[38] Cannon traveled to San Francisco to meet Stanton and Koya Saburō, an official of the Japanese consulate, to discuss both temporal and spiritual opportunities.[39] "Mr. Koya thought it very probable that we might secure permission to preach the Gospel in Japan without any government interference," Cannon reported.[40] The apostle returned to Utah optimistic about sending missionaries to Japan and the possibility of luring the Japanese shipping line to San Diego. He wasted no time in sharing his findings with fellow LDS leaders.[41] Apostle Heber J. Grant noted in his diary, however, that Cannon's business plan was discussed but that the debate over a Japanese mission was postponed, perhaps signaling that the First Presidency did not share Cannon's sense of urgency for the evangelism of Japan.[42] As fate would have it, however, both the railroad deal and missionary opportunity fell apart. The Japanese government chose Seattle, not San Diego, as the *Nippon Yūsen Kaisha* connection city, and Cannon passed away suddenly, his Japan dream dying with him.[43] Other church leaders made no further attempts to begin formal missionary work in Japan until the twentieth century.[44]

The Latter-day Saints also had literary meetings with Asians. Church-sponsored magazines were an important source of LDS education about the peoples and places of the East. During the postbellum period, George Q. Cannon used his apostolic influence and *Juvenile Instructor* editorship to educate the Mormons on the Chinese and Japanese. Throughout the last quarter or so of the nineteenth century, his church-sponsored magazine featured dozens of articles on Asia and its culture. (Unfortunately the authorship of most of the articles is unclear, as no names or sources are given. Cannon likely reproduced interesting articles he encountered in national periodicals without making proper attribution, a common practice in nineteenth-century journalism.) Almost without exception, Cannon's articles presented a favorable view of East Asians but favored the Japanese over the Chinese.

The *Juvenile Instructor* articles were also peppered with references to future LDS missionary work in Japan. For example, one article suggested: "It is not too much to expect that Western customs and the Christian religion will in a few years gain such a foothold in Japan that the folly of idol worship will be entirely unknown amongst its highly intelligent people." Another read: "It is probable that the next few years will effect a still greater improvement in that country, as quite a number of young men from Japan are being educated in the United States, who, of course, will carry home with them American ideals of living.... It is possible they will modify their laws so as to admit of the gospel being preached there, as it will certainly be at some future time."[45]

George Q. Cannon ran nearly a dozen articles featuring Asia during the 1880s.[46] Although most of the articles discussed featured topics on Japanese life, Cannon could not resist plugging Japan as an LDS mission field. Convinced of the fruits of Mormonism, he wrote: "We firmly believe that Japan will yet be successfully visited by the Elders of our Church, and that from that race thousands of obedient souls will yet be gathered to swell the multitudes of those who shall be called to Zion." Contemporary events in Japan seemed to bolster his sentiments. By the mid-1880s, the Asian balance of power was shifting from China to Japan, a sea change that warranted further comment. "Of all the Asiatic nations perhaps Japan is making the greatest strides at the present time in the way of education and an adoption of the inventions and discoveries of modern times. The people of this empire are unquestionably more progressive than their neighbors the Chinese, and the interest that is now being taken in that people by civilized nations is very great."[47] By the late nineteenth-century, Cannon and other church leaders were convinced that Japan, not China, held the key to the evangelization of Asia.

EAST ASIANS MIGRATE TO AMERICA

Since the mid-1850s, when Chinese workers sailed by ship to the Gold Mountain of California and the American West, Asian immigrants have added their own swatches and threads to the patchwork and stitching of American religious history. As Pacific borderlands scholar Laurie F. Maffly-Kipp argues, the story of America's religious past is generally told from a westward orientation, thereby diminishing the contributions and struggles of Asians and Pacific Islanders who immigrated to America from the Pacific basin.[48] The traditional narrative also obscures the domestic contacts and exchanges between Americans and immigrant groups. Tweed and Prothero's third theme, *migration*, helps historians excavate these revealing social and religious encounters at home.[49]

When Americans were first introduced to China they felt threatened, historian Robert McClellan claims. Here was a country that had been around for thousands of years, compared to the youth of the United States. Protestant leader Josiah Strong argued that America's destiny stretched beyond the borders of North America to the Pacific basin, including China. American Protestants rationalized that China needed to be spiritually saved and morally uplifted by their Christian nation. Not surprisingly, Americans described the Chinese as inferior to the Anglo-Saxon race.

They could not imagine China as a great civilization because that undercut the United States' role in their redemption.[50]

Beginning in the mid-1800s, hundreds, then thousands, and then tens of thousands of Chinese workers emigrated to Hawaii and the American West, the majority from China's Guangdong Province. America offered new hope for Chinese beset by natural disasters and financial woes in their homeland. Most immigrants were male laborers, who were either single or who had left their families back in China and planned to return to China flush with money. American business managers viewed the men's lack of family and social attachments as a boon. They could be easily displaced without the tethers of family life. These employers did not hesitate to put the Chinese in poor work environments and exploit them economically. Until the early 1880s, Chinese labor was abundant and little valued. White workers, however, became increasingly concerned over the massive influx of Asian workers who threatened their jobs. Labor organizations pressured Congress to rebuff Chinese immigrants seeking citizenship rights, resulting in the 1870 Nationality Act. The Chinese remained second-class citizens for many decades, bereft of naturalization opportunities. The federal government passed additional legislation in 1875 and 1882, blocking the immigration of Chinese prostitutes and barring the immigration of additional Chinese laborers, respectively. The 1882 Exclusion Act had an immediate impact on Chinese immigration. That year over thirty-nine thousand Chinese immigrated to America; two years later the number had dropped to less than three hundred. Due to worsening social conditions, many Chinese returned to China, opening the door for increased Japanese immigration.[51]

Although Japan emerged from international isolation in the middle of the nineteenth century, its citizens were not free to travel about the globe until 1885, when the Meiji government relaxed its emigration laws. With new Chinese laborers unavailable in the United States, due to the passage of the 1882 anti-Chinese legislation, American business leaders welcomed the sudden influx of Japanese laborers. The immigrant population of Japanese in Hawaii and California swelled as a result. The majority initially worked on sugar plantations in Hawaii. Those who continued east to California worked mainly in the agricultural industry, arriving after the completion of the railroads and the heyday of mining. These immigrants also opened small businesses, working together with Japanese women, who were not yet barred from immigrating like female Chinese. For a time the Japanese were even allowed to own their own land. Nearly twenty-seven thousand Japanese immigrants made their way to America in the 1890s, still a small number when compared to the Chinese migrant population, which amounted to well over one hundred thousand immigrants in the nineteenth century. It would not be until 1908 that the U.S. government would begin to curtail Japanese immigration, as it had Chinese immigration decades earlier.[52]

The Chinese and Japanese immigrant experiences in America were both similar and different. Both peoples hailed from East Asia, the majority coming from lower-class backgrounds. The two immigrant groups had a skewed proportion of men to women. Initially the Chinese and later the Japanese were seen as cheap labor in the aftermath of the Civil War and the end of African slavery. Both immigrant groups were exploited in America as they were not initially given the protection of the U.S. Constitution as "non-whites." In the American West especially, all East Asians endured politically charged "anti-Chinese" and "anti-Japanese" movements. They were linked together as an invading force that threatened white Americans. But the Chinese and Japanese immigrant experience in America also differed in important ways. The Chinese were originally brought to America as part of the "coolie" system of labor. They were indentured workers, essentially slaves, unlike the Japanese who immigrated independently decades later. Immigrants from China arrived in America in the wake of the 1848 discovery of gold in California; the majority was employed in the building of the western railroads. Immigrants from Japan, on the other hand, began arriving en masse after the railroads were largely completed. The Chinese were excluded from immigration starting in 1882, several decades before the Japanese were excluded in 1924. The East Asian groups overlapped, but they had distinct eras of influence and majority status among Asian Americans.[53]

American Protestants began evangelizing in China years after the British Anglicans. The American Board of Commissioners for Foreign Missions in 1829 sent Elijah Bridgman, David Abeel, and Peter Parker to educate and medicate the Chinese, as well as teach them the Good Word. By the mid-nineteenth century, various American Christian groups were laboring in the treaty port cities of Hong Kong, Canton, and Shanghai.[54] It would not be until the 1870s, however, that Protestant representatives began active missionary work in neighboring Japan.[55]

Protestant leaders and laity in the American West were also eager to evangelize the East Asian immigrants moving into their midst. Some home missionaries in California viewed the influx of Asians as a providential means of taking Christianity across the Pacific Rim. Living on the west coast of the Pacific frontier, they anticipated that Asian American converts would return to their native countries with their newfound faith. In a sense, antebellum California and its immigrants seemed a likely Christian springboard to Asia.[56] During the second half of the nineteenth century, Presbyterian, Congregational, Baptist, and Methodist home missionaries and clergy worked with the Chinese in the San Francisco Bay area. Like other American Protestants, these California Christian workers believed that it was their duty as both Christians *and* Americans to spiritually strengthen and socially support the peoples of Asia. They organized schools, provided medical care, offered social services to the Chinese immigrants, and defended them from anti-Asian sentiment.[57]

In his study of Protestant reactions to Chinese immigrants living in the Pacific Northwest during the nineteenth century, historian Daniel Liestman likewise points out the Protestant clergy's concern for Asian immigrants in America. In contrast to much of American society that belittled the Chinese, and later the Japanese, Protestant groups in Washington and Oregon sought to uplift the Asian newcomers. Like their counterparts in California, these men and women hoped that their Chinese and Japanese communicants would ultimately spread the gospel among their fellow countrymen. After the Civil War, American Protestants refocused their energies on both foreign and home missions. Asian immigrants fell under the category of home missions as they were now living in America. A number of Protestant denominations opened home missions specifically for the Chinese beginning in the mid-1870s. The Portland Baptist Mission was one of the more successful programs, others being operated by the Episcopalian, United Brethren, Methodist, Christian Alliance, and Christian (Campbellite) churches, as Liestman documents. These organizations taught English classes, operated Sunday schools, and organized Chinese church services, in an attempt to both Christianize and Americanize their charges. As anti-Chinese feelings increased in the Pacific Northwest, many Protestant leaders and missionaries acted as much-needed advocates for the Chinese. At the same time, other Protestant clergy spoke out against the growing Asian population, which they believed was hurting the morals of their cities and job opportunities for their fellow whites. By the late nineteenth century, with the Chinese population shrinking, some Protestants shifted their attention to the Japanese or just combined their efforts on the two Asian communities. In time, however, due to slower-than-anticipated growth and results, most Protestants lost interest in evangelizing East Asians domestically.[58]

EAST ASIANS IN MORMON COUNTRY

The nineteenth-century migrations of East Asians to the American West constitute a third component of the Mormon encounter with the East. The first Chinese Latter-day Saints were immigrant laborers living in Hilo, Hawaii, who converted to Mormonism in 1854.[59] The following year, church member Alexander Badlam, then living in California, came in contact with a number of Chinese workers. With the encouragement of church leaders in Utah, Badlam drafted a long letter on the Chinese and prospects for missionary work in California among them.[60]

Brigham Young was encouraged by these and additional reports of Chinese immigrants embracing Mormonism in California and the Sandwich Islands. In March 1857, he wrote to his nephew John R. Young, who was presiding over the mission in Hawaii, expressing hope that the radiance of Mormonism might go forth among all peoples, including the Chinese. "The millions of China's population, that now worship, they know not what, have yet to learn of the living & true God, and tho they have turned a deaf ear to them when we sent unto them, they may yet listen to the truth, when proclaimed to them by some of their own nation. I am glad that you have baptized some of them, and pray that the number, intelligence and faith of all such may be increased."[61] But the Utah War of 1857 disrupted LDS evangelism around the world. Young recalled Mormon men of all ages from their missionary responsibilities abroad to help fortify the Utah Territory against federal assault. The missionaries teaching the Chinese in Hawaii and California packed their belongings and returned to Utah. Historian Will Bagley suggests, "This early interest in Asia demonstrated the worldwide vision of the LDS Church, even as it struggled to survive in the Rocky Mountains," a conclusion I will explore later in this chapter.[62]

A number of Japanese immigrants in Hawaii also encountered the members and missionaries of the LDS Church during the final decade of the nineteenth century. Two of these Japanese men, Tomizo Katsunuma and Tokujiro Sato, have "legitimate claim to being the first Japanese Mormon[s]," Shinji Takagi documents.[63] Katsunuma, a well-educated veterinarian, emigrated to Hawaii and even spent time in Utah before joining with the Latter-day Saints, while Sato emigrated to Hawaii and labored with his hands in various industries before, during, and after his conversion to Mormonism.[64] During the first decades of the twentieth century, additional Chinese and Japanese men and women embraced LDS teachings and formed a nucleus of Asian church members in the mid-Pacific.[65]

The migration of Chinese and Japanese workers was not just limited to Hawaii and California. By the late nineteenth century, the majority of

Latter-day Saints lived in North America, due to the church's earlier policy
of gathering to the "American Zion." Most church members lived in Utah,
the stronghold of Mormon country.[66] Settled in 1847 by predominantly
Euro-American Mormons, the state of Utah was and is dominated racially
by whites and religiously by Latter-day Saints.[67] From 1850 to 1960, at least
98 percent of Utahans were white. By 1990 this figure had only dropped to
94 percent. Nevertheless, hundreds of Chinese and Japanese immigrants
made Utah their home during the nineteenth century.[68] (Several Koreans
also worked in Utah mines during the 1890s, but nothing is known of their
backgrounds. The Korean migration to Utah would not begin in earnest
until the first decade of the twentieth century.[69] Moreover, Latter-day
Saints would not have meaningful encounters with the Koreans abroad
until after World War II.[70]) These migrations resulted in regular encounters between Asian and white Mormons and other residents of Utah, from
which we can learn more about LDS racial attitudes toward East Asians.

   Chinese immigrants first arrived in Utah as laborers helping to build
the Central Pacific Railroad, linking Sacramento, California, with Prom-
ontory, Utah, in the years following the Civil War. When the transpacific
railroad was completed in 1869, former railroad construction workers
settled in northern Utah, most in Box Elder County, and continued to
work in the railroad industry. In early Utah, most Chinese railroad workers formed close-knit communities near their places of employment and
apart from white residents. At one point in the late nineteenth century,
Corinne was home to about three hundred Chinese immigrants. Ogden,
Utah's quintessential railroad town as the connection point of several
railroad lines, had over a hundred Chinese residents by 1890. Most of
these Asian immigrants congregated in a growing Chinatown noted for
its unique structures and Chinese businesses. The mining towns of Park
City, Pleasant Valley, and Silver Reef benefited from the contributions of
hundreds of Chinese workers. By 1890 there was a total of 806 Chinese in
Utah. By the turn of the twentieth century, Utah's capital, Salt Lake City,
boasted the most Chinese residents, most of whom lived in Plum Alley,
the state's largest Chinatown.[71]

   The nineteenth-century Euro-American response to the Chinese in
Utah was wide-ranging. As in other parts of the West during postbellum America, the Chinese faced increasing hostility in Utah, especially in
mining areas where they were seen as a threat to other lower-class white
workers. Nevertheless, the Utah Chinese did not face the same level of dis-
crimination that they did in other western states. Some Utah newspapers
even defended the Chinese immigrants during the period of anti-Asian

immigration. Many Utahans viewed the Chinese as benign curiosities to be tolerated and sometimes even celebrated, especially during their holiday festivals. "Most white residents of Utah tended to view the Chinese as a faceless, if not nameless, seemingly indistinguishable group of people who tended to cluster in predominantly white communities," historian Daniel Liestman describes.[72] As the Chinese population expanded, however, some Utah residents viewed the mysterious Chinatowns as dens of iniquity. They were concerned with the gambling, prostitution, violence, and opium smoking that had become, or at least were believed to be, commonplace in these Chinese enclaves. Nativist white labor groups also complained that their members were losing jobs to the Asian immigrants. With mining on the decline, many Chinese switched to service industries including laundries, restaurants, and grocery stores. Some even worked in the medical field, introducing traditional Chinese healing practices to Utah.[73]

Although the Chinese and white inhabitants lived in essentially separate spheres in nineteenth-century Utah, members of various Utah Christian denominations attempted to evangelize the Chinese. Several Protestant churches sought to build relationships with their Asian neighbors through English conversation classes in hopes of eventually introducing Christianity to their students. Lena Wakefield, a representative of the American Home Missionary Society in Salt Lake City, began teaching an English class in 1881. By 1895 the Congregational Church's education outreach enjoyed the attendance of over a hundred Chinese students. Utah Methodists also targeted the Chinese for conversion and in time held services specifically for their growing Chinese communicants. Baptists in Ogden also set up a Chinese Sunday school in the 1890s. For some reason, Latter-day Saints were skeptical of the Protestant evangelism of the Chinese immigrants in their midst. They were unconvinced that Christian educational efforts would result in lasting conversions. Ironically, the normally missionary-minded Mormons did next to nothing to fellowship with and evangelize the Chinese in Utah. The Chinese likewise showed little interest in the LDS faith and continued to worship in the handful of "Joss houses" located in northern Utah.[74]

Hundreds of Japanese immigrants also made their way to Utah during the late nineteenth century and were employed by the railroads and agricultural community. Japanese labor agents, including Yozo Hashimoto and Edward Daigoro, helped recruit additional Japanese to the Intermountain West.[75] By the end of the nineteenth century there were over four hundred Japanese living in Mormon country. This figure would jump to over two thousand residents of Japanese heritage within a decade.[76] During the early years of the twentieth century, the Japanese would take the place of the Chinese who moved from Utah. By 1940 there were 2,210 Japanese to only 228 Chinese living in Utah.[77] Compared to available Chinese immigrant history, scholars have written little on the nineteenth-century Japanese migration to Utah. The fact that the Japanese did not congregate in high-profile ethnic enclaves like the Chinese or face the same type of anti-immigration persecution (until the 1920s) may explain this gap in scholarship.[78]

But we do have some clues as to how the Latter-day Saints interacted with the Japanese immigrants living in predominantly Mormon communities in the West.[79] Drawing on church records, oral histories, and a limited number of written reminiscences, historian Eric Walz explored the Mormon encounter with Japanese immigrants in the late nineteenth and early twentieth centuries. He was surprised to learn that the LDS Church made little effort to evangelize the first and second generation Japanese living in Mormon country, although they would eventually expend tremendous resources to run a mission in Japan. Walz suggests several reasons for the LDS neglect of the Japanese immigrant community. Most Mormons, particularly those involved in agricultural enterprises, viewed the Japanese as a highly desired labor pool, rather than prospective converts. There were a number of Japanese conversions to Mormonism when individual Latter-day Saints looked beyond the laborer stereotype. But it was not until the rise of the second generation Japanese that the two groups met on more equal terms, especially through church programs for children and youth.[80] The Latter-day Saints in Utah, however, did exhibit somewhat greater tolerance to the relocated Japanese Americans in their midst during World War II than most other American religious groups.[81]

While Chinese and Japanese migrations to Hawaii and California led to nineteenth-century evangelistic efforts by the Latter-day Saints, it is surprising that the same cannot be said of similar encounters in Utah. During the nineteenth century, Euro-American Mormon leaders focused their attention on or allocated their church's resources almost completely to the Atlantic world, or the nations and inhabitants of North America and Western Europe. "Mormonism has traditionally taught particularistic doctrines favoring some ethnic groups over others," sociologist Armand L. Mauss writes. "Traditional doctrines have channeled Mormon missionary efforts *toward* some societies (those in northwestern Europe, Latin America, Polynesia, or the North American aboriginal peoples) and *away* from others (for example, societies with large populations of blacks)."[82]

This worldview evolved as a result of contact, exchange, and encounter between Latter-day Saints and other peoples, as well as evolving scriptural interpretations. Mormon missionaries were encouraged to search out the "believing blood" of Israel, typically those with Anglo-Saxon heritage identified in the nineteenth century by many Christians as being connected with biblical lineages. During the mid- and late nineteenth century, the Mormons enjoyed their greatest successes in the North Atlantic world, where they believed the elect could be readily located and converted. They also claimed to discover "believing blood" in populations not traditionally connected with biblical lineages, such as Native Americans and Pacific Islanders, who seemed to be linked to Book of Mormon peoples.[83] Asians, including the Chinese and Japanese, seemingly fell well below the descendents of biblical Ephraim, yet somewhere between the promised seed of Lehi (the Book of Mormon peoples) and the ostracized seed of Cain (those of African descent), by the postbellum era.[84] Asians were, as a result, a low LDS missionary priority during the nineteenth century.

MEETING AND MIGRATION

Interpersonal and literary meetings between the Latter-day Saints and East Asians were a source of information for LDS Church leaders evaluating future East Asian missionary opportunities. Evangelistic encounters abroad helped the isolated Latter-day Saints learn about the Asian world and its peoples to a degree. But they never achieved the level of knowledge sought by American Protestants who were the leading interpreters of Asian cultures and religions in America. Mormon missionaries and travelers did not crisscross the globe during the nineteenth century as investigators of other peoples and faiths. Judging from missionary diaries and extant correspondence, few missionaries showed real interest in Asian cultures and belief systems. Moreover, early LDS missionary opportunities to observe Asian cultures and religions firsthand ended prematurely in the 1850s. The China Mission closed after a month of struggle in 1853 and the East Indian mission was a losing battle that same decade.[85] No LDS missionaries were stationed in Asia between 1856 and 1901.[86] It was also difficult to find in-depth materials on Asia in pioneer Utah libraries.[87] Given the apparent limitations of interpersonal meetings abroad, literary meetings took on added importance. Church periodicals, including the *Juvenile Instructor*, educated the generation of Latter-day Saints who would be responsible for taking the gospel to Japan. The rise of Japan politically, economically, and militarily led Mormon leaders to conclude that the Japanese, rather than the Chinese, were the more progressive people and the nation most likely to give Mormon missionaries the best reception. These impressions were confirmed on at least two occasions when high-ranking Japanese officials assured LDS leaders that their petitions to evangelize in Japan would be successful. Later events proved them right.

East Asian migration to Hawaii and the American West during the second half of the nineteenth century reminded Mormon leaders that there were many peoples, especially in East Asia, that they had overlooked while targeting the Atlantic world with their missionary resources. Nevertheless, general authorities continued to focus on North American and Western European missionary fields. "It was a strange dichotomy that Mormon leaders sent missionaries all the way to Hong Kong in 1853 if they then later ignored the Chinese population which gathered on their doorstep; Plum Alley [Salt Lake City's Chinatown] was only a few blocks from Mormon Temple Square," observes one historian of pioneer Utah Chinese.[88] The same goes for the Utah Japanese. As Armand Mauss explains, the Mormon concepts of scattered Israel and privileged lineages account for much of this paradox. It would take a major decline in missionary success in the Atlantic world, mixed with a heavy dose of millennialism in Salt Lake City, to convince church leaders that it was again time to evangelize in East Asia. The presence of Asian immigrants living near church headquarters was likely a regular reminder to LDS leaders that they had yet to scratch the surface of the Great Commission in Asia. They needed to establish an errand to the East. These encounters between the Latter-day Saints and the Chinese and Japanese would have a major impact on the LDS Church's decision to open an East Asian mission in 1901.

3

Euro-American Mormon Missionary Model

Thus did the Church of the Latter-day Saints [in the nineteenth century]
seek to fulfill the initial obligation given to that church in the very opening
of the New Dispensation, namely, to preach the gospel of the kingdom
to every nation, and kindred, and tongue, and people.

—Brigham H. Roberts, 1930

Nineteenth-century Latter-day Saints developed a unique method of evangelism, which I have tagged the "Euro-American Mormon missionary model." As the label suggests, early LDS missionary work grew out of a Protestant North American and Western European historical context, not the "pagan" Asia-Pacific world.[1] The Mormons' Anglo-centric missionary approach enabled them to enjoy grand success in the United States and Canada as well as in Great Britain, Scandinavia, and parts of continental Europe. Their mode of evangelism and theological claims to primitive Christianity fired the imagination of prospective converts already saturated in biblical culture. The church that started with six members in 1830 ballooned to over 271,000 by 1900, largely as a result of aggressive missionary work.[2] This entrenched pattern of evangelism, however, paradoxically hampered LDS missionary efforts in non-Christian, non-Western nations during the same era.

Although transpacific contacts with Asians, as described in chapters 1 and 2, acted as a catalyst for church authorities to inaugurate a mission to the Japanese, these same contacts and exchanges did not motivate the Latter-day Saints to alter their Euro-American evangelism for future missionary projects in Asia. Christian theologians and evangelists have long struggled with how to export their religious tradition across cultural boundaries, dealing with many of the same challenges that the Mormons faced when they temporarily evangelized in Asia during the 1850s. In modern terms, the nineteenth-century Mormon evangelists "imposed" or "translated" their religious systems in Asia, while other Christian groups "adapted" and "inculturated" their faith traditions. The ill-fated LDS China Mission of 1853 serves as a preliminary case study to illustrate several weaknesses of the Euro-American missionary model when applied beyond the North Atlantic world. Five decades would pass before Mormon leaders again sent missionaries to East Asia.

EVANGELISM AND INCULTURATION

Since the days of the Apostle Paul, Christian thinkers and evangelists have wrestled with how to export their spiritual tradition across national, social, ethnic, and religious boundaries. Many have pondered the relationship between Christianity and culture. Since this new religious movement spread beyond its Palestinian roots, its missionaries have struggled for consensus over what part of their message is core and what is periphery. Can and shall a line be drawn between the two? Are evangelists wise to employ the same approach and message among every people? Or should they tailor their methods and good news to each new group? In the late twentieth century, Catholic and Protestant leaders, theologians, and intellectuals have borrowed vocabulary from the social sciences, especially anthropology, to better articulate these challenges in worldwide Christianity. Interested parties continue to add buzz words such as "globalization," "internationalization," and "localization" to their missiological lexicons. While each of these words has its own specific meanings, they are often used interchangeably by theologians and academicians to describe the universal unfolding of the gospel.[3] Since the late 1970s, missiologists have also employed the term "inculturation" to more precisely explain the dynamic interplay between Christianity and global cultures. Yet its meaning has also become muddied through extended and varied use.[4]

Theologian Peter Schineller offers a series of definitions for inculturation. But he first describes what it is not: "imposition," "translation," and "adaptation." At the same time, he makes clear that these three words point progressively toward the true spirit of inculturation. First, imposition, a word freighted with negative baggage, is not inculturation. This unflattering term describes "a method or process by which doctrines, religious customs, morals, and ways of praying and acting are brought from outside, from a foreign or alien culture and tradition, and imposed or forced upon the new culture. It shows no appreciation, no respect or regard, for the values, customs, and religious traditions of the group that is the object of mission." Those who would impose Christianity on other groups believe that their religious tradition and all its trappings can be easily transplanted across cultural boundaries with little more than some necessary linguistic translation. This is how most evangelism has occurred because of its ease of transfer to new lands and peoples. Second, translation is not synonymous with inculturation, although it moves beyond simple imposition. While translation is often necessary when exporting religious traditions, Schineller warns that it "becomes not only the starting point but the only method." Church representatives just render their system of worship and beliefs into new vernacular with little thought to the needs of the locals and their culture. Third, adaptation moves beyond imposition and translation, suggesting that religious workers try to modify and alter their spiritual system to local cultures. "Yet adaptation has more recently been criticized as inadequate, in fact as a subtle form of imposition, and accused of not truly taking the local culture seriously," Schineller cautions. "Instead of getting inside, critics say, it remains outside or above, and is only willing to make or allow extrinsic, accidental, superficial changes in ways of being Christian."[5]

Schineller then suggests three words, "indigenization," "contextualization," and "incarnation," that embody inculturation. To begin with, indigenization gestures to being native, local, or inside a particular culture, rather than being outside and merely translating or adapting foreign systems. "The indigenization of theology means that the local community, with its own indigenous leadership, has the primary responsibility and task of developing the teaching, the liturgy, and the practice of that local church," he describes. "Outside help may be needed at the beginning and at key stages, but the major work is done by the local church as it develops its own identity based on its own cultural heritage and situation." Next, contextualization suggests an entwining of Christianity with specific circumstances, not necessarily particular cultures, which demands increased religious imagination. Lastly, incarnation implies that Christians "identify ourselves with the culture, people, and history we are part of," just as Jesus did in Palestine. He was part of the Jewish culture, teaching with its metaphors and living its precepts. So inculturation is a theological worldview that combines the positive connotations of indigenization, contextualization, and incarnation, and moves beyond the negative import of imposition, translation, and adaptation. Inculturation, as a concept, is often applied across the Christian experience, especially to evangelism.[6]

The above theo-anthropological concepts and continuum help scholars further delineate the Mormon approach to evangelism and its outcomes. In recent decades, LDS leaders and intellectuals have likewise deliberated over the most practical and effective ways to spread their religious tradition beyond its traditional borders. Contemporary Mormonism is finally dealing with the relationship between Christianity and culture, a discussion that has been raging for centuries within the other branches of the Christian church.[7] LDS scholars are now grappling with the challenges of spreading an American-centric gospel throughout various nations in Asia, South America, Africa, Europe, Australia, and even ethnic conclaves within the United States.[8] It remains to be seen how twenty-first-century Mormonism will adapt to these changing realities and intercultural encounters both abroad and at home. Historians can, however, look to the nineteenth century to see how Mormons dealt with these intercultural issues. Where did Latter-day Saints fall on the evangelistic spectrum between imposition and inculturation and what were the results?

AMERICAN PROTESTANT AND MORMON MISSIONARY ENTERPRISES

The American Protestant foreign missionary enterprise had its beginnings in outreach to the Native Americas during the colonial era. Several notable Puritan missionaries, like David Brainerd and John Eliot, worked with New England tribes to promulgate Christianity. But evangelism to Native Americans was not the driving force of the early colonists. "Protestants in the New World did not conceive of their errand into the wilderness primarily as the expression of missionary fervor," historian Patricia R. Hill explains. "The main function of the church in Puritan eyes was not to convert the heathen without but to regulate the spiritual lives of the saints."[9] Nevertheless, during the eighteenth century, the British Anglicans sent missionaries to America under the banner of the Society for the Propagation of the Gospel in Foreign Parts, and some Quakers and Moravians evangelized outside of Euro-American towns. American Protestants focused their energies on building up local congregations instead of evangelizing the heathens at home or abroad. It would not be until the First Great Awakening (c. 1730–1770) that the missionary impulse would play an increasing role in Protestant thought.[10]

The interdenominational New York Missionary Society, founded in 1796, was America's first Protestant missionary organization. Thereafter, a growing number of likeminded groups worked among Native Americans. The Second Great Awakening (c. 1790–1840) was responsible for the creation of numerous evangelical associations including the American Bible Society, the American Colonization Society, and the American Tract Society. These and other antebellum voluntary missionary societies grew out of theologian Samuel Hopkins's idea of disinterested benevolence, or the notion that one should seek to bless others through the Christian gospel not out of fear of divine punishment or guilty conscience but to please Jesus Christ. As described in chapter 1, students at the Andover Theological Seminary were responsible for the genesis of the American Board of Commissioners for Foreign Missions in 1810, decades after other European powers had sent missionaries to the Pacific world. By the Civil War, American Protestants were evangelizing in the nations of South Asia, Southeast Asia, the Pacific Islands, Latin America, East Asia, the Middle East, Africa, and Catholic Europe. Initially, many Protestant denominations worked together in foreign missions, until the splintering of missionary boards in the postbellum era. But all were driven by the sense of American Manifest Destiny, or the notion that American Christians were responsible for not only the salvation of North America but also the entire world.[11]

Like many nineteenth-century American Christians, the Latter-day Saints believed that the resurrected Christ had commanded his disciples in the Old World to "teach all nations, baptizing them in the name of the Father, and of the Son, and of the Holy Ghost" (Matt. 28:19). Although nearly two millennia had passed since the earliest Christians attempted to meet this obligation, their counterparts in the New World still sought to share the Christian gospel with every nation, kindred, and tongue. The Mormons, despite their poverty, persecution, and eventual displacement to North America's Great Basin region, helped shoulder the ever-present burden of fulfilling the biblical Great Commission.[12] As theological restorationists, in the most literal sense, the Latter-day Saints attempted to recapitulate biblical history. Mormon missionaries saw themselves walking in the footsteps of earlier evangelists like Paul and Timothy.[13]

Latter-day Saints shared much of the same Christian worldview as American Protestants. Millenarianism, for example, influenced the thought and decision making of LDS leaders and laity alike.[14] "Millennialism," historian Grant Underwood argues, "is far more than simply believing that the millennium is near. It is a comprehensive way of looking at human history and an integrated system of salvation. It is a type of eschatology used to refer broadly to people's ideas about the final events in individual human lives as well as the collective end of human history."[15] Specifically, he claims that Latter-day Saints were premillennialists who believed that Christ's Second Coming would usher in the millennium, as opposed to postmillennialists who believed that the millennium would precede Christ's return. He and other scholars refute the conventional wisdom that suggests that premillennialists were not as dedicated to evangelism as postmillennialists. They make the case that premillennialists held their own when it came to missionary work. Underwood gestures to evangelist Dwight L. Moody, who stated that he "felt like working three times as hard" once he embraced premillennialism, and to missionary George Duffield, who challenged antebellum critics who mistakenly claimed that premillennialism hampered the intensity and urgency of the missionary spirit.[16] Like Moody, Duffield, and other millenarian Protestants, the Latter-day Saints engaged the world rather than retreating from it, only to save what they could in the process.[17]

In the months leading up to the formal organization of the LDS Church in April 1830, Joseph Smith claimed a number of revelations that signaled evangelism would soon play a major role in his new religious movement. In February 1829, for example, he received a revelation addressed specifically to his father, Joseph Sr., calling him to preach the gospel (Doctrine and Covenants 4). Over the next several years, Mormonism's founding prophet dictated similar inspired callings for numerous members of his growing flock. It soon became clear that all church members were responsible for spreading the news of the Restoration. Once they were converted they were responsible to warn their neighbors (D&C 88). Latter-day Saints were promised great spiritual blessings, including eternal joy, if they fulfilled their missionary duties and helped save souls (D&C 18). As a result, members of the growing movement felt the need and desire to share what they believed to be the restitution of primitive Christianity.[18]

During the 1830s and 1840s, while the Latter-day Saints gathered and scattered throughout New York, Ohio, Missouri, and Illinois, Joseph Smith continued to encourage evangelism. New converts, the products of missionary work themselves, embraced their missionary responsibilities and went forth on their own, sharing the good news with their family and friends with no formal missionary training. Although some were called directly to the work by revelation, the vast majority simply opened their mouths and shared their message with anyone who would listen. During these early decades, men continued to engage in their own economic pursuits and occupations, as there was no paid clergy in Mormonism. But they took sabbaticals from their worldly responsibilities and devoted themselves to short preaching tours, relying on the financial generosity of others. These early missions usually lasted for several weeks but sometimes as long as a few months, depending on the time of year and the missionaries' professional obligations. In his classic study of North American LDS missionary work, historian S. George Ellsworth labeled this early evangelism model the "freelance missionary system." This corps of nonprofessional missionaries preached wherever they could get a hearing. They evangelized in both public and private spaces. Town squares and street corners, as well as barns and cabins, became the sites of Mormon preaching. Untrained by the Protestant divinity schools of the East Coast, they preached a homespun message, noteworthy for its simplicity. Mormon missionaries typically worked through their existing social networks, approaching family and friends, with whom they already had a tie and, therefore, a better chance of being successful. Nevertheless, these men, like representatives of other Christian faiths, endured the disinterest and often antagonism of their audiences. Freelance missionaries were remarkably successful in antebellum America, Canada, and, increasingly after 1837, in Great Britain.[19]

As the years rolled by, LDS men were increasingly called by church leaders to serve specific missions beyond their own neighborhoods and kin. Joseph Smith assigned apostles from his newly created Quorum of the Twelve to evangelize up and down the Eastern seaboard and Great Britain. (As a side note, the British Mission soon became the church's largest growth center; at one point there were more church members in Western Europe than in North America.) With many of the apostles abroad, by the end of the 1830s, members of the Quorum of the Seventy assumed the duty of calling missionaries. Nevertheless, freelance missionaries continued to staff Mormon missionary fields into the 1840s. When the majority of the apostles returned from Great Britain in July 1841, they assumed the Seventy's responsibility to administer the calling of missionaries. From this point on, the number of formally called missionaries grew and the number of self-called freelance missionaries shrank. Even so, both systems of missionaries—freelance and appointed—continued through the Nauvoo, Illinois, period and the martyrdom of Joseph Smith in 1844. By mid-century over 1,500 Latter-day Saints had served full-time missions.[20]

The Euro-American Mormon Missionary Model

Growing out of the spiritual hothouse of antebellum America, Mormonism developed a unique approach to evangelism that enabled it to spread beyond its upstate New York origins: the Euro-American missionary model. Because early LDS evangelism emerged from a North American and Western European historical context, its missionary methods privileged the West over the East. During the nineteenth century, the Mormons focused their missionary energies on the peoples of the Christian, Western world. They believed that Christ's original gospel had been lost through apostasy until Joseph Smith restored the primitive church in 1830. As a result, all non-Mormon Christians, perhaps even more than the non-Christian "heathens," were in dire need of the message of Mormonism.

American evangelical Protestants, on the other hand, targeted primarily non-Christians living in non-Western lands. Notable exceptions included Native Americans, Hispanic and Asian immigrants, and the members of domestic religious groups they considered deviant, especially the Mormons in Utah. But these evangelistic endeavors generally fell under the rubric of "home," rather than "foreign," missions.[21] (The dichotomy of "foreign" and "home" missions did not exist in the Mormon worldview. All areas outside of Utah were considered simply the "mission field.") As we shall see, American Protestant missionaries had vast experience proselytizing in the Eastern world, unlike the Latter-day Saints. As a result, they, too, advanced their own missionary model, one quite distinct from that of their Mormon contemporaries. Scholars can learn a great deal by comparing the two groups' missionary models, especially by contrasting their evangelistic practices, personal backgrounds, missionary training, financial arrangements, and human deployment.

Evangelistic Practices

By the late nineteenth century, the American Protestant foreign missionary enterprise was reeling from internal debate over the propriety of various types of evangelistic practices. The discussion can be summed up in the phrase "Christ versus culture." On the one hand, more conservative Protestants, led by Rufus Anderson and Henry Venn, fought to do away with English language teaching to the natives and other forms of Westernization. Anderson and Venn's camp believed that missionaries were sent abroad to teach the Christian gospel, not to transform local cultures into Western enclaves. They were concerned that assigning missionaries to foreign lands with specific trades, such as teaching, medicine, or agriculture, undermined the true evangelical purpose. They were proponents of Christ only and resisted the liberal reconceptualization of foreign missions. Conservative Protestants also believed that pluralism and inclusivism were slippery slopes to unbelief. They worried about the lack of testimony of emerging fundamental Christian positions on Biblical inerrancy that mainline missionaries in Asia and their supporters at home seem to have jettisoned during their tenures in the Orient.[22]

More liberal American Protestants, on the other hand, advocated a reinterpretation of Christian evangelistic practices. They argued that Christianization went hand in hand with civilization and advanced a number of criticisms of mainline missionary work as part of their pluralistic agenda. For decades they argued against Anderson's conception of Christian missionary work being centered solely on the dissemination of Christian theology. Early Puritan missionaries like David Brainerd, who provided schools and assisted with Native American farming, provided the model for this alternative approach. Liberals sought to improve both local temporal and spiritual conditions. In other words they advocated culture, then Christ. Many liberal Protestants rejected traditional Christian exclusivism while laboring in East Asia; they were unable to reconcile the displacement of Asian religions with seemingly unwanted and unappreciated Christianity. Rather than abandoning their missions, however, liberal Protestants reconfigured their roles, emphasizing Christ the humanitarian over Christ the teacher. Emboldened by the social gospel, these Protestants viewed the nursing of bodies, the teaching of minds, and the filling of bellies as crucial precursors to the healing of souls.[23]

In contrast to the variety of missionary approaches battling within American Protestantism, nineteenth-century Latter-day Saints focused their missionary practices on unadulterated evangelism, according to their understanding. They focused on preaching Christ, not advancing Western culture, especially not American culture, which they often viewed as the antithesis of their gospel message.[24] Mormon evangelistic practices centered on gospel preaching and teaching opportunities. The men spent much of their time tracting, or canvassing neighborhoods and busy streets while handing out printed leaflets or other literature on Mormon subjects. They would either sell or loan the pamphlets to interested persons and then try to arrange a teaching meeting to discuss unique LDS doctrines. The missionaries also used local newspapers to their advantage, especially since the dailies were often the organs of anti-Mormon rhetoric. LDS writers penned editorials and explanatory essays to defend their cause and spread their message. They also announced preaching meetings through local tabloids. Mormon missionaries held public preaching meetings whenever and wherever they could. They even rented other Christian church buildings to hold large audiences. Some Sundays they showed up at Protestant services and were invited to preach by naïve clergy. After sharing their message of apostasy and restoration, the Mormons were rarely invited back. In some cases, the missionaries arranged for spirited debates with other religious leaders to stir up excitement.[25] Unlike some Protestant missionary organizations, the Latter-day Saints did not typically offer educational or social welfare services in the mission field.[26]

Personal Backgrounds

American Protestant missionaries were grounded in this world but driven by an otherworldly spiritual cause. Missionary service was an optional exercise for Protestant men and women. Foreign missions were demanding undertakings that required incredible commitment and long-term fortitude. Mission boards carefully screened prospective applicants for deep spirituality and evidence of personal conversion. Candidates shared their powerful moments of conversions in their paper applications to demonstrate that they were qualified for the work. The applicants were also expected to feel a specific sense of evangelistic purpose. They needed to feel compelled to work beyond domestic ecclesiastical opportunities. The Protestant missionary model was based on self-selection: one felt called by God, not by an organization. "The single most important factor that transformed the Christian worker into a foreign missionary was his conviction that there was a greater need for his services abroad," historian Valentin H. Rabe explains.[27]

What were the personal backgrounds of these men and women? The greater part of male Protestant missionaries hailed from the smaller settlements of New England and upstate New York. Few came from urban areas and maritime regions; some missionary boards were actually skeptical of candidates from larger cities. In 1880, less than 20 percent of one missionary organization's volunteers grew up west of New England. By the turn of the century, however, things were changing. Missionary volunteers were signing on across the United States, although a growing number called the Midwest their home. Most were born and reared in America, with the exception of only the now-mature children of foreign missionaries born in the mission field. The bulk still left little villages and towns when they embarked on their missionary adventures. They were mainly middle-class Americans who had access to higher education, as we shall see. Few enjoyed wealthy upbringings, and those who did were viewed with some suspicion. For the most part, the foreign missionary enterprise at the ground level was an egalitarian undertaking. The backgrounds of female Protestant missionaries were more standardized, at least for the American Board's volunteers. The typical missionary was an unmarried daughter of a large family from the countryside whose chances for marriage were doubtful. She likely had training as a teacher or nurse and desired to use her talents in foreign lands in the service of Christ.[28] Historian Barbara Welter points out that these women were "filling a role in a field abandoned" by men and "achieving prominence in an institution which was itself declining in prestige."[29]

Quite the opposite of American Protestants, Latter-day Saints did not view evangelism as optional. Mormon men, and women beginning in 1898, were issued unsolicited short-term missionary assignments by church leaders. Those who were "called" to the work were expected to fulfill the assignments regardless of their personal, financial, or physical conditions. They did not participate in the geographic selection or timing of their callings. During the 1850s, the Mormon missionary system became more routinized and institutionalized. Geographically isolated in Utah from other Americans, LDS leaders replaced the freelance missionary system with the more organized appointed missionary system. General authorities began calling missionaries over the pulpit during the church's semi-annual general conferences held in April and October in Salt Lake City. Men were often surprised to hear their names called, but the vast majority responded willingly. A demographic snapshot helps us better understand the backgrounds of the LDS missionaries who served during the 1850s. Their ages ranged between twenty and forty-eight, with the average being thirty-five years old. Given their average age, it is no surprise that most of the men were married with children. About a quarter of these men had previously served at least one mission. Although there was no formally set mission length, they served on average for thirty months. Throughout the 1860s, church leaders continued to call missionaries during general conference, which made the semi-annual event a time of great excitement and anxiety for male church members and their families. The average LDS missionary age increased to thirty-seven during this decade. But most of these men were serving missions for the first time. Male church members increasingly served only one full-time mission during their lifetime, a change from earlier times when many served multiple assignments.[30]

Male LDS missionaries continued to receive their assignments during general conference throughout the 1870s. The length of missionary tenure decreased dramatically to only fourteen months, or less than half the length of the previous decade, easing the burden on family members left at home. The average missionary age increased to forty. During the 1880s, male Latter-day Saints mercifully learned of their missionary assignments by unsolicited letter, rather than the surprise call during general conference. These calls were issued by apostles assisted by members of a missionary committee. The average age of the missionary dropped to thirty-five. Most were still married men with wives and children. Moreover, the mission length increased to twenty-four months. By the late nineteenth century, the majority of missionaries came from the ranks of second-generation Latter-day Saints living in Utah. Few had previous evangelizing experience. The length of mission had been unofficially standardized at about twenty-four months. The age had also decreased to an average of thirty years old. Rather than self-selecting as freelance missionaries, or being called to serve during general conference, or even just receiving an unsolicited letter in the mail like their predecessors, the missionaries of the 1890s were consulted about the possibility of serving a mission by their local ecclesiastical leaders before they were extended formal assignments. A growing number of single younger men were being called to shoulder the work of the Great Commission. But it would not be until 1898 that the first female Latter-day Saints were called as full-time missionaries, apart from serving with their husbands.[31]

Missionary Training

Although most of the early luminaries of the Protestant foreign missionary enterprise were graduates of prestigious New England divinity schools and universities such as Yale, Princeton, and Williams, the majority of missionaries during the late nineteenth and early twentieth century had studied at lesser-known denominational colleges and bible schools. Many were the byproducts of the Student Volunteer Movement or like-minded groups eager to evangelize the world "in this generation." Mission agencies were continually fed candidates from church-affiliated institutions of higher learning. By the early twentieth century, between 87 and 95 percent of Protestant missionaries received formal missionary training and religious education at these church colleges before departing for their fields of labor. Understanding these recruiting dynamics, mission boards strategically created and maintained excellent relations with these schools, including helping to fill their faculties and staffs with missionary-minded men and women. As a group these Protestant missionaries were highly educated, especially when compared to the larger American population: not even 1 percent of white males in America had college degrees at the time.[32] Yet the missionaries did not typically learn the requisite foreign languages until arriving in the field, knowing that they would have years or even the rest of their lives to master the local tongue.

While their professional Protestant contemporaries enjoyed formal and extensive missionary training, the amateur Mormon missionaries received informal and narrow preparation. During the nineteenth century, LDS leaders did not provide a training regimen to the thousands of missionaries ("elders") they assigned around the world. Instead, they expected the elders to learn how to be missionaries as they evangelized. The men learned what they could from more experienced missionaries and asked returning missionaries about evangelism conditions. Some men prepared informally for their callings by studying the scriptures, practicing preaching, and even learning the basics of their foreign language as they sailed across the oceans to their missions. Beginning in 1867, church leaders offered more formal theological training through the reestablishment of the School of the Prophets in Salt Lake City. Joseph Smith had arranged this education program in Kirtland, Ohio, and Nauvoo, Illinois, to help train new church leaders and future missionaries. These classes quickly spread throughout Utah, where male members gathered weekly to study Mormon doctrine and discuss church government and administration. Simple preparation for evangelism was also offered, but it never was the main attraction. Brigham Young discontinued the classes in the fall of 1872. Thereafter, missionaries received informal training through the church's auxiliary organizations, including Sunday schools and the Young Men's Mutual Improvement Association. Despite these educational opportunities, the church's mission presidents bemoaned the lack of training their elders received before arriving in the mission field. Few of the missionaries had any higher education, in stark contrast to Protestant missionaries.[33]

The Mormon elders received most of their training when they reached their mission fields. They learned how to evangelize by watching other missionaries, especially more senior companions and mission leaders. But in some missions, the elders did not always evangelize in pairs, stunting their learning curve. Some studied foreign languages the same way. The elders who lacked language skills were sometimes sent to live with member families who helped them learn the language. Ideally, church leaders paired prospective elders and their language skills, if any, with specific mission fields. Danish-speaking missionaries were generally assigned to Denmark, their Swedish-speaking counterparts were usually sent to Sweden, and so on. Due to the massive immigration to Utah of tens of thousands of European converts, the languages of Western Europe did not prove a stumbling block to the Mormon missionary program. By the late nineteenth century, however, the number of prospective missionaries with native language skills decreased in tandem with the plummeting European immigration.

Aware of the problem, church leaders encouraged immigrant converts to teach their children (future missionaries) their native languages. Nevertheless, LDS leaders did not offer formal missionary training until 1899, when they provided classes at several of the church's educational academies. And these classes focused more on gospel study and the acquisition of social graces and missionary methods than on language training. This haphazard preparation paled in comparison to the missionary schooling of their Protestant contemporaries at divinity schools and missionary colleges. The LDS Church did not offer foreign language classes to its missionaries until after World War II.[34]

Financial Arrangements

The majority of American Protestant missionaries were life-time salaried professionals. They viewed their calling to the work of evangelism as both a spiritual avocation and temporal vocation. Willing to sacrifice lives of potential ease back home, these intrepid men and women left America for their mission fields, where they would make their long-term homes. As they were devoted to full-time evangelism, whether by the teaching of Christ or the advancement of Western culture, they relied on the financial generosity of mission boards and Christian organizations back in America for their support. As the Protestant foreign missionary enterprise swelled in the late nineteenth century, fundraising became a major task of domestic sponsor organizations. Protestant leaders encouraged their congregations and constituencies to give generously to provide financial assistance to their brothers and sisters serving abroad. Like most fundraising operations, however, the bulk of the contributions came from a committed few. In time, women contributed the majority of funds to mission boards. During the heyday of the foreign missionary enterprise, men reasserted themselves as key financial backers. Luther D. Wishard helped launch the Forward Movement in a bid to sustain the growing number of student volunteer missionaries. He and his staff encouraged Protestant businessmen to give of their wealth for the greater good of missions. The Laymen's Missionary Movement was another successful, yet short-lived, Protestant attempt to harness the enthusiasm and funds of successful businessmen, and later businesswomen, for the cause of foreign missions. By the early twentieth century, Americans had overtaken their British counterparts as the most prolific Protestant mission fundraisers.[35]

A notable exception to the typical Protestant missionary financial arrangement was Hudson Taylor's China Inland Mission and the other faith missions his movement spawned in Africa and Asia. He and his supporters eschewed the solicitation of funds, instead relying on the generosity of those who championed his cause and gave voluntarily. While they were not salaried, these missionaries anticipated, or had faith, that God would provide for them. They did survive, and in many ways thrived, but not at the same standard of living as other mission workers abroad.[36]

Unlike the full-time, salaried professional Protestant missionaries, the Mormon elders financed most of their nineteenth-century missions by relying on the New Testament model of traveling without "purse or scrip," meaning evangelizing without cash or personal property (Matt. 10:10; Luke 10:4). They went beyond the "extremism" of Hudson Taylor and relied totally on those they met on a daily basis in their missionary fields. Joseph Smith received several revelations encouraging the reestablishment of this practice (D&C 24:18; 84:78). His successor, Brigham Young, was likewise a proponent of this financial arrangement, having served numerous missions to North America and Great Britain, relying on the financial generosity of others. During the mid-1800s, a majority of Mormon missionaries were married, requiring the monetary maintenance of their families left behind. Given the economic circumstances in Utah at the time, this required great sacrifice by wives and children. Although the men were expected to leave their families for several years in the best financial shape possible, many had to rely on the contributions of fellow church members for their survival. Local church leaders were responsible for making sure these missionary families had funds sufficient for their needs. Church leaders created a short-lived Mission Fund in 1860 to help pay for these expenses. Latter-day Saints were encouraged to donate money, food, goods, and clothing for these temporarily fatherless families. In subsequent decades, church members cultivated missionary gardens and farms to feed these dependents. By the late nineteenth century, however, unmarried young men were displacing married older men as the church's missionary force, so the need to take care of missionary families diminished.[37]

Mormon missionaries traveled domestically and internationally without purse or scrip for much of the nineteenth century. Those traveling abroad often sold their teams and wagons to help pay for their ship passage. Some of the elders also helped defray the cost of their sailing voyages by working odd jobs onboard ship. When they landed in their mission fields they relied on the locals, both church members and those of other faiths, to support their evangelism efforts. By the late 1860s, however, many Mormon missionaries were also benefiting from funds being sent from home. This helped ease the burden on local church members, but some church leaders were concerned that the missionaries might lose their humility and reliance on the Lord if they moved away from traveling without purse or scrip. By the late nineteenth century, the financial arrangements for the Mormon missionary system were a blend of local charity and family and church support. Some missions such as those in Switzerland and Germany had vagrancy laws that kept the elders from relying on community contributions.[38]

Human Deployment

American Protestants evangelized almost exclusively in non-Christian, non-Western nations. The editors of a turn-of-the-century missionary encyclopedia made it clear what constituted a foreign mission: "All Christendom is home to the Christian. To him the non-Christian lands, alone, are foreign lands." They made exceptions, however, for Protestant evangelism efforts in Roman Catholic-dominated countries and for missionary fields in North and South America where non-Christians, or "pagans," exercised influence, such as parts of Canada and Alaska.[39] The American Board of Commissioners for Foreign Missions, America's largest Protestant missionary organization, initially deployed its missionaries to South Asia and the Near East. By the end of the Age of Jackson, however, the American Board oversaw major evangelism campaigns in India, the Sandwich Islands, and the Near East, as well as minor missions in Southeast Asia, Africa, and China. But only the Near East and India remained its star missionary fields by mid-century, while the Sandwich Islands, Africa, and China were given lower priority of human and financial capital. Between 1812 and 1860, the American Board deployed 268 missionaries (out of 841 total) to the Near East (31.9 percent), 218 to India-Ceylon (25.9 percent), 170 to Hawaii and Micronesia (20.2 percent), 99 to East Asia (11.8 percent), and 86 to Africa (10.2 percent).[40]

After the Civil War, however, other American Protestant missionary boards increased their foreign evangelism efforts in East Asia, especially in China and Japan, the latter of which was finally opened to Christian missionaries in 1873. During the last two decades of the nineteenth century, these East Asian nations, together with Korea, were the greatest beneficiaries of the American Protestant foreign missionary enterprise.[41] Between 1890 and 1915 the number of missionaries laboring in China, Japan, and Korea as a region skyrocketed 900 percent. Other foreign missions around the world grew exponentially during the same time period, due in large part to the rise of the Student Volunteer Movement. Moreover, by 1915, 80 percent of American Protestants evangelizing abroad were clustered around the Mediterranean and massed in East Asia. It would not be until the second half of the twentieth century that their ranks would shift to Africa, Latin America, and even Christian Europe.[42]

The global deployment of Mormon missionaries was almost the exact opposite of Protestants during the nineteenth century. Unlike the Protestants, Latter-day Saints focused their resources on the Christian, Western world. In theory, Mormonism was supposed to be a global religious tradition, a message for all.[43] In reality, its missionary program spread unevenly around the world. Much of the lopsided nineteenth-century human deployment was due to LDS racial, theological, and logistical concerns, as described in chapter one.[44] Between 1830 and 1899, Mormon general authorities called and set apart over twelve thousand full-time missionaries. Specifically, they assigned 6,444 (53.2 percent) church members to evangelize throughout the United States and Canada and designated 4,798 (39.6 percent) laity to missionize in Europe, especially in Great Britain and Scandinavia. Mormon authorities sent the remaining 803 (6.6 percent) elders and sisters to the Pacific basin frontier, which includes Asia. But they assigned only 27 (less than 1 percent) elders to Asian nations during the same period. Not a single LDS missionary evangelized in Japan before 1901. In short, they allocated an eye-popping 93 percent of their missionaries to the Atlantic world during the nineteenth century.[45]

The nineteenth-century Euro-American Mormon missionary model differed in important ways from the American Protestant missionary approach (see Table 3.1). First, the Latter-day Saints focused on preaching Christ rather than exporting Western culture, regardless of the latter's benefits. Unlike the Protestants who operated schools, hospitals, and churches, the Mormons tracted, held preaching meetings, engaged in intra-Christian debates, and contacted prospective converts on the streets. Second, Mormon missionaries, especially by the late nineteenth century, came from quite homogeneous backgrounds. The majority were living in Utah when they received their mission calls and most had no formal schooling beyond secondary education. American Protestants, on the other hand, hailed from across the Northeast and Midwest, representing numerous denominations. While LDS women did not formally evangelize until 1898, Protestant females constituted a major force within the foreign missionary enterprise. Third, the LDS elders were typically sent on their missions with little if any missionary training. While some attended theological classes before departing, most learned how to be missionaries once

Table 3.1.

Comparison of the Mormon and American Protestant Missionary Models

Component	Mormons	American Protestants
Evangelistic practices	Christ, not culture	Christ and culture
Personal backgrounds	Homogeneous	Heterogeneous
Missionary training	Informal, narrow	Formal, extensive
Financial arrangements	Short-time, volunteer amateurs	Life-time, salaried professionals
Human deployment	Christian, Western world	Non-Christian, non-Western world

they arrived in their fields, in intensive on-the-job-training. In contrast, most Protestant men and women enjoyed the benefits of higher education. Nearly all received formal missionary training through their mission boards before leaving the country. Fourth, Mormon missionaries were short-timers in their fields of labor, usually staying about two years before returning to their prior vocations. For much of the nineteenth century they traveled without purse or scrip. These amateurs and their families eventually had to pay much of the cost of their voluntary missionary service. On the contrary, their Protestant counterparts often committed the balance of their lives to further the cause of Christ. These professionals were financed through mission board fundraising activities back in America. Fifth, the vast majority of Latter-day Saints labored in the United States, Canada, Great Britain, and Scandinavia, all Christian nations. Conversely, American Protestants served the peoples of the Levant, South Asia, Africa, and East Asia, who knew little, if anything, of Christ.

The Early LDS China Mission:
A Preliminary Pacific World Case Study

Imposing and translating the Euro-American missionary model proved disastrous in the non-Christian, non-Western world of Asia. (The Mormon missionaries never even moved toward adaptation or inculturation during the nineteenth century.) The nearly stillborn LDS China Mission, as described in chapter 1, offers scholars an excellent case study to better appreciate why the normative LDS approach was so poorly suited to evangelize non-Christian, non-Western peoples. Moreover, a preliminary analysis of its struggles helps historians understand why the later Japan Mission would likewise flounder. Both Eastern missions were Mormon firsts: the years 1852 and 1901 mark the beginnings of LDS evangelism in China and Japan. Moreover, the Asian missions struggled to engage their Eastern audiences, leading church leaders to eventually shutter both operations. So how did three components of the missionary model—missionary training, financial arrangements, and evangelistic practices—impact the outcome of the early China Mission?

The elders called to China in August 1852 were expected to evangelize the Chinese without any missionary training, including language acquisition. These men were literally working in the fields one day and designated their church's official representatives to the world's most populous nation the next. They learned of their missionary callings to China, along with everyone else in attendance, at the church's semi-annual general conference. "To day was the Special Conference held for the purpose of sending Elders abroad. There was about 80 or 90 chosen to day to go forth to different parts of the world," Hosea Stout noted in his diary. "Myself, James Lewis[,] Walter Thompson and Chapman Duncan were chosen to go to China. The brethren who were chosen all manifest a good spirit & seem to have the spirit of their Calling."[46]

While they may have been in good spirits in Utah, they lost their enthusiasm once they arrived in East Asia, largely due to their lack of preparation. When the Mormon elders sailed into the Hong Kong harbor, they were struck by the foreignness of their new environment. "All were in a strange land and among strange people," Lewis recounted. "We did not find a cordial welcome."[47] Stout similarly described their tenuous situation as foreigners in China to Brigham Young: "We are strangers in a strange land where darkness covers the earth and gross darkness the people. Here we find a people situated differently from others we have seen and less likely to receive the gospel."[48]

The Mormons' biggest problem was that none of them spoke Chinese. (Unlike the Western European LDS missions that were staffed primarily by native-speaking immigrants, there was not a single Chinese LDS convert until 1854.[49] Church leaders had no other option than to call non-Chinese-speaking men to the mission.) Unlike the Protestant missionaries who arrived in China confidently anticipating to study the language for years, the Mormons despaired. All three men were totally unprepared to preach in the local language. "China is divided into many provinces, each province having a different dialect, not understood by the others.

Their written language is uniform and understood by all, having different sounds to the same character, but the same meaning. Their words are monosyllables and are represented by complex characters," Stout lamented to Brigham Young.[50]

In their defense, it is unclear if they were actually planning on evangelizing the Chinese-speaking locals or if they instead hoped to convert English-speaking expatriates living in the British colony. When the first Mormon missionaries landed in the Sandwich Islands in 1850, for example, they initially focused their attention on the English-speaking Caucasian settlers. It was only after these efforts failed that some of the missionaries felt inspired, and obligated, to preach to the Hawaiian natives. Still, other missionaries abandoned the Hawaiian Mission rather than learn the local language.[51]

Regardless of their initial intentions, the elders in Hong Kong quickly realized their linguistic quandary and anguished over the prospect of learning Chinese. The Latter-day Saints' lack of language training also limited their ability to understand and appreciate the surrounding Chinese culture. Their diaries and letters make it clear that they gained most of their information from foreign newspapers in English and from conversations with other foreigners in Hong Kong. It is possible that some of the information they received was actually misinformation from some foreigners, especially other Euro-American missionaries who did not want the Mormons to remain in the region. Clearly, Stout and his companions were totally unprepared to thrive, let alone survive, in Chinese culture.[52] They realized they needed to hire a Chinese teacher in order to reach the Chinese population of Hong Kong, especially since the small English-speaking populace expressed little interest in their message.[53] But teachers did not come cheap.

The Latter-day Saints in Hong Kong also suffered as a result of their financial arrangements. Before learning of their unsolicited missionary assignments, the men were barely eking out a living in pioneer Utah. "In 1852 I was called on a mission to China with Hosea Stout and Chapman Duncan, this was the great trial of my life while in poverty with helpless children another expected every day. I felt my weakness like Sampson shorn of his locks but my trust was in God my Heavenly Father," Lewis reminisced. After he and his companions said goodbye to their families and friends in the valleys of Utah, they traveled by horse and wagon to California. When they arrived at the Pacific Coast in the spring of 1853, they sent the proceeds from the sale of their wagons and horses to their destitute families back in Utah, thus "starting without purse or scrip as did the apostles of Christ to preach the restoration of the Gospel through the Prophet Joseph Smith," in Lewis's words.[54]

Whereas traveling without purse or scrip gave biblical legitimacy to the elders in Christian North America and Western Europe, the same Euro-American missionary practice proved to be a major liability in Asia. The Mormons found the cost of living in Hong Kong prohibitive and the price of Chinese tutors beyond their meager funds. "To our astonishment we found it as costly living here as in San Francisco. We are totally without means of support by labor, a prospect truly gloomy, causing a complete breakdown of our morale had we not evidence within us that we were sent of God to establish the gospel here," Stout wrote to Young. "The lowest cost of a Chinese teacher will be about twenty dollars a month. We can see no way of sustaining ourselves so as to learn the language."[55] The elders expected financial handouts but the Hong Kong residents were unmoved and withheld their funds. The Chinese and Euro-American inhabitants looked down on the Mormons because of their hapless financial condition, in contrast to the financially independent representatives of other Christian faiths. Recapitulating this New Testament financial system was a major stumbling block to their evangelism of the Chinese in Hong Kong.

Traditional LDS evangelistic practices added to the Mormon elders' lack of success among the residents of Hong Kong. Unlike other Euro-American Christian representatives in Asia, the Mormons did not try to set up schools or offer any social services. The Chinese were not impressed. As millenarians the Latter-day Saints instead focused their efforts on broadcasting the Mormon message. The three men initially attempted to canvass local residents to drum up interest in their message. But few of the people they encountered had any desire to discuss religion and the vast majority refused to engage in spiritual conversations, especially with mendicant missionaries. "Upon other topics they were free and sociable, but felt to wonder at our presumption in endeavoring to establish our doctrines in Asia under the circumstances in which we placed ourselves; for they looked upon any person in a dependent position as worthy of no regard whatever, & beneath their notice," Lewis wrote. "The other [non-LDS] missionaries presented themselves backed by the God of this world, and were received with courtesy and respect, as desirable acquisitions to society; but the servants of the Lord were despised, their company not desired, and their doctrine unheeded even by the lowest caste of the English and America population."[56]

While tracting was one of the mainstays of Mormon missionary work in the Atlantic world, it was ineffective in Hong Kong. The Mormon elders next tried preaching meetings. "In the evening we had a meeting," Stout described. "The first too [sic] which has been held in this dark and benighted land since the dispensation of the gospel has been revealed in the last days."[57] Initially, English-speaking soldiers and other foreigners attended the LDS gatherings, but that soon changed. "The people seemed satisfied yet they said it was not what they expected to hear, for they anticipated an expose of spiritual wives [plural marriage] and so forth," Lewis recalled. As a result, their listeners lost interest when the elders taught the more traditional Christian doctrines of Mormonism. To make matters worse, the editors of the English-language newspapers began publishing articles demonizing Mormonism and polygamy, a practice which ironically was first publicized during the same general conference at which the China Mission was announced.[58] "Our congregations in the mean time were reduced to a cipher—no one attending. We then began to visit the people individually, so that we might clear our garments, and bear a faithful testimony, after having traveled so far," Lewis later described. "Our endeavors to teach the way of life and salvation was unheeded by the Americans and English" of Hong Kong.[59]

The Euro-American missionary model, which flourished in the Christian Atlantic world, floundered in non-Christian, non-Western Hong Kong. After about six weeks in China the LDS missionaries lost hope.[60] They were discouraged and at a loss as to how to proceed. "We feel that we have done all that God or man can require of us in this place," one elder lamented. "We have preached publickly [sic] and privately as long as any one would hear and often tried when no one would hear."[61] After only weeks in Hong Kong they determined to temporarily abandon their missionary labors in China.[62] While the contemporaneous Taiping Rebellion and the harsh tropical climate contributed to their despondency, it was the missionaries' inability to localize traditional missionary practices that truly led to their retreat. Their lack of language and cultural training along with their anachronistic financial arrangements stand out as some of the leading causes of their discouragement in Hong Kong. Before, during, and after the Mormons' short stint in Hong Kong, American Protestants continued to build up Chinese churches in the East.[63]

Granted, the Mormons did enjoy evangelistic success with some peoples of the Pacific during the second half of the nineteenth century. But these were Pacific Islanders, not Asians. Protestant and Catholic missionaries had largely colonized and Christianized the Hawaiians of the Sandwich Islands and Maoris of New Zealand prior to the arrival of the

Mormon missionaries. Therefore, these and other peoples of the South Pacific can hardly be considered as religiously or culturally distant as the inhabitants of Asia. Moreover, the LDS representatives in Polynesia and Australasia were able to overcome the weakness of the Euro-American missionary model in the Pacific world, as historian Laurie F. Maffly-Kipp helps us understand. Unlike in Hong Kong, the LDS evangelistic practices meshed well with the traditional cultures. The Mormon style of preaching and worshiping was less formal than that of other American churches. As opposed to the Protestants who relied on books to help teach the natives, the Mormons emphasized the telling of stories, the singing of hymns, and the enjoyment of the gifts of the spirit. The natives took pleasure in their cultural continuities with the Latter-day Saints. The personal backgrounds and lack of missionary training of the Mormon missionaries actually worked to their advantage in the Pacific, unlike in Hong Kong. In contrast to the Protestants who were learned and considered themselves refined, the visitors from Utah lacked formal learning and the haughtiness that sometimes accompanies education. The Mormon missionaries were also so poor that they had to live like the natives, unlike the Protestants who kept their distance from the locals and were unwilling to adopt their food or habits. The islanders, unlike the Chinese, were impressed with the humility of the Mormons, who treated them with greater respect than other Euro-Americans. Living with the locals also enabled the Latter-day Saints to quickly acquire the local languages and learn local customs. The Latter-day Saints were persecuted by other Christian groups, including the Protestants. Paradoxically, this maltreatment set the American Mormons apart from the Christian establishment in the eyes of some Pacific islanders. As "outsiders" they became insiders.[64] Yet the reverse was true in China.

MORMON EVANGELIZATION

To truly appreciate the development and the distinctive features of the nineteenth-century Mormon missionary model (evangelistic practices, personal backgrounds, missionary training, financial arrangements, and human deployment), it is helpful to compare them with the American Protestant evangelism experience. In summary, the LDS missionaries believed that missionary practices necessarily centered on Christ, not culture.[65] Their Protestant counterparts were split into various factions, some arguing for Christ and others arguing for culture as the heart of their missionary work. The Mormons came from homogeneous personal backgrounds while the Protestants emerged from more heterogeneous circum-stances. Missionaries from Utah received informal missionary training whereas evangelists from various Protestant missionary boards benefited from formal preparation. The Latter-day Saints evangelized as short-time, volunteer amateurs at the same time as life-time, salaried professional Protestants. Lastly, Mormon elders almost always evangelized in North America and Western Europe. American Protestants, in contrast, labored in non-Christian, non-Western countries. While there are exceptions to any model (in this case, nuances in every mission and era), this typo-logical comparison highlights how differently the Mormons approached evangelism in the nineteenth century.

Finally, there is no question that the nineteenth-century Mormon evangelism approach was geared toward the conversion of other Euro-Americans. Nor is there any doubt that they were incredibly successful evangelizers in the North Atlantic world, as a result.[66] Nevertheless, their emphasis on converting other Euro-Americans, at the expense of Asians, Africans, and Latinos, had an unintended consequence: Mormons never learned how to rework their approach to non-Christian, non-Western audiences. During the nineteenth century, Latter-day Saints seemed con-tent to impose their traditional missionary model, giving little thought to what we now call inculturation. It would not be until after World War II, and the true beginnings of Mormon globalization, that LDS leaders and missionaries would substantially retool their missionary model for their varied international investigators.

HOSEA STOUT. In 1852, President Brigham Young called Stout and several companions to evangelize in China. Ill-prepared, they only remained in Hong Kong for several weeks before returning to Utah. *Courtesy Church History Library, The Church of Jesus Christ of Latter-day Saints.*

IWAKURA TOMOMI. In 1872, Iwakura Tomomi, Japan's Minister of the Right, led a group of Japanese government officials on a year-and-a-half tour of the United States. The Iwakura Mission, as it would become known, made an unplanned stop in Salt Lake City in February 1872. *Courtesy Church History Library.*

WALTER MURRAY GIBSON. In 1861, Gibson left Salt Lake City with the intent of founding a Japanese mission; he made it only as far as the Sandwich Islands (Hawaii). *Courtesy Church History Library.*

GEORGE Q. CANNON. During the last three decades of the nineteenth century, Elder George Q. Cannon was an advocate for opening a mission in Japan. *Courtesy Church History Library.*

ABRAHAM H. CANNON. In 1895, Elder Cannon proposed to church leaders a plan for a railroad linking Utah with San Diego, making it easier for missionaries to reach ships bound for Japan. *Courtesy Church History Library.*

LORENZO SNOW. During the administration of President Snow, church leaders increased their attention toward Japan. *Courtesy Church History Library.*

TOMIZO KATSUNUMA. One of the first Japanese Latter-day Saints, he was baptized in Logan, Utah, on August 8, 1895, and eventually moved to Hawaii where he worked as a U.S. government immigration agent. *Courtesy June Stageberg.*

TOKUJIRO SATO. A Japanese immigrant living in Hawaii, he was baptized there in about 1892, making him one of the first Japanese Latter-day Saints. *Courtesy June Stageberg.*

BETWEEN AMERICAN AND JAPANESE FLAGS. The first four missionaries to Japan at a missionary benefit dinner in Salt Lake City in summer 1901. Standing (left to right): Horace S. Ensign, Alma O. Taylor. Seated (left to right): Heber J. Grant, Louis A. Kelsch. *Courtesy Church History Library.*

APOSTOLIC DEDICATION OF JAPAN SITE. Horace S. Ensign, Louis A. Kelsch, and Heber J. Grant at the dedication site in Yokohama, Japan, 1901. Alma O. Taylor took the photograph. *Courtesy John W. Welch.*

EARLY LATTER-DAY SAINT MISSION HOME IN TOKYO. For many years the early Japan Mission was headquartered in this building in a suburb of Tokyo. Missionaries also lived here while evangelizing in the area. *Courtesy Church History Library.*

ELDERS OF THE EARLY JAPAN MISSION. The unmarried missionaries called to Japan in 1902. Left to right: John W. Stoker, Erastus L. Jarvis, unidentified woman, Frederick A. Caine, and Sanford W. Hedges. Photograph taken ca. 1902. *Courtesy Church History Library.*

HEBER J. GRANT FAMILY IN JAPAN. Left to right: Heber J. Grant, Mary Grant (daughter), and Augusta Grant (plural wife) in Japan, ca. 1902. *Courtesy John W. Welch.*

MISSIONARY MEALTIME IN JAPAN. Alma O. Taylor (far left), Heber J. Grant (center), and others enjoying traditional Japanese cuisine. *Courtesy John W. Welch.*

Alma O. Taylor. Taylor served one of the longest proselyting missions in the history of Mormonism, serving as a missionary and mission president in Japan from 1901 to 1910. This photograph was taken in Tokyo, Japan, ca. 1906. *Courtesy Church History Library.*

Frederick A. Caine. Beginning in summer 1905, Elder Caine assisted Japan Mission president Alma O. Taylor in translating the Book of Mormon into Japanese. *Courtesy Church History Library.*

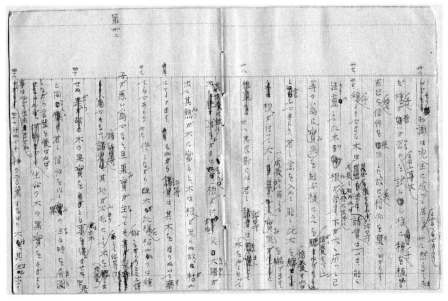

Japanese Book of Mormon text. Page from Alma O. Taylor's translation of the Book of Mormon (Alma 32:36–41) into Japanese. *Courtesy Church History Library.*

LATTER-DAY SAINT MISSIONARIES AND MEMBERS. Mormon elders and sisters and unidentified Japanese members in Osaka, Japan, May 13, 1917. *Courtesy Church History Library.*

JAPAN MISSION PERSONNEL WITH ELDER DAVID O. MCKAY. Japan Mission special conference, January 1921. Standing (left to right): Irwin T. Hicken, Deloss W. Holley, Howard Jensen, Joseph S. Payne, Lowring A. Whitaker. Sitting (left to right): President Joseph H. Stimpson, Mary E. Stimpson, David O. McKay, Hugh J. Cannon, Myrl L. Bodily, and Owen McGary. *Courtesy Church History Library.*

STIMPSON FAMILY IN JAPANESE DRESS. Studio portrait of Joseph and Mary Stimpson, together with their three children, in Japan, dressed in traditional Japanese kimonos, ca. 1921. Stimpson served as president of the Japan Mission from 1915 to 1921. *Courtesy Church History Library.*

SUNDAY SCHOOL GATHERING IN JAPAN.
Elders with Japanese Sunday school children in Tokyo, ca. 1920s.
Courtesy John W. Welch.

POSTWAR CHURCH LEADERSHIP.
Standing (left to right): W. Paul Merrill, President Edward L. Clissold, and Guy A. Hart.
Clissold served as Japan's first mission president (1948–1949) upon the church's official return
after a twenty-four-year absence from the country. *Courtesy Church History Library.*

II

Twentieth-Century Challenges in Japan

4

Opening the Japan Mission

If the time has come for Elders to go to Japan, let Japan be penetrated. After a while perpahs an opening may be made in Korea, and in Manchuria, and in China, and these lands be penetrated by the Elders with this message of salvation, as soldiers of Christ. Our young men go to the Philippines and to Cuba, and they have been willing to lay down their lives for their country. Young men from this State have done so, and have thus shown their patriotism. Let us in like manner show our patriotism to the kingdom of God and for the salvation of Jesus Christ, our great leader.

—George Q. Cannon, 1900

Nearly five decades passed after the closing of the early China Mission in 1853, before Mormon leaders again called missionaries on an evangelistic errand to Asia. Observers have drawn parallels between the original "errands" of seventeenth-century Puritans and nineteenth-century Latter-day Saints.[1] Ralph Waldo Emerson labeled Mormonism the "after-clap of Puritanism" for good reason.[2] The imagery and language of their undertakings does seem analogous. While the Puritans sailed in wooden vessels across the liquid Atlantic desert, the Mormons pulled hickory handcarts the width of American's Great Plains, each to build their respective "cities on a hill." Moreover, both second- and third-generation Puritans and Mormons, because of emerging doctrinal diversity, economic enterprise, and political pluralism in New England and the Great Basin, struggled to translate their ancestors' theocratic visions into everyday realities. As a result, the two groups toiled to retain their original sense of mission and identity as they assimilated into America. Although John Winthrop and Brigham Young led their followers away from the established church in an attempt to save it, subsequent generations were forced to look outward, not inward, for relevance.[3]

Intellectual historian Perry Miller suggests that Cotton Mather and his Puritan contemporaries were anxious and "lament[ed] over the declension of [their generation], who appear, page after page, in contrast to their mighty progenitors, about as profligate a lot as ever squandered a great inheritance." The sons and grandsons of the original Puritans struggled with their identity, not with "the stones, storms, and Indians," Miller writes.[4] Beginning in the early nineteenth century, the Puritan descendents, or a subset of American Protestants, rechanneled their sense of failure into a renewed sense of errand. Their errand to the world would be its evangelism. They felt obligated, as both Americans and Protestants, to "save and renovate the world," in the words of historian William R. Hutchison.[5] In other words, nineteenth-century American Protestants transformed their ancestors' "city on a hill" into a mandate to spread their brand of Christianity throughout the non-Christian, non-Western world.[6]

Similar lamentations—"that all adventures are over, that no great days and no heroism lie ahead"—bleed through the writings of second- and third-generation Mormons living in Utah at the turn of the twentieth century. The West had shrunk in relative size and in the popular imagination. These young men, born in the safety of Utah, far from the earlier persecutions of Ohio, Missouri, and Illinois, desired their own errand and wilderness. As with the Puritans, a sense of purpose was this crowd's problem. But the golden age of LDS missionary success in Great Britain and Scandinavia had ended; existing foreign missionary fields had lost much of their romance as a result. So it is not surprising that in 1901, when church leaders announced the opening of the inaugural mission to the peoples of Japan, most Latter-day Saints in Utah rejoiced. Had church members been aware of the difficulties endured by other Christian missionaries in Japan, however, and the challenges that lay in store for those elders and sisters who would be called to East Asia, their enthusiasm for their new errand to the world would likely have been tempered.

CHRISTIANITY IN JAPAN

Roman Catholicism encountered Japan in the sixteenth century, when Portuguese ships carrying Jesuit missionaries landed on Japanese shores. Years earlier, Portuguese sailors discovered Japan for the West. This contact between East and West was made possible by the confluence of the Age of Discoveries (the Pacific world was finally explored by Europeans) and the Protestant Reformation (the Counter-Reformation movement led to the rise of the missionary-minded Jesuit order). Jesuit priest Francis Xavier arrived in Japan in 1549, after learning about the island nation from a Japanese man named Yajirō, who was later baptized, in Malacca. But after living through two years of a Japanese civil war, Xavier determined to evangelize instead in China. Cosme de Torres assumed the leadership of the Catholic Church in Japan. One decade after the Jesuits began evangelizing the Japanese, the order reported that there were six thousand Christian converts. By the beginning of the seventeenth century there were about three hundred thousand *Kirishitan* (Japanese Catholic Christians). According to Catholic records, the number of converts more than doubled by the 1630s, the result of mass conversions of the feudal retainers of *daimyō* (feudal lords) who also converted to Catholicism.[7]

During these decades of growth, however, Christianity in Japan came under attack. In 1587, Toyotomi Hideyoshi, the reigning Japanese leader, issued an expulsion order for all Christian missionaries. Within a decade, the government had executed a number of Catholic representatives and Japanese Kirishitan. When Hideyoshi passed away, Tokugawa Ieyasu seized control of the country and instituted the governing Edo bakufu. In 1614 the Edo government issued another expulsion order for all Western missionaries and prohibited the practice of Christianity throughout the island nation. Over the next two centuries, the Kirishitan experienced tremendous persecution. Government officials demolished all church buildings and martyred thousands of converts and remaining missionaries. Countless other Kirishitan were tortured until they renounced their beliefs and embraced traditional Japanese religions. During the seventeenth-century reign of Shogun Tokugawa Iemitsu, the oppression of Catholicism intensified. So did the nation's desire for political isolation.[8]

Beginning in 1639, the Tokugawa shogunate introduced a policy of national seclusion, which limited trade relations with China, Korea, and the Netherlands. It did this to gain absolute control over its foreign relations and establish the government's internal and external authority. It would not be until 1858 that the Edo government would again allow European powers to trade with its merchants. By the early 1800s, the shogunate's policy of *sakoku* (closed country) had deepened to the point where foreign culture and trade were essentially limited to the Japanese populace and some Dutch merchants. About this time, the Dutch were being challenged for their supremacy in Asia as other Western nations began to act on their colonial ambitions. Russia began sending its ships and men to Hokkaidō in the 1790s to try to engage in trade with the Japanese. Britain continued to expand its colonial influence into India, Malaysia, and China. These and other outside threats encouraged the isolationist Japanese government to close the borders even more tightly. In 1825 the Tokugawa government issued its Expulsion Edict, which mandated that foreign ships coming close to its shores would henceforth be fired upon.[9]

The Dutch, Russians, and British were not alone in their expansionist policies. By the middle of the nineteenth century, the United States, with citizens now in Oregon and California, also turned its attention to Asia. In 1852, President Millard Fillmore dispatched Commodore Matthew Perry to Japan to open diplomatic and commercial relations. In July 1853, Perry and his infamous black ships initiated the first direct U.S. contact with Japan by sailing into Edo Bay, now Tokyo Bay. His visit and demands for treaty relations were received with mixed reactions from the various Tokugawa factions. The following February, Perry returned with a larger naval fleet to coerce the Tokugawa government to sign a treaty to normalize relations. Made official on March 31, 1854, at Kanagawa, now Yokohama, the treaty required Japan to open two of its ports—Shimoda, Shizuoka Prefecture, and Hakodate, Hokkaidō—to American ships and trade and allow an American consular agent to live in Shimoda. In the following years, the Japanese shogunate entered into similar agreements with the British, Russians, and Dutch. Japan's era of national seclusion had ended.[10]

In 1858, American consul Townsend Harris negotiated and expanded upon the provisions of the earlier Kanagawa Treaty on behalf of the United States. Known as the Harris Treaty, it stipulated the opening of Edo, Kobe, Nagasaki, Niigata, and Yokohama to foreign trade; placed Japanese tariffs under international control; fixed import duties at low levels; and established extraterritoriality for foreign residents living in Japan. It also allowed the reintroduction of Christianity, although missionaries were not welcome until 1873, when the Meiji government revoked the prohibition against evangelism in Japan. Other Western powers soon demanded similar accords. These unequal agreements, the Ansei commercial treaties, weakened the shogunate's domestic and international power; many Japanese believed they demoted their country into a near-colony of the West.[11]

During the centuries when Christianity was officially prohibited in Japan and its practitioners made to recant or suffer death, a number of Kirishitan banded together and created an underground church organization, modeled after informal Jesuit associations. These Japanese determined to practice Catholicism, although they mixed their beliefs with Japanese religious traditions out of necessity. In order to eradicate these subversive groups, Japanese government officials led a series of anti-

Christian purges on a sporadic basis until 1868. Nevertheless, the underground Kirishitan movement amazingly survived until the Meiji period and the reintroduction of Christianity to Japan. These *kakure Kirishitan* (hidden Christians) developed a syncretic form of Christianity.[12]

Roman Catholics were the first Christian group to resume missionary work in Japan after the nation began to open up to the West. In 1844, Theodore-Auguste Forcade, a Catholic missionary, arrived in modern-day Okinawa, where he remained for two years. It would be another decade before Catholic representatives reached Honshū. In 1862 they opened the first Catholic meeting house in the treaty port of Yokohama, to the annoyance of some Japanese leaders. During the nineteenth century, the French Catholic missionary groups spent most of their time training Japanese clergy and locating the kakure Kirishitan. Many of these underground believers embraced their leadership but some decided to retain their interpretations of Catholic practices and never rejoined Catholicism. "The general trend of Roman Catholicism for most of the Meiji period was to ignore political developments and movements for social reform in favor of building a community of believers centered on the priesthood and isolated from mainstream society," historian Helen J. Ballhatchet summarizes.[13]

Russian Orthodox missionaries also labored among the Japanese during the nineteenth century with impressive success. Father Nikolai was the driving force behind the mission. Before traveling to Japan he studied the language, started the translation of religious texts, and prepared an insightful plan for the evangelism of the Japanese. He baptized his church's first converts in 1868. The next year Nikolai returned to Russia, where he secured greater financial support for his mission. In the years that followed, he and his assistants were able to grow local churches. The Orthodox Church was attractive to the Japanese for a number of reasons, including the charismatic leadership of Nikolai and the church's ties to the West. Moreover, the rituals and furnishings of its houses of worship were evocative of Buddhist temples. Nearly its entire staff was Japanese, which helped the Orthodox Church better understand the surrounding culture and religions. But finances remained a thorn in the mission's side, as did its lack of Russian support staff. These problems had been eclipsed, however, by the late nineteenth century, when political relations frayed between Russia and Japan. The two nations finally broke ties during the first decade of the twentieth century, damaging the status of the Orthodox Church in Japan.[14]

The Protestant evangelism of Japan commenced with the arrival of American Episcopal missionary John Liggins in 1859. Within a decade there were Protestants laboring in all of the treaty ports. Unlike the Roman

Catholic and Russian Orthodox missionaries, the Protestants remained aloof from Japanese society, seeking to maintain their Western lifestyles. As we shall learn, the Protestants emphasized education and social welfare reforms in Meiji Japan. As a result, they exerted an inordinate amount of influence on Japanese society, while championing the Westernization of Japan as an outgrowth of Christianity. A number of Japanese Protestant converts, like Uchimura Kanzō, became well known in educational and government circles. Japanese converts also helped Protestantism move beyond the treaty ports to rural areas unfamiliar with Christianity after 1873. Protestant growth was rapid during the 1870s and 1880s until the rise of Japanese nationalism. While Roman Catholicism and Russian Orthodoxy presented a united front to the Japanese, the denominational rifts within Protestantism hampered its growth and appeal, despite several failed attempts to create a unified Protestant Japanese church.[15] By the turn of the twentieth century, Christianity had secured a strong, yet small, toehold in Japan.

JAPAN AS A POTENTIAL MISSION FIELD

Unlike their Christian counterparts who began evangelizing in Japan immediately following the Asian empire's official "opening" to the outside world in 1853, American Latter-day Saints waited nearly five decades—until 1901—to commence missionary work among the Japanese. Moreover, as described in chapter 2, Mormon leaders made no attempt to missionize the East Asians, including a small number of Japanese, living in their midst in the American West during the nineteenth century. While social, linguistic, and political realities all seemingly factored into this decision, so did LDS theological conceptions of race and lineage. It would take a dramatic drop-off in missionary success in the North American and Western European mission fields, coupled with a renewed sense of millenarian urgency, to persuade LDS leaders to finally look east instead of west at the beginning of the twentieth century.

During the nineteenth and early twentieth centuries, Latter-day Saints understood the world and its ethnic groups in terms of the Bible and Book of Mormon scriptural narratives. According to sociologist Armand Mauss, nineteenth-century Mormon constructions of lineage played a major role in Latter-day Saint self-understanding and evangelism priorities. Most Euro-American church members believed themselves to be direct descendants of one of the twelve tribes of biblical Israel, and especially favored Ephraim, whose offspring was responsible for gathering the remnants of the House of Israel in the last days. While the light-skinned seed of Ephraim enjoyed a privileged role at the top of the LDS racial hierarchy, the dark-skinned descendants of Old Testament Cain and Ham were seemingly cursed, and therefore unworthy to hold the Mormon priesthood until the late twentieth century. Toward the top of these two extremes were the Native Americans, held to be part of an ancient Israelite diaspora in the New World (Manasseh and Ephraim), as well as the Jews or offspring of Judah. Then there were the descendants of the other Israelite clans, those who had been scattered and "lost" across the globe, who likewise were to receive the promised blessings of the Abrahamic covenant in the end of days. Beneath the favored Israelites but over the condemned Cainites and Hamites stood the "Gentiles," who could enjoy the full blessings of the Abrahamic covenant through accepting the message of Mormonism.[16] Conspicuously missing from this racial hierarchy was thoughtful consideration of the peoples of East Asia.

Historian Norman Douglas makes the case that LDS leaders prioritized the allocation of the human and financial missionary capital according to this ethnic ladder that evolved as Mormon elders and sisters evangelized across the world, especially throughout the Pacific basin frontier. The first missionaries called to teach the gospel in the Sandwich Islands (Hawaii), China, India, and New Zealand in the 1850s, for example, initially understood their mission to be focused on the Euro-Americans living in these lands, not the native Pacific Islanders or Asians, until they met with failure. "Rather than being led to the islands originally because of a deep-seated conviction that the Polynesians were descendants of Lehi [patriarch of the Book of Mormon peoples], the Mormons' attempt to allocate to the Polynesian a place in Mormon scripture and to view themselves as custodians of the keys to the islanders' spiritual kingdom was a rationalization of and a compensation for their initial lack of success with the white of various island groups," Douglas argues.[17]

Celebrated missionaries like Addison Pratt in French Polynesia and George Q. Cannon in the Sandwich Islands quickly turned their attention to the indigenous inhabitants of their respective Pacific mission fields. Symbolic "branches" of the House of Israel were thereafter discovered as missionaries, members, and leaders came in contact with these Pacific Islanders. "During the second half of the nineteenth century, the blood of Israel, especially of Ephraim, seemed particularly abundant in those parts of the world in which most Mormons could trace their own ancestors, as well as among those aboriginal peoples whose ancestors were featured in the Book of Mormon," Mauss maintains.[18] Elders in Hong Kong and Bombay likewise followed suit and soon shifted their attention to their native Asian charges during the 1850s, until church leaders recalled all missionaries from Asia for the remainder of the nineteenth century.

Latter-day Saints became increasingly curious and ambivalent about the relationship between the House of Israel and the peoples of Asia. For example, George Jarvis, a Latter-day Saint serving in the British navy off the East Asian coasts in the 1850s, tried to evangelize in Japan while at port in Yokohama and became interested in the lineage of the Japanese. Almost five decades later, in 1902, while serving as a patriarch in the St. George Utah Stake, Jarvis pronounced a blessing on the head of his son Erastus who had just been called to serve in the Japan Mission, that he would be able to "learn the origin of the Japanese people," in reference to their scriptural lineage. George Jarvis also told his son that he believed that Hagoth, a Book of Mormon seafarer, might have landed on the Japanese coast, so Erastus should keep a lookout for a "typical Israelitish altar, high up on the bluff, west of Yokohama harbor" when he disembarked in Japan.[19]

As early as 1887, some Latter-day Saints were interested to learn of the possibility of Israelite blood coursing through the veins of the Japanese. In an unsigned letter reproduced in the widely read *Millennial Star* periodical, a non-LDS traveler related his experiences coming in contact with Nicholas McLeod, a non-Mormon Scottish expatriate working in Asia, while both men were living in Japan. During the late 1870s, McLeod self-published several books in Japan theorizing that the Japanese people were actually Israelites.[20] Like McLeod, the writer believed that the Japanese were literal descendents of Jacob, the patriarch of the Israelite nation, who had immigrated to the isles of East Asia as "lost tribes." An LDS editor added a footnote to this recital that suggested that the Book of Mormon might hold the key to understanding the great diaspora of Israel throughout the Pacific Basin frontier, including Japan. "It is probable that these people were drifted to the islands of the Pacific Ocean and inhabited them. It was doubtless in this manner that the Sandwich Islands were peopled, as also other islands and even Japan, as there is a great similarity between the American Indians, Sandwich Islanders, the Maories [*sic*] in New Zealand and the Japanese."[21] Years later, a *Millennial Star* editorial with an identical title followed the same line of reasoning:

> It is well known that scholars are at a loss to account satisfactorily for the ancient history of Japan. That some of the descendants of Jacob should have found their way to Japan, after the breaking up of the Assyrian empire, is not improbable. Israelites have been found in China, preserv-

ing much of the old tradition and religion, and it is by no means incredible that some of that race should have crossed over to the Japanese islands, and there become a factor in the development of the country and the nation. Israel was scattered throughout the world, in order to act as a leaven, preparing all the nations of the earth for the last dispensation.[22]

In ensuing years, a number of researchers have written on the similar subject of Israelite blood being spread throughout Asia, including Japan.[23]

Following the death of President Wilford Woodruff, Lorenzo Snow was sustained as Mormonism's fifth prophet-president in September 1898. His short administration (1898–1901) was marked by the church's improving financial position and heightened international outreach. At the time of Snow's selection, the church owed an almost overwhelming $2.3 million to creditors. This debt was the result of the U.S. government's seizure and mismanagement of church property during the anti-polygamy Edmunds-Tucker Act of 1887 episode as well as LDS debt-financed public works projects in the 1890s. Seeking a solution to the church's financial dire straits, Snow reemphasized the paying of tithes. The financial crisis came to a conclusion by the beginning of the new century, as a result, and church leaders began thinking about new opportunities.[24] Under Snow's direction, Mormonism entered the twentieth century with 283,765 members, 967 wards and branches, 43 stakes, and 4 temples. In addition, nearly a thousand men and women were evangelizing in over a dozen mission fields.[25] However, the vast majority of these members, congregations, and edifices were located in North America, and they did not represent the world's population. Up to this point LDS missionary work and resources were mainly focused on the nations of North America and Western Europe, while the countries of Asia, for example, languished in spiritual darkness, in the Mormon mind.

Disturbed by this trend, President Snow determined to shift his church's attention to the nations of East Asia, South America, and Eastern Europe. Church authorities believed that Christ's Second Coming was nigh, due to a resurgence of millennialism, and felt that they needed to fulfill the Great Commission in lands heretofore untouched by Mormon evangelists.[26] They had not sent missionaries on an evangelical errand to Asia, the world's most populous continent, since the 1850s. In Snow's mind, the central responsibility of the Quorum of the Twelve Apostles was "to warn the nations of the earth and prepare the world for the coming of the Savior," not to overly busy themselves with stake and ward duties, the responsibilities of stake presidents and bishops.[27] LDS Apostles had been much more involved in foreign missionary work before external and internal stresses forced their retreat to the Great Basin during the 1880s and 1890s. In 1837, Joseph Smith sent several apostles to the British Isles, where they labored with great success. Apostle Heber C. Kimball was the first mission president in Europe. Brigham Young sent a number of apostles to open new missionary fields in Europe, just three years after the first pioneers reached the Salt Lake Valley.[28] Snow believed that his lieutenants needed to refocus their energies outward, not inward, to fulfill their errand to the world, just as their apostolic predecessors had done for much of the nineteenth century.

President Snow was not a lone voice in the First Presidency regarding the declining LDS missionary enterprise at the start of the twentieth century. First Presidency counselor George Q. Cannon was likewise concerned with his church's flagging missionary program. He believed his church was "expending means and time with deficient [conversion] results" in the British Isles and other parts of Europe as it entered the new century.[29] Rather than harvesting thousands of European converts each year, LDS missionaries were now barely gleaning hundreds of new members. Moreover, changing political, economic, and social circumstances in Europe continued to diminish some of the earlier appeals of American Mormonism. These new missionary realities encouraged Cannon and others to also advocate the opening of new missionary fields in countries where the "believing blood of Israel" might yet be uncovered.[30]

George Q. Cannon expressed his millenarian vision of twentieth-century evangelism in the October 1900 general conference. "I have had resting upon my mind now for some time a feeling to call upon the Latter-day Saints and tell them that the coming of the Lord is near, even at our doors," he declared. LDS missionaries were no longer enjoying the returns that they once did and time was running out; individual elders were only baptizing about two people a year. "I would not dare to tell you how much money is spent as well as time to do this," Cannon complained. As the Latter-day Saints were commanded by scripture to warn all of the nations, he, too, promoted a reallocation of evangelism resources away from underperforming missionary fields. "Hundreds of Elders now in the missionary fields might leave this nation, and go to peoples who have never heard the sound of the Gospel," he suggested. "Oriental lands now untouched by the Elders of the Church have to be penetrated and the honest souls sought out." Snow's counselor viewed Japan as the toehold needed for the Mormon expansion into Asia. "If the time has come for Elders to go to Japan, let Japan be penetrated. After a while perhaps an opening may be made in

Korea, and in Manchuria, and in China."[31] Church authorities were taking more notice of the East.

OPENING OF THE JAPAN MISSION

Japan loomed large on the horizon of new LDS evangelism possibilities during 1900. Rather than orchestrating the evangelism of hundreds of Chinese and Japanese immigrants living within miles of their offices at church headquarters, however, the First Presidency determined to take the gospel directly to East Asia. A series of nineteenth-century encounters with East Asians both at home and abroad convinced Mormon authorities that Japan, not China, should be the church's Eastern priority. Accordingly, on February 14, 1901, during a weekly meeting of the Council of the First Presidency and Quorum of the Twelve, George Q. Cannon announced the establishment of the Japan Mission and called Apostle Heber J. Grant, a second-generation Latter-day Saint, to be its president.[32] Over the next several months, Grant selected three missionary companions: Horace S. Ensign, Louis A. Kelsch, and Alma O. Taylor. The Mormon errand to the Asian world had commenced.

Many Latter-day Saints in Utah were delighted when the First Presidency publicized the creation of the Japanese mission field. Historian Leonard J. Arrington describes the thrill in Utah over the mission as "somewhat analogous to excitement over early space flights."[33] The Salt Lake City *Deseret Evening News* reported that the announcement of the Japan Mission had "aroused no little interest" in Mormon circles.[34] In the months leading up to the departure of the elders to Japan, church members and other Salt Lake City citizens feted the elders on several occasions. Although all missionaries were sent off with some sort of farewell party, it is clear that the opening of a new mission by an apostle garnered more excitement and caused more celebration than usual. The First Presidency even sponsored a benefit concert for the Japan Mission in the Tabernacle.[35] Nearly a dozen Salt Lake City Japanese residents hosted another farewell party at the LDS Twenty-first Ward chapel, where Japanese and American flags hung side by side. "The evening's entertainment concluded with general hand shaking and expressions of good will on the part of the Japanese to the Mormon Elders who were about to leave for the Orient," one reporter described.[36]

Despite the nearly tangible buzz in Utah over sending missionaries to Japan, there was disagreement among some Latter-day Saints over the propriety of evangelizing East Asians. In the weeks leading up to the April

1901 general conference, some church members expressed concern about Mormonism's prospects among the Japanese, a people who seemed to some beyond the reach of the "believing blood" of the House of Israel.[37] "We know not what is in store for this Church in the Empire of Japan," First Presidency member Rudger Clawson admitted.[38] Apostle John W. Taylor tried to diffuse the ingrained theological and racial belief that only the descendants of the House of Israel, who most Latter-day Saints assumed the Japanese were not, would be receptive to the gospel. "Some of you have heard that Elder Grant is going to Japan, and you begin to query in your minds, Is this nation of the house of Israel? Is it a proper thing for Elder Grant to go to Japan?" Apostle Taylor declared that "there is no nation on the face of the earth but will hear the everlasting Gospel; ... Then our minds may be set at rest in regard to Elder Grant going to Japan."[39]

But some Mormons remained uneasy about a mission to a supposedly non-Israelite nation. Two months after Grant and his companions landed in Japan, church authorities readdressed these fears during October 1901 general conference. "People have asked the question whether or not Brother Grant would be successful in Japan, and whether the Gospel would gather people from other nations," Apostle Matthias F. Cowley related. "Such a question need not be asked, for it was answered this morning in the revelation read by Apostle Smoot, where it says in relation to Zion, 'And there shall come unto her out of every nation under the heaven.' We need, therefore, have no concern whatever about that."[40] It would be up to the Japanese people to demonstrate their receptivity to Mormonism, and thereby assert their biblical birthright to the promised blessings of the House of Israel in the last days.

Language acquisition was another concern. Determined to familiarize himself with Japanese linguistics before his missionary arrival in the land of the rising sun, Japan-bound missionary Alma O. Taylor contacted Paul Carus, a Buddhist sympathizer and founder of Open Court Publishing, whom he had met the previous year while studying to be a mortician in Chicago. Carus had been instrumental in introducing many Americans to Eastern faiths like Buddhism and Hinduism through his publications. Carus encouraged Taylor to contact the Reverend Nishijima Kakuryo, a leader of the recently created Buddhist Mission of North America, who was then living in San Francisco. Nishijima and his mentor Sonoda Shuye had arrived in northern California in September 1899, as missionaries for their Jōdo Shinshū Buddhist faith, and opened the Hongwanji Branch Office on Polk Street in San Francisco. Over the next several months the two Japanese priests offered study classes and public lectures on Buddhism, eventually organizing Young Men's Buddhist Associations in nearby Sacramento, Fresno, and Vacaville, and issuing a newsletter. For their efforts Nishijima and Sonoda are regarded as the founders of the Buddhist Churches of America.[41] On June 14, 1901, Taylor wrote to Nishijima hoping that the Buddhist priest might help him locate some Japanese language study materials. The young Mormon missionary explained that neither he nor Carus could locate suitable primers in Salt Lake City or Chicago. Could Nishijima help? Taylor made clear why he needed to learn Japanese—so that he and his missionary companions could teach the message of Mormonism to Nishijima's Buddhist countrymen once they arrived in Japan later that summer. This would be the first of five letters that Taylor and Nishijima would exchange.[42]

Nishijima responded to Taylor's missive by first apologizing that he was unable to provide the requested language study materials from San Francisco: "If there were plenty of time before you left this country I would have sent to some book store in Tokyo for the books." The Buddhist priest then discussed Taylor's pending missionary assignment to his fellow Japanese. "You say in your letter that you are about to go to Japan to teach our people with the true Spirit of Christianity which is not taught by the hundreds of so called Christian sects upon the earth to-day; and I am very glad for it," Nishijima began. The missionary from Japan further declared that he harbored no ill will toward any other religion and wished that all religionists would "be just as brothers and sisters, and be in harmony and peace" as faith in general elevated the character of adherents. Even so, Nishijima expressed his concern that Mormonism, widely despised by Christians in America, "teaches men the unlawful life of polygamy which will debase them instead of lifting." He warned Taylor that if he and his LDS missionary companions were to advocate plural marriage in Japan they would be met with "severe condemnation" by both Christians *and* Buddhists alike. Nishijima then admitted that he had never really studied Mormon doctrine or practice and was ignorant of its contributions to mankind. "If you really belong to this sect and intend to teach it to our people," he concluded, "I wish you would be so kind as to tell me how you will benefit our people who are in the state of dullness and ignorance, by your own way of living of which all other Christian sects are so much despising?" Nishijima enclosed a copy of his periodical *Bukkyō Seinenkai Kaihō* (Young Men's Buddhist Association Newsletter) and invited Taylor to respond to his concerns.[43]

Taylor replied to Nishijima's dispatch in typical missionary fashion: "I respond cheerfully to your question as to how the religion of 'Mormonism' will be a benefit to the people of your fatherland."[44] He then extolled the basic tenets of Mormonism, including the sanctity of LDS homes, the loving leadership of faithful Mormon parents, and the industrious pioneering nature of the Latter-day Saints. After offering a general history of the LDS faith, Taylor addressed Nishijima's concerns about Mormon plural marriage. "It seems to be the general idea that 'Mormonism' has but one doctrine—the doctrine of polygamy," the eighteen-year-old Latter-day Saint began. "The people of the world who are not thoroughly acquainted with the 'Mormon' idea of polygamy; and know of it only from circulated reports (which are mostly rumors) have the horrifying thought, that the 'Mormons' are eaten up with passion; and that their homes are worse than the brothels of harlots; that their girls are given to men to satisfy their fiendish lust; indeed, that they are more like beasts than human beings." Taylor then launched into an impassioned theological defense of plural marriage, although he contended that Mormon polygamy was a moot issue in the twentieth century since its practice had officially ceased in 1890. "We are *not* going to Japan to preach polygamy, for it is a dead issue, and new polygamous relations are not being entered into among the 'Mormons,'" he declared. Little did Taylor and his companions realize how "alive" the issue of plural marriage still was until they arrived in Nishijima's native country weeks later.[45]

DEPARTURE FOR JAPAN

On July 24, 1901, Apostle Heber J. Grant and his three missionary companions prepared to do some trailblazing in Japan. They had purposefully scheduled their departure to coincide with Pioneer Day, a religious holiday in Utah commemorating the vanguard company of Mormon pioneers entering the Salt Lake Valley in 1847. The youngest member of the evangelism quartet, Alma O. Taylor, expressed enthusiasm as he contemplated his pending separation from his loved ones. "This being the day of starting on my mission to Japan, it is one of excitement and work," he reflected in his journal. "With most people, the thoughts of leaving relatives and friends for so long a time as I may be gone on this mission, would be very sad but with me this contemplation of the labor lying before me is so pleasant that I say good-bye to all with joy."[46]

That evening, after the Pioneer Day parades and fireworks, the missionaries and their families and friends assembled at the Salt Lake train depot to say their final goodbyes. Then the elders boarded the Oregon Short Line train bound for the Pacific coast. "It was quite an auspicious day to make a start; it being the 54th Anniversary of the pioneers entering the Salt Lake Valley. I felt that inasmuch as the Gospel had never been preached in Japan and that we were to be the first to sound the Gospel cry to that nation; that we were indeed going pioneering on pioneer day," Taylor noted.[47] Grant also described his feelings: "I was never happier in my life and there was never a feeling of deeper gratitude in my heart than there was last night as our train pulled out of the depot." But he continued with soberness: "I can with difficulty realize that I am on my way to Japan and may not see my loved ones at home for a number of years."[48] The train pulled out of the Salt Lake City depot at 11:10 p.m. The twentieth-century Mormon errand to the East had begun.

The missionaries traveled north by train to Ogden, Utah, where they caught their rail connection to Vancouver, British Columbia. After making their way to the harbor, the quartet boarded the *Empress of India*, a six-thousand-ton steamship operated by the Canadian Pacific Railway Company. This steamer, together with the *Empress of Japan* and the *Empress of China*, sailed routes connecting Vancouver to Hong Kong, Yokohama, Kobe, Nagasaki, and Shanghai.[49] After two weeks at sea the elders finally caught sight of the Japanese coastline on August 12, 1901. That afternoon they waited onboard ship in the Yokohama harbor, where they were examined by quarantine doctors. Pronounced healthy, they were allowed to disembark at the Yokohama docks. Grant and his cohort then passed through the customs house and made their way to their lodging at the Grand Hotel.

The Mormon elders were dazzled by the new sights and sounds they encountered. Alma Taylor captured a number of observations in his journal that first day. He and his companions were especially impressed by the Japanese *jinrikisha* (human-pulled carts) and the laborers who conveyed them under their own power from the wharf to their hotel. "They trotted at a good rate all the way and did not seem out of breath at all," he noted. "The fact that humans are thus worked seems almost impossible but before night I saw hundreds and hundreds of these rikisha men and many others who were pulling freight carts on which there was as much as 1000 lbs." Taylor continued to be wowed by his new environs that evening. From the veranda of his hotel he looked out over the bay and was entranced by his surroundings. "Seeing also the apparel and manners of the people, I indeed felt 'A stranger in a strange land.'"[50] Louis A. Kelsch likewise recalled his first observations of Japan. "It seemed to us when we arrived that we were indeed strangers in a strange land, for everything was strange unto us. The people, their customs, their habits, their food—all were strange. We could not speak to the people, only through interpreters, except to those who were able to understand the English language."[51] But the elders were excited to be on Japanese soil poised to preach the gospel in a new land.

The missionaries' initial exuberance at being in Japan was tempered a few days later, however, as they watched their ship sail from the harbor. Taylor wrote, "With longing eyes we stood on the shore and watched as it moved gently out of the harbor, and we felt as though we were parting with a dear friend. But," he continued with his characteristic optimism, "still we were happy in the thought that we had come to this land for the purpose of winning souls unto Christ."[52] Missionary work among the Japanese would prove difficult and frustrating to Taylor and his companions, however. During their first weeks in East Asia, the four men busied themselves with various responsibilities, including responding to a barrage of anti-Mormon press that greeted their arrival. But the missionaries were excited by the number of Japanese who seemed interested in learning more about their faith, including influential newsmen. "Is it the prayers of the Saints that is causing the Lord to turn the hearts of this people unto us his servants? Is it that this nation is famished for the word of God, and have been seeking for it but found it not because it was not in their midst?" Taylor wondered in his journal. "Is it that the blood of Israel flows so freely in their veins that they recognize immediately the voice of the good shepherd and their hearts leap with joy when they hear his call?"[53] The young missionary's initial optimism would be tempered over the next several years when Japanese conversions to Mormonism proved scarce.

So it is not surprising that Apostle Grant and his evangelism companions were also taken aback by the controversy their arrival in Japan stirred up in the Japanese press. As Japanese studies scholar Sarah Cox Smith documents, Mormonism "was portrayed as ridiculous and indeed laughable in its doctrine but with an uncanny, almost eerie, power to attract believers. Many perceived it to be a threat to Japanese culture. In a sense, the Latter-day Saint doctrines had been translated—or rather, mistranslated—by Japanese and resident Christian writers long before the missionaries ever set foot on Japanese soil." Some Japanese were afraid that Mormonism, specifically its teachings and practice of plural marriage, would set back the recent social advancements of Japanese women and threaten Meiji enlightenment. A number of magazine and newspaper articles were written in opposition to Mormonism in the decade before the Utah-based faith arrived in Japan in 1901.[54] And what began as a trickle of printed pieces on the Latter-day Saints morphed into a flash flood of editorials and essays, both in opposition to and in support of Mormonism, for a solid month after their appearance in Yokohama. "More than a dozen newspapers in the dominant commercial city of Osaka, and no less than twenty major regional newspapers throughout the country devoted considerable space—often on front pages—to articles and editorials reporting or otherwise commenting on the arrival of this new Christian sect with unusual doctrines," scholar Takagi Shinji chronicles. Between August 13 and September 10, 1901, at least 160 newspaper pieces were written about Mormonism and the quartet of Latter-day Saint elders boarding in Yokohama.[55]

APOSTOLIC DEDICATION OF JAPAN

On Sunday, September 1, 1901, just two weeks after arriving in Japan, Apostle Heber Grant and his companions left their hotel in Yokohama's foreigner district and walked for a good twenty minutes until they located a grove of trees that offered them privacy on a hillside overlooking the Yokohama harbor. They looked forward to spending some time together outside of their lodging, where the controversy in the press might be forgotten for a few hours. Wearing light-colored summer suits to help them endure the blazing heat, the four men sat down in a circle and opened their prayer meeting by singing, "We Thank Thee Oh God for a Prophet." Grant and Louis Kelsch both offered opening prayers on this momentous occasion and they were all kneeling by this point. Horace Ensign and Alma Taylor then offered their own prayers, petitioning God for strength and wisdom to fulfill their missionary charge, and for Grant to be inspired in his apostolic opening of Japan for the preaching of the gospel. They continued kneeling in a circle as their leader offered his official dedicatory prayer.[56]

Since the earliest days of Mormonism, LDS leaders and laity have cultivated a unique Christian understanding of the concept and importance of priesthood dedicatory prayers.[57] Tad R. Callister defines dedication as "the act of devoting or consecrating something to the Lord, or 'setting apart' something for a specific purpose in building the kingdom of God. It is a priesthood function performed through an official and formal act of prayer." He further suggests that for Latter-day Saints, these hallowed prayers both "call down the powers of heaven to establish a sacred space or time in the furthering of the desired purpose" and "consecrate the participants, focusing their souls upon the meaning of the dedicated object or act," thereby fusing the secular and the sacred, "and the blessings of God are invoked so that the powers of heaven and earth are joined to bring about works of righteousness."[58]

Joseph Smith himself set the precedent for the dedication of physical objects. He likely drew on the biblical precedent of the dedication of Solomon's temple (1 Kings 8:22–53), when he consecrated a future temple site in Missouri in 1831, the completed Kirtland Temple in 1836 (D&C 109), and portions of the Nauvoo Temple before his martyrdom.[59] Smith also oversaw the consecration of olive oil for the blessing of the sick and afflicted (James 5:14), as well as for use in the anointing ritual in both the Kirtland and Nauvoo temples (D&C 109: 35; 124:39). He further made it clear that lands could be dedicated, by those with proper authority, for "divinely appointed purposes." Keeping his own counsel, Smith sent Apostle Orson Hyde to dedicate the Holy Land for the gathering of the Jews and the construction of a future temple in Jerusalem, a prayer that has been offered a number of times by subsequent apostles, which in turn set precedence for multiple dedications of lands for the preaching of the gospel.[60]

Joseph Smith taught in Kirtland, Ohio, that global evangelization was the special responsibility of the newly constituted Quorum of the Twelve. "They are the Twelve Apostles, who are called to the office of the Traveling High Council, who are to preside over the churches of the Saints, among the Gentiles, where there is a presidency established; and they are to travel and preach among the Gentiles." He continued: "*They are to hold the keys of this ministry, to unlock the door of the Kingdom of heaven unto all nations, and to preach the Gospel to every creature.*"[61] During a dedicatory service of the Kirtland Temple, he reemphasized this special responsibility: "I then called upon the quorums and congregation of Saints to acknowledge the Twelve Apostles, who were present, as Prophets, Seers, Revelators, and *special witnesses to all the nations of the earth, holding the keys of the kingdom, to unlock it, or cause it to be done, among them*, and uphold them by their prayers, which they assented to by rising."[62] This is why President Lorenzo Snow was so anxious for Grant, a member of the Quorum of the Twelve Apostles, to open the Japan Mission in 1901.

Grant's apostolic dedicatory prayer was unlike any Christian prayer previously offered on behalf of the nation of Japan, although it began ordinarily enough. Grant asked the Lord to hear his words, expressed thanks that they had arrived in Japan safely after crossing the Pacific, gratitude that they had testimonies of the gospel and that they were privileged to be asked of the Lord's prophet to go to Japan as "messengers of life and salvation unto a people who had never heard the Gospel." He then asked that their sins might be forgiven. Grant next dedicated the nation of Japan for the preaching of the gospel, the gathering of Israel, and "establishment of righteousness upon the earth." He next rebuked Satan, in the name of

Jesus Christ and by the authority of his priesthood, and his hold over the minds of the Japanese and any efforts to thwart the rise of Mormonism in Japan. He also praised God that the Japanese had been preserved from the "power of the Great and Abominable Church," likely the Catholic Church in early twentieth-century LDS thought, and expressed his opinion that God had blessed the Japanese "with sufficient knowledge to see the shallowness of the man-made Christianity which was sought to be introduced among them." He also prayed that the Lord might soften the hearts of the Japanese as a people so they might accept the message of Mormonism.

Interestingly, Grant also prayed that the Three Nephites, translated beings described in the Book of Mormon, would visit the Mormon elders in Japan and assist them in their missionary labors. Continuing on with his Book of Mormon theme, Grant spoke of the peoples of the Book of Mormon, the Nephites and the Lamanites. Recalling Grant's words, Taylor recorded that the apostle

> spoke of the righteousness of Lehi and of the great faith of Nephi in doing whatsoever the Lord commanded him. Also spoke of those, who because of iniquity, had been cut off from among the Nephites and cursed with a dark skin like unto the Lamanites their brethren, and said we felt that through the lineage of those rebellious Nephites who joined with the Lamanites, that the blood of Lehi and Nephi had been transmitted unto the people of this land [Japanese], many of whom have the features and manners of the AMERICAN INDIANS. Asked the Lord that if this were true, that he would not forget the integrity of his servants Lehi and Nephi and would verify the promises made unto them concerning their descendants in the last days, upon this people, for we felt that they were a worthy nation.

Apostle Grant concluded the ceremony by reading a copy of another dedicatory prayer given sixty years earlier on the other side of the world, by a fellow Mormon apostle. On assignment from the Prophet Joseph Smith, Apostle Orson Hyde had traveled from Nauvoo, Illinois, to Jerusalem to dedicate the Palestine region for the prophesized literal gathering of the Jews. On October 24, 1841, Hyde scrambled up the Mount of Olives and there, overlooking the city of Jerusalem, dedicated the area "for the gathering together of Judah's scattered remnants." Brothers Grant, Kelsch, Ensign, and Taylor concluded the dedication by "expressing the feelings of our hearts and telling of our love for each other and our earnest desires and determination to labor with all the zeal which we possessed for the success of the work of the Lord in this land," according to Taylor. After singing two more hymns the missionaries closed their dedicatory meeting with prayer.[63]

ERRAND TO JAPAN

In the missionaries' minds, the Japan Mission was now officially open for the preaching of Mormonism. During their first few months in Japan, however, the four elders enjoyed little evangelism success. But they became convinced that at least some of the Japanese were related to Native Americans, and thereby descendants of the Book of Mormon peoples. This same phenomenon occurred elsewhere during this period. "With the turn of the twentieth century, however, the varied missionary outreach of the church began to produce evidence of the blood of Israel in other parts of the world, where the gospel was starting to be well received. These include in Latin America, southern and eastern Europe, Russia, Asia, New Zealand, and various Pacific islands," Mauss explains.[64] "These and other LDS mission leaders and missionaries thus became advocates, as it were, for extending literal Israelite identity to a great variety of peoples, some quite exotic by comparison with Anglo-Ephraimites of Utah. In the process, 'believing blood' came to be found almost everywhere the missionaries went."[65]

For example, that first December the LDS elders in Japan became acquainted with Christian author Takahashi Gorō. "He has the face of An American Indian and a head that is perfect in proportion," Alma Taylor noted on one occasion.[66] A few days later the same missionary noted of Takahashi: "He impressed us as being a descendent of the Lamanites for we had never seen a face so much like the faces of the American Indians since our arrival in Japan."[67] The following February Taylor described meeting with several famous Japanese newspapermen: "It was indeed interesting to look into the faces of these gentlemen and study the lines of their features. The editor, whose coal black hair hung in beautiful locks around his shoulders, looked all the world like an Indian brave dressed in citizens clothes."[68] During the early years of the Japan Mission, elders continued to believe that some of the Japanese were of Book of Mormon ancestry and held out hope that they might find the "believing blood" of Israel among the inhabitants of Japan.

Most of their time was spent studying Japanese or in defending, rather than sharing, their faith. Finally, a young Shinto priest by the name of Nakazawa Hajime began to show interest and eventually desired to be baptized. On March 8, 1902, six months after the priesthood dedication of Japan, the four elders hired a small rowboat and oarsman to ferry their Japanese convert and an interpreter out into Tokyo Bay. Of the retained boatman Taylor wrote: "He was not a small Japanese and his coal black hair which was nearly two inches long stood straight up from his forehead that crowned one of the most perfect Indian countenances that we have been privileged to behold in this land, and I felt that we were really in the presence of one in whose veins flowed the blood of the great Lamanitish nation or the blood of that stalwart seed, the Jaredites."[69]

Once they reached the requisite depth for immersion, Grant and Nakazawa lifted themselves over the boat's frame and into the salty water. Clasping Nakazawa's right wrist with his left hand, Grant raised his own right arm to the square and performed the first Latter-day Saint baptism by immersion in Japan. "All was peace, and Apostle Grant's words were spoken slowly and with marked distinctness," one missionary recorded that evening. "Our bosoms swelled with emotion as the words of the prayer fell upon our ears and we could have shouted with thanksgiving when the waters parted and enveloped within their rippling folds one of God's children, who soon came forth from that 'burial with Christ' unto a new life, having taken upon himself the covenant of the everlasting gospel." He continued: "It can only be left to the imagination of others the feelings which passed through my mind and heart, for this was the first time for me to witness the initiation of a convert into the fold in the mission field, and it was with the deepest sentiments of brotherhood that I welcomed this soul into the chosen fold of the Father. . . . We began the day with four members . . . and ended with five."[70]

Over the next twenty-three years, the sons and daughters, as well as grandsons and granddaughters, of Mormon pioneers, would labor to fulfill their church's missionary errand to the Japanese. But conversion scenes like this one would be few and far in between. And many Japanese who were baptized by Mormon elders would later cut their ties with the American religion, including Nakazawa. Despite the earlier trans-Pacific encounters with the Chinese and Japanese, which led to the First Presidency's announcement of the Japan Mission in 1901, these same mappings, meetings, and migrations did not lead church leaders to reformulate their evangelical outlook or practices for an Asian audience. While their church's Euro-American missionary model was well suited for the evangelism of Christians in the North Atlantic world, it was too provincial to missionize in East Asia where the inhabitants spoke Japanese, Chinese, and Korean and where the people practiced Buddhism, Shinto, and Daoism. Believing they could merely impose and translate their religion in non-Christian Asia, the missionaries floundered. The Latter-day Saints anticipated business as usual in the East; they seem to have forgotten the hard lessons learned in China, India, Siam, and Burma during the 1850s by the time of the opening of the Japan Mission in 1901.

5

Mormon Missionary Practices in Japan

*There is a fascination in missionary work among a pagan people that is not known
by missionaries in Christian lands. The Japan mission gives the opportunity
to appreciate the work of St. Paul among the ancient pagans,
and to taste with him the joy and satisfaction that come with
the conversion of souls from the altars of idolatry.*

—ALMA O. TAYLOR, 1910

The eighty-eight Latter-day Saints who evangelized in Japan between 1901 and 1924 saw themselves, like Hosea Stout decades earlier in Hong Kong, as strangers in a strange land.[1] But their sense of estrangement from the East went much deeper than the new sights, sounds, and smells that greeted them in Yokohama harbor. From the day they arrived in Japan until the day they returned to America, these men and women were unsure how to evangelize in a non-Christian, non-Western nation. Neither the LDS collective memory nor the sum of Mormon experiences could provide them with the solution. Fewer than two dozen Latter-day Saints had ever served missions in Asia by the time the Japan Mission was established (all during the 1850s), and none had ever evangelized in Japan.

Mormon general authorities were sympathetic to the plight of the fledgling Japan Mission. The church's ruling body wrote to a mission president in Japan: "We fully appreciate the fact that you have difficulties to encounter in the Japanese Mission that are not met with in any other mission in the Church."[2] On another occasion, First Presidency counselor Anthon H. Lund opined: "The method of preaching the Gospel to a people that do not believe in the true God is, of course, much different from the way we preach it to those who are believers in the Bible, and in Christ as the

Savior of mankind."[3] These quotes demonstrate that the Latter-day Saints were aware of the exceptional challenges to their traditional missionary approach among the non-Christian Japanese. Nevertheless, Mormon missionaries in Japan and leaders in Utah struggled to devise fundamentally new evangelistic practices for East Asia that actually worked. Lund's declaration notwithstanding, the LDS method of preaching the gospel to the Japanese was generally similar to the way Mormons evangelized the Lutherans in Scandinavia or the Catholics in Maryland. Japan remained a strange land to the LDS missionaries during the early twentieth century.

The Japan Mission (1901–1924) coincided with the heyday of the American Protestant foreign missionary enterprise (1880–1930).[4] Continuing a Mormon-Protestant comparison, this chapter contrasts the two groups' evangelistic practices.[5] While the Protestants emphasized spiritual and secular education first, social welfare activities second, and Christian literature third, the Mormons' focus was quite different: they stressed personal contacting first, Christian literature second, spiritual and secular education third, and social welfare activities last. Even when the Mormons tried to modify their traditional evangelistic practices, they ended up mostly entertaining the Japanese or further exoticizing their American church. The two groups' practices echo their philosophical orientations. The Protestants advanced Christ and culture, while the Mormons underscored primarily proselyting activities, according to the Euro-American missionary model. Lastly, I compare the evangelistic results of these two groups. The Mormons, who merely imposed or translated their message, struggled to make headway in Japan over the next twenty-three years; they baptized only 166 Japanese, many of whom had fallen away by the time the Mormons closed the mission in 1924. In contrast, American Protestants were comparatively successful, converting tens of thousands of Japanese to Christianity during the late nineteenth and early twentieth centuries, because their evangelistic approach and practices were more adapted to Japanese society. But it must be noted that Christianity never became numerically significant in Japan during this period.

PROTESTANT EVANGELISTIC PRACTICES IN JAPAN

Historian Cyril H. Powles identifies differing patterns of missionary approach by American Protestants, Roman Catholics, Russian Orthodox, and global Anglicans in Japan during the late nineteenth century. He suggests that Protestants had a "dialectical" approach to Japanese culture. They objected to Japanese tradition and viewed Buddhism and Shinto as pagan and therefore theologically bankrupt. Ancient cults needed to be destroyed. Moreover, they regarded Japanese culture as antiquated, something to be replaced. They wished for the Westernization, or better yet Americanization, of Japanese civilization. In contrast, the Catholics embraced a "dualistic" approach to Japanese culture. During the nineteenth century, all of the Roman Catholic missionaries stationed in Japan hailed from France, and they soon outnumbered the Protestants. Catholic missionaries believed that the church and Japanese culture could coexist; although the latter was inferior, the two were not in opposition. The Orthodox Church's "absorption into culture" approach to Japanese culture is Powles's third categorization. The Orthodox missionaries supported native cultures and expanded into new areas by absorbing into local cultures rather than coming out in opposition. As a result, the Orthodox missionaries evangelized in local languages and sought to become part of Japanese culture. Finally, Powles argues that Anglicanism had an "affirmation of variety" approach to Japanese culture. They upheld traditional institutions, while at the same time maintaining their own identity. They did not involve themselves in local politics and were careful to let the Japanese be Japanese.[6] Not surprisingly, their evangelistic practices reflected these varied worldviews. A comparison of American Protestant and Mormon evangelistic practices among the Japanese helps scholars understand why the two groups had such different missionary results.

Spiritual and Secular Education

Education was the most emphasized Protestant evangelistic practice in Japan. "The missionaries sought to induce a particular type of Christian experience, obtain assent to a certain theological statement, stimulate the growth of certain attitudes and behavior, and organize the believers into churches that within a minimum length of time would become self-supporting," historian Winburn T. Thomas explains, and schools seemed the most effective way to achieve these aims.[7] Protestant missionaries focused their Christian education efforts on the youth of Japan, yet they also offered primary and kindergarten classes in some areas. Although many students were initially interested in learning English, a good number soon demonstrated curiosity about Christianity, as the missionaries anticipated. Mission schools spread throughout all of the treaty ports and eventually to the Japanese countryside. Presbyterian, Episcopalian, Methodist, and other Protestant missionary organizations subsidized the expensive Japanese schools, believing that education would help them achieve their missionary objectives. By 1883 there were nine boys' mission schools and fifteen girls' mission schools. A number of well respected Protestant high schools and institutions of higher learning, including Dōshisha University and Aoyama Gakuin, were established in later years. The missionaries offered a combination of secular and spiritual learning to their Japanese students. Schooling led to some Japanese entering the ministry and helping to grow the native church. Even those students who did not embrace Christianity entered Japanese society with high regard for Protestant ideals and education.[8]

In addition to these traditional schools, Protestant missionaries also operated Sunday schools in Japan. These classes were usually run by local churches and drew good crowds. Unlike the more formal schools that taught the sacred alongside the secular, Sunday schools were primarily religious learning opportunities involving scripture, hymns, and lessons. Other missionaries held Bible study groups. Some even taught outside of Christian schools, at public and private Japanese schools and universities. A few Protestant teachers, like agriculturalist William S. Clark in Sapporo, became well-known educators in Japan. Outside of the classroom they helped establish local churches and Christian programs. On occasion, some Protestants collaborated with local Japanese governments to set up schools. However, when Christianity fell out of vogue in the 1890s, these types of schools came under anti-Christian attack. "Schools then were of primary importance in the policies and programs of the mission agencies and churches," Thomas suggests. "The history of Protestantism in Japan would have read quite differently but for the universal desire for knowledge on the one hand, and on the other the willingness and the competency of the missionaries to avail themselves of the opportunity which Japan's zeal for education afforded."[9]

Social Welfare Activities

It would not be until the beginning of the twentieth century that social welfare activities became a hallmark of Protestant evangelism in Japan. In time, these activities would feature more prominently than even Protestant educational efforts. Unlike many Chinese and other Asians who looked to Western missionaries for medical care and training, the Japanese were early adaptors of Western medicine and the most technologically advanced people of the Asia-Pacific world. Moreover, the Protestants in Japan were trying to establish native churches that fundraised internally. Paying for expensive medical missions from America was not in line with these objectives. Nevertheless, some Christian physicians opened up the way for educators and evangelists when Westerners were still viewed with suspicion. Missionaries like J. C. Hepburn, John C. Berry, Arthur H. Adams, and Henry Faulds all practiced medicine in Japan for a time. An interdenominational Protestant group established the Akasaka Hospital in 1886. Representatives from the American Board of Commissioners for Foreign Missions, the American Episcopal mission, and the United Presbyterian Church all offered healthcare at one point. By the end of the nineteenth century, with Japan producing plenty of its own German-trained physicians, the need for American Protestant doctors was negligible.[10]

This is not to say, however, that missionaries in Japan eschewed other social welfare activities during the early years among the Japanese. One Protestant group established the Nurse's Training School in Kyoto, which later became part of Dōshisha. Some sought to help Japanese orphans. The Okayama Orphanage was an outgrowth of this social reform. Teaching classes and holding worship services in prisons became another expression of social welfare, especially by Japanese converts. A number of prisoners eventually converted to Christianity as a result. In time, American Protestants tried to "elevate" Japanese morals by fighting against prostitution, the practice of concubinage, and alcohol and tobacco abuse. Protestants formed temperance societies and women's Christian groups to combat these social ills. By the late nineteenth century, Protestant missionaries "were developing a conscience and sense of obligation" in Japan—at least about the need for the Japanese to adopt Christian mores and values.[11]

Christian Literature

In addition to educational and social welfare activities, Protestant missionaries also distributed several types of Christian literature to the Japanese as part of their evangelistic activities. A Japanese translation of the Bible was of primary importance to scripture-centric Protestants. J. C. Hepburn, the author of a path-breaking Japanese-English dictionary, led the charge by initiating an interdenominational translation effort and doing much of the translation work himself. The resulting Permanent Translation Committee shouldered the responsibility of translating both the Old and New Testaments. The Japanese New Testament was published in 1880, while the Old Testament was not published until 1888. The missionaries were assisted by a number of Japanese scholars. In subsequent years, Bible societies and individual missionaries offered their own colloquial translations of the New Testament.[12]

Protestants also produced a plethora of tracts, a second type of Christian literature. Some of the earliest tracts were translations of existing English- and Chinese-language documents, while others were written specifically for the Japanese, such as *Sanyōbun* (Three Essential Documents) and *Kami no ōinaru ai* (The Great Love of God). Missionaries, including James Hepburn, J. D. Davis, and others produced tracts in Japanese on nearly every Christian subject. Missionaries also authored or translated hundreds of devotional books for Japanese consumption. In time, Japanese converts began writing their own religious literature. Mission periodicals were a fourth category of Christian reading material missionaries used to evangelize. A number of Protestant denominations published their own magazines, including *Shichinichi zappō* (Weekly Miscellany) and *Fukuin shimpō* (Gospel News). Over three dozen such publications were being distributed by 1894. Japanese converts were especially involved in these efforts. English-language materials form the fifth category of literature used to evangelize in Japan. Many of the early Japanese Christians were learned men and women who were interested in studying all things Western, including the English language. Missionaries were able to engage the curious as well as their converts through books written in English. The final type of evangelistic literature was the hymnal. Missionaries used hymns in their worship services but with uneven results. "The thirst of the Japanese people for knowledge, and their ability to read, facilitated the presentation of the Christian message through the written word," Thomas summarizes.[13]

The dialectical American Protestants focused their evangelism energies on those activities congruent with their approach to Japanese culture. Seeking to advance both Christ and Western culture, they offered spiritual and secular education to eager Japanese students. American Protestants sought to uplift Japanese society by aiding orphans and prisoners, as well as by leading the temperance charge against alcohol and tobacco consumption. Protestant missionaries also made Christian literature, including translations of the Old and New Testaments, easily accessible to the Japanese. As Table 5.1 demonstrates, the Protestant and Mormon emphases on leading evangelistic practices in Japan were quite different, although there was some obvious overlap, such as Christian literature. While the Protestants focused on education and welfare efforts, the Mormons emphasized personal witnessing and the distribution of tracts and other printed materials, as we shall see.

TABLE 5.1. Comparison of American Protestant and Mormon Evangelistic Practices in Japan in Descending Order of Emphasis

AMERICAN PROTESTANTS: CHRIST AND CULTURE	MORMONS: CHRIST, NOT CULTURE
Spiritual and secular education	Personal contacting
Social welfare activities	Christian literature
Christian literature	Spiritual and secular education
	Social welfare activities

MORMON EVANGELISTIC PRACTICES IN JAPAN

The Latter-day Saints shared some of the evangelistic beliefs and practices of their Christian contemporaries in Japan, while simultaneously maintaining their own missionary approach. I suggest that the Mormons had an ambivalent approach to their church's only Asian mission field, based on my reading of journals, letters, and mission records. The Euro-American LDS leaders, missionaries, and members viewed Japan as did most other Westerners: as an exotic locale, different from all they had experienced. When interviewed by a reporter about his assignment to open the Japan Mission, Elder Heber J. Grant admitted that it had "a good deal of the 'unknown quality' about it."[14] With respect to Japanese culture, the Mormons were most like the Anglicans, who sought to preserve their own identity while encouraging the Japanese to do as they pleased, as long as it did not conflict with specific moral practices, such as drinking alcohol or sexual immorality. Although the Latter-day Saints viewed Japanese society as morally decayed, they did not get involved with social programs that sought to uplift Japanese life, as the Protestants did. The Mormons did not try to be absorbed into Japanese culture like the Orthodox, nor were they like the Protestants, who found little value in Japanese culture and traditions. Still, the Mormons were concerned with Buddhist and Shinto religious practices, which they deemed distracting to potential converts unable to let go of old ways. When it came to Japanese politics and government, the Mormons were most similar to the Russian Orthodox: they did not get involved. Both religions had no problem rendering to Caesar what was Caesar's, including political control in Japan.

As one would expect, each Christian tradition's missionary practices were a reflection of how its representatives viewed the Japanese culturally, spiritually, and politically. The Roman Catholic, Russian Orthodox, Anglican,

Protestant, and, in time, Mormon missionaries offered what they believed the Japanese needed most. While the American Protestants successfully evangelized the Japanese by providing spiritual and secular education, engaging in social welfare activities, and producing Christian literature—a Christ and culture approach—the Mormons proceeded in Japan as they always had in the Atlantic world through a Christ, *not* culture approach: the evangelistic practices of the Euro-American missionary model.

Personal Contacting

In contrast to American Protestants, the Mormons emphasized personal contacting over all other evangelistic practices in Japan. They were there to preach what they believed to be the restoration of primitive Christianity. As one reads the diaries, letters, and reports of the missionaries who labored among the Japanese, it becomes clear that tracting and missionary work were nearly synonymous. They also held street meetings, where they were able to engage passersby in conversation. The Mormons also promoted magic lantern lectures, leveraged their status as Americans in a variety of contacting situations, and engaged in sporting activities that brought them into proximity with other foreign Christian organizations. But when the missionaries tried to augment their traditional personal contacting practices, they entertained rather than converted the Japanese.

Tracting

The missionaries in Japan began evangelizing the Japanese by tracting Tokyo neighborhoods. Although the missionaries usually boarded in pairs for economic reasons, they typically spent long days by themselves, canvassing neighborhoods and talking to people on the streets. The missionaries viewed tracting as an art form to be mastered. A. Ray Olpin, laboring in the Osaka conference, wrote a fascinating article describing the nuances of tracting in Asia. "When entering a Japanese home, the formalities reach their height," he explained to his American audience. "Since the object in tracting is to leave a favorable impression with the people, so that they will investigate the truths contained in the free pamphlet, the Latter-day Saint missionary must be exceedingly careful, not only in his actions but in his talk, making himself as insignificant as possible, without destroying his prestige." Olpin then gave readers "a faint idea of the artistic part" of tracting in Japan.[15]

Newly arrived missionaries in Japan were often stressed by their early tracting opportunities. John L. Chadwick related one of his initial can-vassing experiences. "We decided to go out tracting in the afternoon, so after dinner we each took forty tracts and started out with a queer feeling down to our shoes. I got through with the first house all right, but I didn't have such good luck the next time for I tackled an old man and he scart [sic] what little Japanese I did know out of me, but after that I got along alright."[16] Four months later, tracting remained a nerve-wracking experi-ence for him. Working by himself, Chadwick had to "face the music alone" and get "the life scart [sic] out of me" again. He recalled that it took "all the courage I had left to go in" to a Japanese home to discuss his tracts. But "[a]fter going to the first few houses I got bold and wasn't afraid to go in any of the houses," he wrote with newfound pride.[17]

Seasoned Mormon missionaries had a variety of experiences while going door-to-door in Japanese neighborhoods. Although the surviving evidence does not allow firm conclusions about reception, it seems that for the most part the Japanese expressed indifference to their message. On occasion, however, the residents were less neutral. For example, Sanford W. Hedges described the following negative experiences to his friends in America. "We found people at first willing to listen to us and to accept our tracts, but in a few moments this kind feeling changed into bitter con-tempt for us. People then refused to accept our tracts, and would not give ear to one single word. At one house, the door was slammed so quickly in my face that I did not know what struck me. I did indeed feel very queer." Although Hedges also shared some positive experiences tracting in the same neighborhood, he lamented the indifference, and the occasional animosity, of the people toward his message. "Doors close on us, people refuse to listen to us, and slander from passersby has been our lot of late. Were it not for the knowledge I have of the message of life and salvation that I bear, I would want to come home immediately."[18]

The elders and sisters were sometimes annoyed by the Japanese response to their efforts. "While out tracting, I met a man who had been to America, Germany, England & other places studying. Never in my life have I seen a person so conceited as he. He would ask me a question and then before I could get through with the answer he would be off on some-thing else," one elder seethed. "I left feeling that I had just had a conflict with an arrogant fool whose own experiences had puffed him up so high that he referred to the ordinary educated Japanese & Americans & people of all countries as ordinary chaps not to be respected for their attainments by people like himself who have been abroad & graduated from the great schools of the world."[19] But these infrequent disturbing experiences were moderated by the daily monotony of going door to door, engaging hardly a soul in meaningful conversation.

Tracting in Japan tested the faith and patience of the missionaries. Most Japanese would politely accept the free LDS literature but showed little interest in engaging in religious discussion. While the elders and sisters distributed hundreds of thousands of tracts to Japanese residents, they saw little return on their investment of time and effort. Even when they were invited into homes while tracting, the younger missionaries struggled to respond to questions or know what to say in Japanese. Sometimes other distractions thwarted productive missionary discussions. One elder recorded in his journal that after spending one afternoon tracting he was finally invited into one of the homes. "I was invited in and had a nice talk, although I didn't feel at ease as I had a large hole in my sock and tried to keep it covered up."[20]

There were also logistical challenges to tracting. The missionaries were assigned to specific geographical areas, referred to as conferences, with prearranged housing in major cities. The elders and sisters were quite efficient in canvassing large neighborhoods, but only because they rarely were able to engage residents in meaningful gospel conversations. In other words, they covered a lot of ground but had very little success. Between 1901 and 1924, missionaries laboring in the Tokyo conference tracted the following cities, towns, and villages: Tokyo, Yokohama, Asagaya, Chiba, Hōjō, Funakata, Nago, Nagano, Naoyetsu, Nakano, Chikura, Sendai, Chōshi, Shizuoka, Okawa, Bōshu, Miyakamura, Mito, and Morioka; between 1906 and 1924, missionaries in the Sapporo conference tracted Sapporo, Toyohira, Teine, Asahikawa, Yochōmachi, Iwanai, Muroran, and Otaru; between 1911 and 1924 missionaries in the Osaka conference tracted Osaka, Tsuruhashi, Ikeda, and Onomachi; and between 1907 and 1922 missionaries in the Kōfu conference tracted Kōfu and Iwasa.[21]

Although it seems obvious that the missionaries should have moved on to new locations, their mobility was actually limited as they could ill-afford to abandon hard-won converts in established conferences, like Tokyo, Sapporo, Kōfu, and Osaka, for new fields of labor. Frequent relocation involved the cost of moving to a new residence, uprooting all friendly connections, and forsaking obligations such as English conversation classes. Even if they were to visit neighboring communities apart from their base of operations, they would be limited in how they could nurture and retain new converts, a process that proved difficult even when physical proximity was available. As a result, missionaries continued to canvass many of the tired areas with the same disappointing results.

It was difficult for the missionaries to keep motivated in the face of Japanese indifference, especially when they found themselves in neighborhoods that had already been tracted out. By 1907 the Mormons viewed even Tokyo, Japan's most populous city, as overtracted. "The elders have labored hard and have been over the available parts of the city with gospel tracts and the resident parts they have visited two or three and sometimes four times, but there has been practically no response from the people and they count only one who, at present, seems to be investigating the gospel with the proper spirit," one mission president lamented.[22] They faced the same problem to a greater degree in less populated areas. James A. Miller, president of the Sapporo conference, bemoaned his evangelism prospects in Hokkaidō's largest city: "This city has been tracted five times since the conference was organized a little over five years ago. We are now tracting it for the sixth time."[23] Alma O. Taylor likewise recorded his disappointment with the residents of Chiba. "After breakfast went into the Sangawa district to do some tracting but found in making my second calls that the people had simply accepted my first tract but not even looked at it in a majority of cases. At two or three places I saw the tracts I distributed lying on the dirt pile or in the chicken yard. Rather encouraging!"[24] Within a few months he had worn out what little welcome he might have had: he had canvassed every home in the area three times.[25] He soon moved back to Tokyo.

During the sweltering summer months (in Honshū) and the freezing winter months (in Hokkaidō), the missionaries were hard-pressed to sustain their unproductive tracting efforts. In June 1904, for example, the heat became so oppressive that the missionaries in Tokyo gathered to discuss the prudence of summer tracting, especially when they felt they could use the time more effectively translating LDS works into Japanese. One missionary recorded that "a council was called to consider the advisability of suspending regular missionary work, that is, visiting from house to house and seeking conversations with the people, during the hot months and devote ourselves exclusively to the translation of the Book of Mormon and other literature necessary to the future activity of this mission."[26] In subsequent years, however, mission leaders urged their charges to continue canvassing local neighborhoods in hope of finding willing listeners. After presiding over a mission conference, one mission president wrote in his journal: "I sought to impress upon the minds of the elders the necessity to work with great zeal, for the time for the proclamation of the gospel is growing short. The signs of the Second Coming are multiplying and the nations must have an opportunity to accept or reject the gospel."[27] When he visited the mission in 1921, even Apostle

David O. McKay encouraged the missionaries to tract several hours each day until a more effective practice was discovered.[28] Despite its status as the quintessential LDS evangelistic practice, tracting was largely unproductive in Japan.[29] Few baptisms resulted from thousands of manpower hours of canvassing neighborhoods.

Street Meetings

Street meetings were another method by which the elders and sisters spread their message in Japan. Although missionaries in North America and Western Europe had held street meetings since the earliest days of Mormonism, their subsequent counterparts in Japan were slow to adopt the practice. Nevertheless, it is clear that a handful of elders were familiar with this practice. For example, when the original quartet passed through Oregon en route to Japan in 1901, they met other LDS missionaries who invited them to attend a street meeting in downtown Portland. Singing hymns and preaching on a street corner was a "new and novel experience" for Apostle Heber J. Grant and Alma O. Taylor.[30] In contrast, Horace S. Ensign and Louis A. Kelsch had previously served missions in the United States where they learned how to hold open-air preaching gatherings. Fear, not ignorance, seems to have been the barrier to embracing the practice. It was one thing to go door to door handing out tracts; it was quite another to stand on a street corner with limited Japanese and try to entertain a local crowd.

One of the earliest references to street meetings in Japan is found in John L. Chadwick's journal, when he noted in August 1905 that Alma O. Taylor, president of the mission, had broached the idea of holding street meetings in Iwanai "but we dont [sic] care to," he confided.[31] Chadwick was likely terrified at the prospect of preaching on street corners, as he had been in Japan less than a year and could not yet speak Japanese with confidence. The missionaries held the first of countless street meetings in Japan two years later, in October 1907. During a visit to Sapporo, Taylor tried to figure out a more effective way to advertise their Sunday services. "Feeling that our preaching meetings should be better attended I decided to announce them on the public highways of the city. Accordingly I took Elders Seely, Roskelley, Cutler and Marriott and went out on the streets," he related. "We sang to mandolin accompanyment [sic] until a large crowd gathered and then announced our meetings. We did this on eight prominent corners. This is the first time I have participated in any kind of a street demonstration in Japan. I naturally felt rather shaky at first but before [we] were through I became attached to the experience."[32] That November Taylor held another street meeting of sorts in front of the Yochōmachi preaching station. "There was quite a number of people came out to hear but they didn't seem to have courage to come inside. There were only ten people inside but twice the number outside so it was sort of a street meeting with the preacher on the inside."[33]

Street meetings remained a novelty in Japan for years. In 1910, Moroni S. Marriott bucked convention and traveled for several weeks around Hokkaidō holding street meetings, relying on the financial donations of others. His mission president, Elbert D. Thomas, rightly noted that Marriott had "just completed a missionary journey which is indeed unique and different from the average" but incorrectly suggested that he was the first missionary to preach the gospel to the Ainu, the aborigines of northern Japan.[34] Moreover, Marriott falsely assumed he was the first missionary to hold a street meeting among the Japanese. "Tonight I decided to try a street meeting.... The people came together in a hurry," Marriott wrote to Thomas. "I told them about the Bible and God. It has been a new experience for me."[35] Although Marriott had in fact held the first street meeting for Ainus, he was neither the first to evangelize them nor was he the first to hold a street meeting in Japan: that designation goes to Taylor. Marriott was likely confused because LDS street meetings were still rare at this point—a fact that would soon change.

During the second decade of the mission (1911–1921), especially during the presidential tenure of Joseph H. Stimpson, street meetings became one of the Japan Mission's most popular ways to evangelize. "One feature of the work here now is the street meeting work that is being carried on vigorously. It would sure be an inspiration to any of the people of Zion to attend one of these meetings," Stimpson wrote to Apostle David O. McKay. "Many people are attracted by the sight of a foreigner standing on the street and speaking in the native tongue. So we never lack a crowd, and though some only stand for a short time, some listen through the whole meeting and buy our books after the meeting is over. We never have less than 200 or 300 present."[36] His missionaries likewise extolled the practice of street meetings. During the spring and summer of 1919, missionaries in the Sapporo conference "held a series of fourteen open air meetings in one of the busiest thoroughfares of the city, the district of the night shops and pleasure houses," according to Pearl M. Lee. "They have been blessed with success, having had an attendance of from fifteen attentive listeners to two hundred at a time. The crowd has been very respectful, sometimes almost reverently so, and at times particularly stable for such meetings, many standing quietly through the whole service. This has provided a means of distributing a number of Church works." Still she admitted that it was "a peculiar experience to preach to an alien company in an alien tongue, on the streets of a foreign city."[37] "Street meetings are proving to be a most efficient method of arousing interest and spreading the gospel," A. Ray Olpin exclaimed in 1920.[38] The Japanese were more willing to accept tracts on the street than at their homes: this way they did not have to let outsiders into private spaces.[39]

Magic Lantern Lectures

Mormon elders and sisters also used technology—magic lanterns—to grab the attention of the Japanese. The magic lantern, or rudimentary slide projector, was invented in the seventeenth century by Athanasius Kircher, a German priest who projected graphic images of the Devil on a screen to alarm audiences. His device was the forerunner to the motion picture projector.[40] By the end of the nineteenth century, Mormon missionaries in the Pacific world were evangelizing by way of magic lanterns. For example, Ezra F. Richards, president of the New Zealand Mission, entertained and taught the local Maoris and white settlers with magic lantern slides of church history images.[41] Likewise, mission president Edward J. Wood used the avant-garde projector in Samoa to dispel the notion that Latter-day Saints in Utah "lived as semibarbarians outside the bounds of civilization." Convert baptisms swelled as Samoan chiefs invited Wood and his lantern show to their villages.[42] And missionaries in Australia pooled their money to purchase a magic lantern, under the encouragement of their mission president, Fred E. Barker.[43]

It is unclear when LDS missionaries in Japan began using similar picture shows, but by 1910 they were employing them often. That year mission president Elbert D. Thomas disclosed that Moroni S. Marriott had traveled throughout Hokkaidō. "He has taken with him a magic lantern, with a full set of life of Christ pictures, pictures of the Prophet Joseph Smith, and some of other Church leaders, temples and scenes from Utah, and hundreds of tracts and books."[44] Thomas then related that Marriott had success with his magic lantern. In one Ainu village about one hundred adults and a number of children gathered to watch the lantern pictures and then visited for two hours about religion.[45] Edwin J. Allen Jr. also described how he and his companions in Hokkaidō showed moving picture exhibitions on gospel themes such as the life of Christ. One missionary provided background organ music; another operated the magic lantern projection machine; a third lectured on the images being presented to the audience. They held these presentations in the evenings when it was dark so the machine would project a good picture.[46]

These picture exhibitions were initially well attended but audience members often fell asleep in the darkness. There were other drawbacks to the magic lantern lectures besides a snoring audience. John L. Chadwick described an accident that occurred when two Japanese boys tried to operate the lantern projector. "They had carvite to make a light with and having never used it before the[y] put to[o] much in and we had quite an exciting time when the[y] light the gas. It burnt one boys face and it made us fly around for a while."[47] While it is clear that magic lanterns were used for a time in the Japan Mission, the transportation, care, and operation of the projectors seem to have limited their use. Finally, more impressive secular picture shows were becoming available throughout Japan during this time. While the more technologically primitive Ainus (and Pacific Islanders) were still impressed by the magic lanterns, the more technologically advanced Japanese were increasingly unmoved.

Foreigner Status

The American missionaries also leveraged their status as foreigners to their missionizing advantage. While they were largely ignored as religious representatives, they were embraced as western curiosities. The missionaries were amused by the interest the Japanese took in them as specimens of the West. John L. Chadwick recorded in his journal a number of times that people would stare at them. "The people stand and stare at us as we go along the road, and bro. Seely is a wonder to them."[48] On another occasion Chadwick wrote: "The people stand and gaze at us as we pass along the road we seem to cause quite a bit of interest." He and his companions were sometimes the first Caucasians some Japanese had ever seen.[49] As a result, the Mormons were often invited to provide musical entertainment at nonreligious gatherings. On other occasions they were asked to present secular lectures. But they tried to stay on message, unbeknownst to their hosts, as we shall see below.

In the spring of 1903, for instance, the missionaries were invited to the opening of a local girl's school. While flattered, the missionaries realized that it was Horace S. Ensign's renowned singing voice, not their gospel message, which garnered the summons. When they arrived they were treated as honored guests. "We found about one hundred girls prettily grouped on a sidehill awaiting our arrival, and what do you think they were waiting for? They were waiting to have us in a picture that was about to be taken of them," Sanford W. Hedges gushed. Ensign, a former standout of the Mormon Tabernacle Choir, opened the day's festivities by performing a classic LDS hymn, "O Ye Mountains High." Substituting singing for preaching, he and the other Latter-day Saints shared the message of Mormonism in English song, a detail likely lost on the non-English-speaking Japanese audience.[50] Hedges reported that as soon as Ensign began, "loud applause rang forth from the audience; when he came to the chorus, we all joined in, and that took the house by storm." The missionaries chalked up the secular outing as evangelism success.[51] On this and many other occasions, music offered the Latter-day Saints access to heretofore inaccessible audiences, but with unclear results.

The American Mormons also were willing to accept the invitations of Japanese friends to lecture on nonreligious themes. Perhaps they figured that any exposure was good exposure. But the Japanese seemed to offer the invitations not because of the Mormons' religious beliefs but because of their foreigner status. They wanted to be entertained, not evangelized. J. Ray Stoddard was living in Kōfu and serving as conference president when he and his companions were requested to speak at a neighboring village's Young Men's Association. "Having been invited to lecture," he explained, "we gladly accepted." They knew, however, that religion was off-limits. According to Stoddard they "were informed that no church doctrine of any kind would be allowed, as the building in which the meeting was to be held, was a government school building, and the school laws were to that effect." In response, the elders determined to lecture on proper health practices, a natural segue into discussing the LDS health code known as the Word of Wisdom. They arrived in Asakami as promised. "Here we were greeted, entertained and fed by the highest officials of the place. A few minutes later we found ourselves on reserved seats before an audience of old, middle aged and young, numbering seven hundred and fifty souls," Stoddard wrote. During the program Bryan L. Wright spoke on "The Physical Man," Joseph S. Pyne discoursed on "The Word of Wisdom," and Stoddard concluded with "The Mental Man." After the meeting, Stoddard reflected on their participation, pleased that they had shared their church's health code, albeit indirectly. "I am thankful to be a member and an ambassador of a Church whose doctrines include all goodness and all truth. It is a religion for every occasion, and although at times we may not be allowed the privilege of applying the name, yet it is the truth of the gospel of Christ."[52]

Sporting Activities

Mormon missionaries also competed in sports as groups, often as a way of interacting with other foreigners, in an attempt to improve their church's image and relations with the international community in Japan.[53] In early 1912, Elbert D. Thomas explained to *Improvement Era* readers his mission's involvement in a local baseball league. Realizing that his letter and enclosed pictures of missionaries dressed as baseball players might raise eyebrows back home, he admitted that Latter-day Saints playing for the Tokyo-America Baseball Team was "a phase of missionary experience that is a little out of the ordinary." He made it clear, however, that they only practiced or played games on Saturdays and generally competed against Japanese university or club teams and against their rival, the Yokohama-American Baseball Team.[54]

Moreover, their teammates were Christians from other denominations. "The team is also interesting from another standpoint. For instance, in a late line-up there were a Baptist, an Episcopalian, a Presbyterian, a Quaker, a Methodist,. and a 'Mormon' missionary; a United States army officer, an attaché of the American embassy, a secretary of the American embassy, and an American electrical engineer. All are the best of fellows." Thomas also mailed a number of charming photographs of the missionaries suited up in baseball attire. One showed H. Grant Ivins (catcher and elected captain for 1912) and the Reverend E. C. Lloyd (missionary teacher of the American Episcopal Church, pitcher and captain for 1911). Other pictures featured Jay C. Jensen (outfielder and first base), James A. Miller (first base and outfielder), Elbert D. Thomas (infielder), and Robert H. Barton (pitcher).[55] Playing on such a team gave his missionaries and the church positive exposure to the foreigner community, especially among other expatriate Christian opinion makers. But it did nothing for their evangelism efforts of the Japanese, other than reinforce the Mormons' foreignness.

To come to the point, the various Mormon personal contacting practices were largely ineffective in Japan. While missionaries tracted with remarkable success in the North Atlantic world, they struggled in Japan as the Japanese were hesitant to invite strangers into their homes, especially Christian foreigners who often struggled with the language. Moreover, the Mormons exhausted neighborhoods due to their sedentary organizational structure: they were practically anchored to specific geographic regions like Tokyo, Osaka, Sapporo, and Kōfu, where they had established conferences and rented apartments. Street meetings overcame some of the problems associated with tracting. The elders and sisters distributed greater amounts of literature to Japanese pedestrians on street corners because the stakes were so much lower: the Japanese could sample the literature without any commitment. Nevertheless, it was difficult for the Mormons to follow up with the Japanese who accepted the literature and then walked away. The missionaries had little luck contacting passersby once they made the initial exchange. What worked so well for the Mormons in New England and Scandinavia failed in Japan.

Struggling to innovate, the staff of the Japan Mission tried to leverage the technology of magic lantern lectures, which were being used in other Pacific missions. For a time, the missionaries packed along their religious slideshows in hopes of garnering interest in Mormonism. But the Japanese were not nearly as impressed with these multimedia presentations as were the Pacific Islanders. Those who attended often fell asleep in the darkness or left merely entertained, not spiritually edified. The missionaries' attempts to leverage their status as Americans also had negligible results. Although they gained access to Japanese groups and events through their singing ability or English oratory skills, gospel teaching opportunities rarely resulted. Japanese patrons seemed to view Mormon missionaries as entertaining foreigners, not as religious representatives. Finally, playing on baseball teams did help improve relations between the Mormons and other American Christians. Yet I have found no evidence of any conversions that resulted from these and other sporting activities. Such participation merely highlighted the Latter-day Saints' exoticness. Even when the Mormons did flex the Euro-American missionary model's traditional personal contacting practices, the results were less than satisfactory. They entertained the Japanese, rather than engaging them in their spiritual message.

Christian Literature

The Latter-day Saints' second (and related) area of emphasis was on the production and dissemination of Christian literature. Unlike the Protestants who considered only the Bible to be scripture, the Mormons had three additional books of scripture that could be translated into Japanese. They also authored and translated dozens of tracts tailored to the Japanese, in perhaps the mission's strongest attempt to move beyond merely imposing their message in Japan. In addition, the missionaries made available in Japanese a variety of popular LDS devotional books. Although the Japan Mission never had its own periodical, the elders and sisters distributed the church's *Improvement Era* magazine to investigators and members who could read English. The missionaries also translated several dozen LDS hymns for the Japanese in a hymnal that went through several editions. The Latter-day Saints decided to translate their message rather than waiting for it to be translated by others.[56] On the other hand, the LDS literature failed to engage the Japanese on a meaningful level as it betrayed the Mormon's lack of understanding of Japanese culture and religion, never reaching the level of inculturation.

Scripture

When the Japan Mission opened in 1901, the LDS scriptural cannon consisted of four major volumes: the Bible (both the Old and the New Testaments), the Book of Mormon, the Doctrine and Covenants, and the Pearl of Great Price, known together as the "standard works."[57] Mormon missionaries benefited from the biblical translation work of earlier Christian missionaries, especially James C. Hepburn and others, who had translated the Old and New Testaments into Japanese.[58] The Latter-day Saints determined to likewise translate the Book of Mormon into Japanese. Missionaries, with the help of local members, had already translated the unique Mormon scripture into Danish (1851), German (1852), French (1852), Italian (1852), Welsh (1852), Hawaiian (1855), Swedish (1878), Spanish (1886), Maori (1889), Dutch (1890), Samoan (1903), Tahitian (1904), and Turkish (1906), before the Japanese version was available.[59] Alma O. Taylor and Fredrick A. Caine, together with several church members and Japanese literary scholars, completed the translation that was published in 1909.[60]

The missionaries used the Japanese Book of Mormon regularly in their evangelism. But as Terryl Givens suggests, LDS representatives advocated the additional book of scripture as a sign that the heavens were open, rather than expounding its contents to nonmembers.[61] This held true in evangelizing in Japan. Mission president Joseph H. Stimpson emphasized the utility of the scriptural text in the conversion process of the Japanese during a mission conference in 1920. "Accumulations of evidence, external and internal, proving the divinity of the book were brought forth, and the best methods of getting the sacred volume more generally among the people was discussed," one elder noted. "The value of this Nephite scripture as an instrument in effective missionary work is recognized by all the missionaries and Saints."[62] Stimpson's successor, Lloyd D. Ivie, likewise encouraged the missionaries to feature the Book of Mormon more prominently in their evangelism during a mission conference. "All went away determined to get the work of the Lord before the people, and we feel that it is through the Book of Mormon and its inspired teachings that the long sought-for peace is going to come to this war-tired world," Aldo Stephens related. "A slogan was adopted at the conference, in which Saints and missionaries alike showed interest. It referred to the placing of the Book of Mormon before the people during the coming year, and it was resolved to place 500 copies in the homes of the people."[63]

Once the Book of Mormon was available in Japanese, the mission leadership turned its attention to a third book of LDS scripture: the Doctrine and Covenants. Latter-day Saints view this book as a collection of revelatory statements and declarations made by Joseph Smith and his prophetic successors. Mission president Elbert D. Thomas assigned Japanese church member Shirai Jōji the translation project in April 1910. He eventually finished the entire Japanese translation and turned it over to the mission leadership. In 1921 Mission president Lloyd D. Ivie wrote the First Presidency asking for permission to have it published, but they "did not feel the time was ripe" for an additional book of scripture for the Japanese. His successor, Hilton A. Robertson, took Shirai's scriptural translation back to America when the mission was temporarily closed in the summer of 1924 and deposited it with the First Presidency in Salt Lake City, where it was subsequently lost. The Doctrine and Covenants would be retranslated and finally published in Japanese after World War II.[64]

Mormonism's fourth standard work is the Pearl of Great Price. In 1851, Franklin D. Richards, president of the British Mission, published this collection of scripture and literature. Decades later Apostle Orson Pratt helped publish the first American edition of the book, which was canonized by Latter-day Saints in 1880. It consisted of selections from the book of Moses, the book of Abraham, Joseph Smith–Matthew, Joseph Smith–History, and the Articles of Faith. Unlike the Book of Mormon and Doctrine and Covenants, the Pearl of Great Price was not completely translated until after World War II when Satō Tatsui was assigned the project and completed it, along with his new translations of the Book of Mormon and the Doctrine and Covenants, in 1957.[65]

Missionary Tracts

After months of studying the Japanese language, Heber J. Grant and his missionaries felt it was time to start writing tracts in preparation for active missionary work.[66] Grant wrote the mission's first tract in 1903, *An announcement concerning the Church of Jesus Christ of Latter-day Saints*, for the mission's first preaching meeting.[67] Later that year he published a second tract, *Matsu Jitsu Seito Iesu Kirisuto Kyōkai ni kansuru kinkyū rinkoku* (The Church of Jesus Christ of Latter-day Saints: An Urgent Message).[68] Grant's youngest companion, Alma O. Taylor, was the mission's most prolific author. He wrote over half a dozen tracts for the mission, along with translating the Book of Mormon. His first attempt resulted in the tract *Thou Shalt Have No Other Gods before Me*, but the other missionaries and their Japanese friends suggested it was too negative toward native Japanese religions and encouraged him to rewrite the tract. He reworked and published the tract as *Ikeru shin no Kami* (The True and Living God).[69] In successive years, Taylor wrote and translated a number of tracts specifically for the Japanese, including *Kami wa imasu ka?* (Is There a God?) and *Matsu Jitsu* (Latter-day Saints).[70] He also authored two tracts to address plural marriage: *Morumon Kyōkai to ippu tasai* (The Mormon Church and Polygamy) and *Tasai shugi no osore nashi* (Have No Fear of Polygamy).[71]

Frederick A. Caine, along with helping with the Book of Mormon translation, translated one of the most used tracts in Mormon history as *Waga Eikoku Kyōkai wo sarite, Matsu Jitsu Seito Iesu Kirisuto Kyōkai ni haireru riyū* (My Reasons for Leaving the Church of England and Joining the Church of Jesus Christ of Latter-day Saints).[72] First published in Liverpool, England, by the LDS British missionaries, this tract seems to be a strange choice for the non-Christian Japanese. One historian suggests, "This tract would be as effective as the distribution by a Jōdo Shinshū priest in America of a tract titled 'Why I Left the Nichiren Shōshū Sect and Joined True Pure Land Buddhism.'"[73] In actuality, several Japanese Anglicans converted to Mormonism, including two of its staunchest members. The missionaries found that it was easier to teach Christians of other faiths rather than Buddhists who had no conception of Christianity.[74]

John W. Stoker wrote *Shinkō* (Faith) and Sanford W. Hedges wrote two tracts for the mission, *Kitō no hitsuyō* (The Necessity of Prayer) and *Matsu Jitsu Seito* (Latter-day Saints).[75] Noted author Apostle James E. Talmage wrote several tracts specifically for the Japan Mission, including a play on the Buddhist and Shinto traditions, *Hito wa Kami no keitō wo yūsu* (Man in the Lineage of God) to be used in Sunday school classes.[76] Joseph F. Featherstone was also involved in the tract writing process, eventually authoring and translating *Iesu Kirisuto no ryakuden oyobi shimei* (The Brief Life of Christ and His Mission).[77] Missionaries wrote and translated two tracts to advertise the publication of the Japanese edition of the Book of Mormon in 1909: *Morumon Kei to wa nanzo ya?* (What is the Book of Mormon?) and *Kami no shinshōsha naru dai shoseki: suguru hyakunen no chūsei ni arawaretaru shoseki no o* (A Great Book that Is a New Witness

for God: Greatest Book to Come Forth during the Nineteenth Century).[78]
One of the last tracts to be translated into Japanese was *Jinmin no tokuchō*
(Characteristics of the Citizens of God), by Nephi Jensen in 1920.[79]

These missionary tracts can be divided into three categories. First are
those pamphlets that were written for other missions and merely translated into Japanese, such as Caine's *My Reasons for Leaving the Church
of England and Joining the Church of Jesus Christ of Latter-day Saints* and
Jensen's *Characteristics of the Citizens of God*. Second are those tracts that
were written by missionaries in Japan, just for the Japan Mission, which
generally summarize traditional Mormon messages, including Taylor's
Latter-day Saints, Stoker's *Faith*, Hedges's *The Necessity of Prayer*, and
Featherstone's *The Brief Life of Christ and His Mission*.[80] Third are those
rare essays that were written by missionaries in Japan, just for the Japan
Mission, which actually tried to meet the Japanese on their own religious
and cultural ground. The best example is Talmage's *Man in the Lineage of
God*, which was written at the request of a mission president who hoped to
draw parallels between Mormonism and the teachings of Buddhism and
Shinto. "We believe that man may advance in righteousness and become
more nearly perfect; even as the followers of Buddha teach, that by the
'Holy Path' or by the 'Pure Path' men may walk in the light and become
Buddha," Talmage wrote. "My brothers of *Shinto*, or *Kami-no-michi*, you
profess to follow the 'Way of the Gods' as your name declares. Your holy
Kami were the creators of the heavens and the earth, the sea and all things
that in them are. We hold that the Godhead is a Trinity comprising the
Eternal Father, Jesus Christ the Son, and the Holy Ghost; that by the power
of the Godhead were the worlds made; and that man is the child of Deity."
While Talmage's tract was a rare step toward inculturation, there is no
record of how his tract was received.

Devotional Literature in Japanese

The American missionaries also made devotional literature available
to Japanese investigators and church members. The earliest such volume
was an apologetic defense of Mormonism written specifically for the Japan
Mission by a well known Japanese Christian, Takahashi Gorō. His 1902
book *Morumon Kyō to Morumon Kyōto* (Mormonism and Mormons),
never captured the interest of the Japanese, however.[81] Convinced that they
needed to tell their own story, especially given the outpouring of anti-
Mormon literature during the early years of the mission, several Mormon
elders wrote and translated books they hoped might be of interest.[82] Mis-

sion leaders asked Erastus Jarvis to translate George Q. Cannon's popular biography of Mormonism's founding prophet, *The Latter-day Prophet:
History of Joseph Smith*, but health problems prevented him from making
the volume available in Japanese.[83] The mission's first book publication was
John W. Stoker's translation of Edward H. Anderson's popular history of
Mormonism, *Matsu Jitsu Seito Iesu Kirisuto Kyōkai ryaku shi* (A Brief History of the Church of Jesus Christ of Latter-day Saints) in 1907.[84] Additional devotional volumes in Japanese include Barney C. Taylor's *Kirisutokyō
ni okeru daisekkei* (The Great Plan: The Christian Way) and Lloyd D. Ivie's
compilation of mission president Elbert D. Thomas' sermons, *To shi sekkyō
shū* (Mr. To's Preaching Book).[85]

English Language Texts

In addition to the tracts translated or written for the Japanese, the
American elders and sisters also distributed the English language LDS
periodical, *Improvement Era*, as a method of evangelism. The missionary department in Salt Lake City mailed copies of this publication to
every mission in the world. The missionaries in turn shared them with
investigators and converts. "We feel that you are doing much good in the
publication of the Era, for it has many inspirational writings, talks and
instructions. It is one of the greatest helps in missionary service we have,"
Ernest B. Woodward wrote to *Improvement Era* officials. "We have a great
number of students who can read and speak the English language, and to
these its great message 'carries over'; but they are only few and we feel certain that if thousands of others could get in touch with it, the message of
truth would prosper in this nation."[86] The missionaries also ordered boxes
of devotional literature in English for use in their English conversation
classes, including William A. Morton's classic *From Plowboy to Prophet*.[87]
The missionaries may have ordered this last text as it was the widely popular (in Utah) apologetic biography of Joseph Smith, who they hoped their
students might find interesting.

Hymnals

In October 1903, mission president Horace S. Ensign, a celebrated sing-
er for the Mormon Tabernacle Choir, invited Alma O. Taylor to assist him
with the translation of some hymns from the *Deseret Sunday School Hymn
Book*. Missionaries living in Hōjō had just organized a children's Sunday
school class and were hoping to have some of the LDS hymns translated

into Japanese for their use. Taylor asked several Japanese friends for their opinions of his rudimentary Japanese translations. Church member Naka-zawa Hajime reviewed three songs, but with questionable results. The for-mer Shinto priest tried to put the songs into verse form, a difficult task for anyone, especially someone new to Christianity who lacked literary training. One Japanese critic "stated that the language was not good" and remarked, "I forget the vulgar words while listening to your rendition of the music."[88] In response, Taylor hired several Japanese poets and literary critics, including Iwano Hōmei, Kawai Suimei, and Owada Takeki, to help with the translations. During the lengthy process, the Mormons were also not shy about adopting the translations of other Christian groups as long as they felt the doctrinal claims were sound.[89]

In May 1905, the first LDS Japanese hymnal was published as *Matsu Jitsu Seito sanbika* (Psalmody of the Japan Mission of the Church of Jesus Christ of Latter-day Saints).[90] The hymnal's sixty songs were printed on white paper and bound in black cloth with gold lettering. One missionary described the new hymnal as "[s]ongs for the use of the saints in their sac-rament and other meetings, songs for the children of the Sunday Schools, songs for use when performing the ordinances of the Gospel and songs for general missionary use."[91] Ensign spent the final weeks of his mission teaching the American missionaries and Japanese members how to sing the songs correctly.[92] New editions of the hymnal were published by the mission in later years.

Although the Mormons traditionally evangelized elsewhere with great success through the production and distribution of Christian literature, the Japanese seemed rather unmoved by their efforts and publications. Protes-tants in Japan had already made the Bible readily available to the Japanese and the additional books of LDS scriptures failed to capture the imagina-tion of the Japanese, in the case of the Book of Mormon, or remained unpublished in Japanese, in the case of the Doctrine and Covenants and Pearl of Great Price. As Laurie F. Maffly-Kipp makes clear, other Pacific peoples embraced the Book of Mormon because the Mormons suggested that they were part of the historical story and beneficiaries of its promises. The LDS book offered Pacific Islanders, the purported children of Lehi, a remarkable heritage overnight.[93] But the Japanese never became part of the scriptural story.[94] Nevertheless, the Mormons did translate traditional missionary tracts for the Japanese and authored several pamphlets specifi-cally for the Japanese. Although some of these were important attempts to adapt the missionary model, the tracts were written and translated by lifelong Mormons who had little understanding of Japanese religions and culture. Although eventually made available in Japanese, they betrayed the Mormon sense of superiority and worldview. The same goes for the devotional literature, English periodicals, and various hymnal editions. The LDS literature did not move into inculturation, except in rare moments.

Spiritual and Secular Education

Spiritual and secular education, the Protestants' most emphasized evangelistic practice, was a distant third for the Mormons. The Latter-day Saints organized a number of well-attended Sunday schools in each of the mission's four conferences. For a time it seemed that these spiritual schools might hold the key to their evangelical success. However, few Japanese students ever converted to Mormonism as a result of attendance, and mission leaders eventually shifted their resources elsewhere. The same can be said of Bible study and English conversation classes. It is important to note that with the exception of the language classes, the Mormons did not teach secular subjects as did the Protestants. No Mormon elder or sister ever became seriously involved in the education system of Japan. As a result, they never had the student following the Protestants did.

Sunday Schools

Missionaries organized the first LDS Sunday school in Japan on August 17, 1902, one year after opening the mission. Apostle Heber J. Grant presided over the organizational meeting at mission headquarters in Tokyo. Horace S. Ensign was named superintendent and Frederick A. Caine was called as secretary. Also present were elders Alma O. Taylor, Sanford W. Hedges, Erastus L. Jarvis, John W. Stoker, and Joseph F. Featherstone, and sisters Augusta W. Grant, Mary Grant, Mary W. Ensign, and Marie S. Featherstone. This school seems to have been primarily for the American missionaries, as there were few interested Japanese students at the time. After selecting the officers, they decided to study the *Articles of Faith* by James E. Talmage.[95]

By October 1903, Caine and Jarvis, laboring in Hōjō, a small town about sixty miles south of Tokyo, had organized another Sunday school specifically for Japanese students.[96] The following month other missionaries reorganized the Tokyo Sunday School for their young Japanese friends. That first Sunday, eighty-nine children between the ages of three and fourteen years arrived at the mission headquarters. Sitting on the floor, they learned LDS hymns and listened while Taylor spoke on the life of Christ.

After the meeting, the children assembled near the garden and had their picture taken. That Christmas the elders and sisters hosted the mission's first annual Sunday school Christmas party. Over 120 children and 25 adults attended.[97] These numbers are all the more remarkable because the missionaries typically struggled to gather a dozen Japanese to any church meeting. In time, the missionaries taught Sunday school in all of the mission conferences. John W. Stoker, John L. Chadwick, and Justus B. Seely, for example, organized a Sunday school in Sapporo in October 1905. By the end of 1907, there were 24 boys and 50 girls on the Sapporo Sunday school rolls. But only one of the children came from an LDS home.[98]

Most of the missionaries became convinced that the only way the Japanese would be converted was to teach them while they were children, rather than waiting until they were grown and socialized into Japanese traditions. Consequently, many elders and sisters viewed the Sunday schools as one of the most promising evangelistic practices. For example, when mission president Horace S. Ensign wrote a short article on the history of the Japan Mission, he emphasized the success of their Sunday schools. He noted that "a special effort has been made to interest the young and rising generation in the things pertaining to the kingdom of God." He continued: "The Lord has blessed the Elders with a knowledge that it is necessary for them to establish Sunday schools and Religion classes for the instruction of the youth; for it is extremely difficult, seemingly, for the adults to cast off the shackles of Buddism [*sic*] and Shinto. The superstitions and myths surrounding the teachings of these sects cling to the people like a child to its mother." According to Ensign, the missionaries in Japan "rejoice exceedingly to hear the little tots repeat the simple prayers...and to learn that some of the children are saying these prayers night and morning in their homes."[99]

A year later, Ensign reported back to Utah that the Sunday schools in Japan were thriving. "The children are deeply interested in their studies, and it does my heart good to hear them recite the story of the birth and mission of the Savior," he related. "We are now teaching them the first principles of the gospel, and it is gratifying to see how they understand them." The Sunday schools had enabled the missionaries to make many Japanese friends, both young and old.[100] They hoped that these social relationships would lead to spiritual conversions. Ensign's successors continued to pour resources into the Japanese Sunday school program. The First Presidency praised their efforts. "We congratulate you on the success that you are meeting with in the Sunday School work, for we have no doubt that it will be through that means chiefly that the Gospel of Jesus Christ will find root upon good soil and bear fruit in due time," they wrote in March 1907. "We have ever felt that the establishment of the Sunday School among the Japanese children was done by inspiration from the Lord."[101]

Mission president Elbert D. Thomas concurred with his predecessors' and his leaders' esteem of the Sunday schools. In response to an inquiry by George D. Pyper, general secretary of the LDS Sunday Schools, Thomas discussed the practice of Sunday schools in Japan from a comparative perspective. "The system of missionary work carried on in Japan by both Greek and Roman Catholic Churches, is at least in theory, Sunday School missionary work, and their success is considered I think, the most lasting among the Christian Churches here." He continued: "Their work is done entirely through the schools and they are satisfied to wait for the children to grow up to become converts. They do practically no work at all among those older than children who are not of their faith. The Catholic with his centuries of experience, knows that lasting results are brought about slowly and by grinding in well the fundamentals." Thomas concluded that the Mormons should continue to sponsor Sunday schools in Japan, like the Orthodox and Catholic churches.[102]

While the Latter-day Saints concentrated their Sunday school efforts on the young, Thomas was hopeful that their evangelism efforts would also draw in the parents and older generations. "Parents are reachable through their children and they become friends generally, if not investigators. The stories of the Gospel are carried in interesting little bits into households by the children." He then explained to Pyper that parts of Mormonism meshed well with Japanese culture. "The moral, ethical, manly, parent-respecting part of our religion fits Japanese Bushido spirit perfectly and while parents do not care for the devine [sic] part of the Gospel, they like their children to learn the other, and have no objection to their believing the devine [sic] if they wish, and really are pleased at what their children learn." Thomas and his missionaries believed that their efforts would produce future conversions. "It will only be a matter of time for the results of the Sunday School to show themselves in our 'Baptisms performed' column." Thomas, like his predecessors and successors, believed that Sunday schools were only legitimate evangelistic practices if they produced spiritual conversions.[103]

But subsequent mission leaders questioned the effectiveness of Japanese Sunday schools. Joseph H. Stimpson was especially concerned by the decrease in Sunday school attendance. In a letter to all of the missionaries he cautioned that something needed to be done to revive the mission's flagging Sabbath program. "The Sunday School Report has been sent in.

It showed a decrease in membership and also in number of schools over the last year. This decrease has been going on for a number of years. We ought to keep this in mind and if the Sunday Schools are worth keeping up at all they ought to be worth working up in attendance."[104] He later responded to Val W. Palmer's question of what should be done with the struggling Sunday schools in the Osaka conference. Stimpson confessed that he had growing doubts about the efficacy of Sunday schools as an evangelizing tool, due to the small number of resulting conversions. "Often the question of the real good of our Sunday Schools comes to light. We have the student from 7 to maybe 12 years of age and, it seems, loose [sic] them forever. Of course I do not think Sunday School work a failure but I have heard much said about the real lasting effect that it does not have. So it may be a good decision to close your Tsuruhashi School for a while."[105]

Over time, Sunday schools proved to be an ineffective finding, teaching, and conversion practice in the Japan Mission. Although large numbers of children and youth regularly attended the LDS Sabbath classes, they rarely converted to Mormonism. (There may have been Japanese children who wanted to embrace Mormonism but were unable to gain parental permission.) The Japanese children and their parents knew they could enjoy the activities of Mormonism without the responsibilities of membership. The American missionaries were friendly curiosities who provided gifts and Western-style holiday cheer. When one church leader toured the mission he observed the Sunday schools with mixed emotions. He noted that the seasonal entertainment "could not have been rendered more skillfully in any ward [congregation] in Zion," but was saddened when he realized that the Japanese children and their parents were there to celebrate the Christmas holiday, not the Christ child. "It appeared that neither parents nor children had participated in the entertainment because of any sympathy for the Gospel. They had come either for amusement or gifts or both."[106]

Bible Study Classes

The missionaries also taught other religion classes targeting Japanese adults. In the years prior to the 1909 publication of the Book of Mormon in Japanese (and sporadically thereafter), the missionaries held Bible study classes, in both Japanese and English, on weeknights. One elder described a typical class in his journal:

From 8:00 p.m. held a meeting for the purpose of considering our teachings concerning God, Jesus Christ, and the Holy Ghost from a Bible standpoint. Nine were present. I prayed, then spoke of Christ's prophecy concerning the downfall of Jerusalem etc. and its fulfillment as recorded in history: making this as a point in favor of the truth of the Bible writings. I then had those present read from the scriptures many passages explaining their meaning and pointing out their relation to the subject (Godhead) when ever they needed such additional comment.[107]

Although the missionaries prepared for their teaching assignments, their letters and journals reveal their ongoing disappointment with the sparse attendance. They readied lessons from the Bible like "Deliverance of the Israelites from Egyptian Bondage" and "Apostasy and the Primitive Church."[108] Alma O. Taylor lamented the lack of interest for his Bible discussions: "Ever since the 1st of June, I had been trying to get enough people out on Wednesday nights to hold such a meeting, but on former Wednesdays only one[,] two, or three came."[109] Years later he was still struggling to recruit students: "After supper I expected to teach the English Bible Class, but no one came except Mr. Wakabayashi."[110] It was discouraging to the elders and sisters when few Japanese investigators attended their Bible study classes.

While getting people to show up was a major challenge for the missionaries, sometimes they struggled with their hard-won students. On occasion their pupils started arguments which disrupted the class. John L. Chadwick, for example, helped run the Sapporo conference Bible study class. One evening they were studying the New Testament when the following incident occurred. Everything seemed to be going smoothly until a Japanese man took issue with Christ's admonition that men should go the second mile with their oppressors. "Why a man would be foolish to give his goods after he had been sued and had his coat taken away from him," the student exploded. He then told Chadwick "that this part of the Bible was what the Japanese didn't like and that it was impossible for a man to love his enimes [sic], he said that man was just the same as a beast because the[y] fought." At this point other students joined the fray until order was restored.[111] Some lessons were more successful than others. One of the biggest challenges was ascertaining the real interest of the students, as in the case of English classes. The missionaries were never sure why their investigators attended: was it to learn English, to study the Bible, or to learn about Mormonism? In other words, were the classes an effective way of finding potential converts?

English Conversation Classes

The teaching of English conversation classes was one of the few innovations in the Japan Mission to the Euro-American missionary model. From the earliest days of the mission, the Japanese seemed more interested in learning English than studying Mormonism. They understood the utility of speaking English as their country continued to westernize, yet, in the minds of the missionaries, the Japanese failed to appreciate the spiritual benefits of Mormonism. As a result, a number of Japanese befriended the English-speaking missionaries under the pretense of studying religion. "We have some students call who come for nothing but to practice their English, and who pretend to be interested in the Gospel, but they stop coming as soon as the Elders commence to explain the gospel in the Japanese language," Heber J. Grant wrote to a fellow apostle in Utah. "I have been amused to hear Bro. [Alma] Taylor talk an entire evening to a Japanese in his own language, and have him [the Japanese] talk in English in reply to all that Bro. Taylor says."[112]

To the missionaries' chagrin, the Japanese continued to request English lessons—even when they had little or no interest in Mormonism. Mission president Horace S. Ensign stressed that the missionaries "should not allow our time to be occupied in long conversations with those who come to us for the sole purpose of learning English."[113] Alma O. Taylor summed up the feelings of many when he recorded his encounter with a woman proposing to study English to aid her in her spiritual quest. "While we were eating breakfast a woman came wanting to know if we could teach her English and she stated that she desired to study Christianity and become a Christian. No doubt she does if it will help her in her English. There are too many such students of Christianity. But few ever amount to anything."[114]

The lack of conversions among Japanese students was the central issue. After becoming mission president, Taylor was even more skeptical of their intentions and even harsher in his condemnation. "We are not here to teach English, but to teach the gospel to the Japanese in their own tongue," he instructed Joseph P. Cutler in Sapporo. "When anyone can understand the gospel in English and we can explain better in English than in Japanese then preaching in English is profitable. Under no other circumstances is English good. No elder will make a success of his work until he teaches in Japanese." Still, Taylor encouraged Cutler to be "kind and helpful" to those seeking help with their English, so as not to hurt goodwill.[115] And when young ladies asked for English lessons, Taylor kindly turned them over to the sister missionaries for classes.[116]

Nevertheless, the missionaries did find some value in teaching English under the right circumstances. For instance, they used language lessons to build relationships with dignitaries whom they hoped would later help their church's cause. "In the evening Mr. Mori the private secretary of the Minister of Finance came to get an hour's practice in speaking English. This gentleman is a friend of our friend Mr. Tokoyo and at the request of Mr. Tokoyo we have consented to help Mr. Mori whose position requires that he shall be familiar with English," Taylor explained.[117] On another occasion, he conceded that the missionaries could benefit personally from exchanging English lessons for Japanese tutoring: "A young man named Katō who is now living with General Kawamura in Harajuku came to see if we would not teach him English. I arranged for him to assist Elder Roskelley in Japanese and for Elder R. to assist Mr. Katō in return in his English."[118]

More important, the missionaries held regular English conversation classes throughout the mission and came in contact with a number of students who joined the church, including Fujiwara Takeo, who later led the mission for a time.[119] "We have many young men who attend our English classes; some in order to learn English, and others who are really desirous of hearing the teachings of the gospel. Among these are many very intelligent young men," Amasa W. Clark of the Tokyo conference noted.[120] For a while they even held weekly English Bible classes to cater to these educated learners in parts of the mission.[121] Yet it is important to note that the missionaries taught English to find and teach prospective converts, not to promote linguistics or secular learning. Unlike the Protestant schools, the Mormons' English conversation classes were spiritual, not secular, ventures.

In brief, unlike the Protestants who championed secular *and* spiritual education for the Japanese, the Mormons emphasized spiritual Sunday schools and Bible study classes in Japan. During the first half of the mission, elders and sisters organized Sunday schools wherever they were stationed. While their classes were well attended by Japanese children and youth, mission leaders eventually questioned their effectiveness as a conversion tool. Few students or their family members ever joined the church. The students seemed to enjoy the interaction and entertainment the American missionaries offered more than the spiritual message. English-language classes were also a mixed bag: the missionaries struggled to understand if the Japanese were there to learn English or to study Mormonism. They were often frustrated by the students' subterfuge. While many American Protestants also taught in the national school system, the

Mormons did not see secular education as their mission, thereby missing out on a possible opportunity to build strong relationships with a variety of Japanese constituencies.

Social Welfare Activities

The Mormons' least-emphasized evangelistic practice was involvement in social welfare activities. The social gospel struggled to take root in Mormon theology before, during, or after the Japan Mission.[122] Although they worked with individual investigators and church members to adopt the moral standards of Mormonism, the Latter-day Saints rarely got involved in social causes, with the exception of natural disaster relief. They were in Japan to preach the gospel, not to uplift or Westernize Japanese society.

Humanitarian Outreach

Unlike Protestant missionaries who focused their efforts on improving both the spiritual and the temporal lives of their Japanese charges, the Latter-day Saints in Japan generally eschewed worldly improvement for spiritual conversion. They did, however, use humanitarian outreach projects as a way to improve their church's image in Japan as well as meet potential converts. Mission president Alma O. Taylor, for example, attempted to mix humanitarian service with evangelism on several occasions. In September 1905, he and Frederick A. Caine visited the Red Cross Hospital in Tokyo and preached to the convalescing soldiers, the ultimate captive audience, for two hours. "It is very monotonous for the soldiers to remain in the hospital without any special change or recreation, so the authorities of the place are, so we were told, pleased to have Christian preachers or others come and talk and sing to the wounded," he explained. "It was quite a beneficial visit and while it was with peculiar feelings that I entered the room where the wounded were lying I soon felt at home and enjoyed myself very much."[123] The duo returned two weeks later and again held church services for the patients. But they were unable to find or teach any new gospel students so they abandoned their efforts at the hospital.[124] They were in Japan to warn the spiritually sick, according to their premillenialist theology, not to heal the physically injured.[125]

On several occasions, the missionaries in Japan and church leaders in Utah donated funds for Japanese disaster relief. In early 1906 the missionaries in Tokyo determined to aid famine victims in northern Japan. In addition to feeding the hungry, they hoped to improve the beleaguered image of Mormonism in Japan. The First Presidency donated two hundred yen on behalf of the Utah church. The missionaries and members in Japan also collected donations for the cause. Alma O. Taylor met with officials in Tokyo to discover where to donate his church's famine relief contributions. He then distributed 120 yen to Sanford Hedges, who was living near the famine victims, with instructions on how to distribute the money to the best advantage of the hungry and his church.[126] That February the missionaries even solicited funds from their non-LDS Sunday school students. After discussing the dire situation with their young friends, the missionaries gave each child an envelope in which to make a small donation.[127]

Near the end of February, Taylor tried to meet with the Japanese Minister of Education to suggest how the Japanese could likewise raise money through their school system for the famine victims. Although the minister and his private secretary were not available, he met with a representative and recommended that all of the Japanese school children be asked to donate a few yen for the famine victims "on one day thus bringing the attention of the entire nation to the scheme and making nearly every family in Japan a party to the relief of the distress, and teaching millions of people a lesson in sympathy and sacrifice." Taylor then showed the Japanese staffer the envelopes that they had used and described "how gladly every child responded to the request for help."[128] The president of the Japan Mission next visited the mayor's office, where he discussed the matter with one of the mayor's aides and then made his way to the *Jiji Shinpō's* office, where he handed over the collected funds, thirty-six yen, to its editor and famine relief coordinator. "The editor took special note of the manner in which the money was collected and states that he desired to give it special notice," he recalled.[129] Days later the *Jiji Shinpō* ran a "short complimentary account of the way in which our contribution from the Sunday School for the famine sufferers was collected."[130] Taylor was pleased: the mission's effort benefited both the famine sufferers and the church's image.[131]

So while the American Protestants became well known and regarded in Japanese society for their social welfare activities, the Mormons rarely involved themselves and their resources in causes they considered outside of their immediate evangelistic responsibilities. Unmoved by the social gospel, the LDS missionaries largely viewed humanitarian outreach as a way to improve their church's public image and to generate additional evangelistic opportunities. As a result, the Japanese never looked to the Mormons as moral or social leaders.

COMPARING EVANGELISM RESULTS

There is no question that Mormon missionaries and leaders on both sides of the Pacific viewed the Japan Mission as a challenging place to evangelize. Mormonism's Euro-American missionary model, especially its evangelistic practices, was largely ineffective in Japan, as missionaries tried to generally impose and translate their gospel message in Asia. How effective were Mormon missionaries and their evangelistic practices in Japan in comparison with their peers in other LDS missions? In 1924, the LDS Presiding Bishop's office, under the direction of Heber J. Grant and his counselors, compiled a series of statistical reports on the church's worldwide missions. What they learned about their only Asian evangelizing outpost was not encouraging.

The Japan Mission, which averaged only eleven converts per year, was the lowest baptizing LDS mission in the world between 1920 and 1923. Of the North American missions, California annually averaged 150.5 converts, Central States 477.8 converts, Eastern States 126.3 converts, Hawaiian 230.5 converts, Mexican 189.5 converts, Southern States 659.3 converts, and so on. In Western Europe, the British, Netherlands, and Swedish missions all baptized over 75 converts annually. Even the other Pacific basin missions outpaced the annual conversions of Japan: Australian 51.5 converts, New Zealand 110.8 converts, Samoan 156.0 converts, Tahitian 40.0 converts, and Tongan 59.8 converts.[132]

Granted, the Japan Mission had one of the smallest evangelism forces of any LDS mission in the world. Yet a comparison of the average number of converts baptized per missionary in Japan with all other missions yields the same dismal result. The average missionary in Japan baptized only 0.8 converts per year, while their peers in other missions baptized an average of 5.05 converts per year. Again, the Japan Mission ranked dead last globally.[133]

The Japan Mission was Mormonism's least productive missionary field, but how did it compare with American Protestant missionary efforts? Despite the assertions of some Mormon historians, statistical data demonstrates that LDS missionaries were less successful than their Protestant counterparts in Japan.[134] While only about a dozen Japanese converted during the first thirteen years after Japan opened its doors to the West (1859–1872), nearly five thousand converted the following decade (1873–1882), once Japan was officially open to Christian evangelism.[135] By 1901, when the Latter-day Saints arrived in Japan, there were over twenty thousand Protestant Japanese converts, divided into Presbyterian, Methodist, Congregational, Episcopal, American Baptist, Southern Baptist, Disciples of Christ, and Seventh-Day Adventists.[136] Moreover, this nineteenth-century evangelism success was *not* due to large numbers of Protestant missionaries during these early years. The American Baptists and Disciples of Christ combined had only a few dozen missionaries stationed in Japan at any given point during the 1880s, yet they were able to convert the Japanese at greater rates than subsequent Latter-day Saints, due in large measure to their evangelistic practices.[137]

LDS missionaries in twentieth-century Japan enjoyed a number of practical and strategic advantages unavailable to the Protestants in the nineteenth century. When the Mormons arrived in 1901, they benefited immensely from the work of the Protestants who had introduced the Japanese to Christianity, including providing essential translations of the Old and New Testaments, as previously described. Moreover, the Latter-day Saints were able to travel freely throughout all of Japan, not just the foreign treaty ports, thanks to the 1899 renegotiations of the unequal treaties. Nevertheless, Protestant denominations continued to grow in Japan during the early twentieth century, while Mormonism struggled to convert and retain Japanese members during the same period.[138]

A comparison of Mormon and Protestant mission statistics for the first quarter of the twentieth century documents that Mormon missionaries were less effective than their Protestant contemporaries. Although the LDS elders eventually baptized 166 Japanese converts, thirteen were excommunicated, several passed away, a handful moved outside of the four established mission conferences, and one emigrated to Hawaii.[139] When LDS leaders closed the mission in 1924, Japan had only a dozen or so active churchgoers, after twenty-three years of work.

In contrast, Japanese Protestant membership in these eight denominations exceeded one hundred thousand members by 1925, despite the fact that their missionaries faced the same cultural challenges as the Latter-day Saints. Of course, by the time the first LDS missionaries arrived in Japan, the Presbyterians, Methodists, Congregationalists, Episcopalians, American Baptists, Southern Baptists, Disciples of Christ, and Seventh-Day Adventists had been actively working among the Japanese for years or even decades. Still, the Seventh-Day Adventists, who arrived in 1896 (just five years before the Latter-day Saints), enjoyed greater evangelism success than their LDS counterparts.[140]

Granted, Protestant denominations generally had more missionaries in Japan than the Latter-day Saints during the first quarter of the twentieth century. Faster-growing denominations like the Presbyterians, Methodists, Congregationalists, and Episcopalians had the most evangelists and ordained nationals. But even the slower-growing American Baptists,

Southern Baptists, Disciples of Christ, and Seventh-Day Adventists, who had comparable (or even fewer, in the case of Seventh-Day Adventists) missionary numbers to the Mormons, far outperformed their LDS counterparts. The Mormons in Japan did not enjoy equal or greater success than contemporary Protestants.[141]

STRANGERS IN A STRANGE LAND

Unlike American Protestants, who adapted their missionary approach for the Japanese, Latter-day Saints remained largely strangers in a strange land during the first quarter of the twentieth century as they imposed their message in East Asia. Doing missionary work in Japan was a novel concept to these eighty-eight Latter-day Saints. Mormon missionaries did not reach the shores of Japan until 1901, over seventy years after the church was organized. Throughout the first sixteen decades of Mormonism, general authorities allocated less than 1 percent of their missionary force to the East. Aside from Africa (with the exception of white South Africa), no other inhabited continent was as overlooked by LDS leaders as was Asia.[142] The missionaries' personal writings indicate that most were never truly at ease in Asia. Many felt isolated, and some even experienced estrangement from their Great Basin homes and families while they evangelized the Japanese. While Mormon leaders and missionaries on both sides of the Pacific realized that Japan was a unique missionary field, different from all they had experienced over seven decades, I have argued that they strained to localize the Euro-American missionary model to their Asian audience, especially their evangelistic practices.

The millenarian Mormons evangelized the Japanese just as their predecessors missionized Americans, British, and Scandinavians. While the Protestants stressed the importance of providing education, social welfare programs, and Christian literature to the Japanese, the Mormons emphasized the reverse. Seeking solely to preach Christ and not to advance Western culture, they spent most of their time and resources personally contacting and witnessing to the Japanese by tracting, holding street meetings, offering magic lantern lectures, playing the role of foreigner, and participating in sporting activities. Next, the Mormons poured massive resources into providing their own religious literature, similar to their American counterparts. They translated additional books of scripture, authored dozens of tracts, translated devotional literature, disseminated English church periodicals, and produced a series of hymnals. Unlike the Protestants who captured the minds and hearts of the Japanese through spiritual and secular education, the Mormons offered only Sunday schools, Bible study classes, and church-centric English conversation classes. In contrast to the Protestants who became well known for their social welfare activities by the early twentieth century, the Latter-day Saints did next to nothing to advance Western culture or social reforms among the Japanese. The Mormons, who basically imposed or translated their message, struggled to make headway in Japan, while the American Protestants converted tens of thousands of Japanese, due in large part to their greater willingness to adapt their missionary approach to the needs of East Asia.

6

Temporary Retreat from Japan

In consideration of existing conditions in Japan and because of the almost negligible results of missionary effort in that country since the mission was opened in 1901 the matter of the temporary closing of the mission and the withdrawal of the missionaries who are laboring there, has long been under consideration by the Presidency and the Council of the Twelve. At a meeting recently held it was decided that this action should be taken without further delay.

—LDS First Presidency, 1924

"I know that the Latter-day Saints have been greatly interested in the mission I was called to preside over, and I regret I am not able to tell you that we have done something wonderful over in Japan," Apostle Heber J. Grant lamented in October 1903 general conference. "To be perfectly frank with you, I acknowledge I have accomplished very little indeed, as the president of that mission; and very little has been accomplished— so far as conversions are concerned." Nevertheless, the apostle held out hope for his church's only Asian missionary field: "I have the assurance in my heart there will yet be a great and important labor accomplished in that land."[1] But progress remained elusive throughout his lifetime. Still, he retained an interest in the progress of the fledgling Japan Mission he helped establish. November 1918 marked both the end of World War I and the death of church president Joseph F. Smith, Lorenzo Snow's successor. According to precedent, Grant, the senior member of the Quorum of the Twelve Apostles, assumed the office of church president.

President Grant finally decided to take his church's only Asian mission off ecclesiastical life support in 1924, twenty-three years after he opened it as an apostle. The First Presidency closed the Japanese operation that

June. Grant, like Presidents Lorenzo Snow and George Q. Cannon, did not feel his church had the luxury of pouring limited resources into underperforming missionary fields indefinitely. By the time the mission closed, Latter-day Saints in the American Mountain West had turned their attention away from Asia. When the hapless missionaries returned to Utah, the pomp and circumstance surrounding their predecessors' send-off was noticeably absent: silence, not brass bands, heralded their return. Although separated by time and theology, second- and third-generation Mormons, like their Protestant counterparts, struggled for relevance as they labored in Asia.

American and Japanese scholars, as well as church members on both sides of the Pacific, have since debated the First Presidency's decision to temporarily close the Japan Mission. Historian R. Lanier Britsch offered a thoughtful analysis in 1970. He argued that the mission's problems could be broken down into several types. First, some difficulties including "language, missionary approach, culture, scarcity of missionary numbers, long tenure, and failure to attract many converts" plagued the mission from start to finish. Furthermore, "international problems, such as the Japanese exclusion laws that were passed in the United States, the near-closing of the Tonga Mission at approximately the same time, the failure to acquire any real property, and the great Tokyo earthquake of 1923 all flared up during the final years of the mission." He identified "the dimension of inspiration which guided the First Presidency, and the general aspect of psychological distress or defeatism which plagued missionaries in Japan, and Church leaders in Salt Lake City," as the third major type of problem faced by the mission.[2] Over the past three decades, no other scholar has written on the demise of the Japan Mission or evaluated Britsch's conclusions.

While the calculus of closure is difficult to ascertain for the Japan Mission, some factors seem to have played a much bigger role than others in the mission's demise. chapter 5 makes the case that the "almost negligible results" of the Japan Mission were largely the byproduct of its leaders and missionaries imposing or translating their gospel message to the Japanese, in keeping with the traditional Mormon evangelistic practices. The missionaries made some, but not nearly enough, effort to understand Japanese culture or adapt their message to their Asian audience, based on their ambivalent approach to missionary work in Japan. Analyzing the final years of the mission through the framework of the Euro-American missionary model yields a clearer understanding of the church's temporary retreat from Asia. The homogeneity of the missionaries' personal backgrounds, lack of missionary preparation, and costly financial burdens, together with the church's relative neglect of the Japan Mission's need for human resources—the remaining components of the Mormon missionary approach—compounded these problems. Unable to move truly beyond the Euro-American missionary model, the Japan Mission was less successful than other LDS mission fields worldwide, and it floundered in comparison with intra-country Protestant efforts. "Study the history of our missionary career ever since the Church was organized and I will venture to say that we hitherto have made very little progress among any people except those who come, as we claim, either pure or mixed from the House of Israel," Assistant Church Historian Andrew Jenson concluded in April 1913 general conference. "We have not had success among the Latin or Oriental races, or among the Chinese or Japanese. There may be some of the blood of Israel among them, but so far we have discovered but a very little."[3]

During the early 1920s, however, there were two external factors that may have led Mormon leaders to further reassess the wisdom of continuing evangelism in Japan. First, the devastating 1923 Tokyo-Yokohama Earthquake captured the world's attention, including that of LDS authorities and missionary families in Utah. Nevertheless, I will suggest that the tremors seem to have inspired, rather than discouraged, LDS missionaries in Japan who believed they enjoyed divine protection in contrast to the incorrigible Japanese. Second, worsening international relations between the United States and Japan impacted the mission. The political strain between the two nations resulted in sporadic moments of discomfort for the Latter-day Saints in Asia, but had little overall influence on the mission's progress until mid-1924. Although both events had a negative bearing on the Japan Mission—they precipitated a sense of crisis—neither doomed the missionary field. Ultimately, church leaders instead closed the mission because of the poor evangelistic results.

After the Second World War, however, several missionaries offered an additional interpretation of why the mission was shuttered. They proposed that their prophet-president foresaw the destruction of Japan during the Pacific war and saved the missionaries from similar fate. But I will suggest that Heber J. Grant made his decision to close the mission based on more pragmatic considerations. Ultimately, it was the failure of the Latter-day Saints to fundamentally modify their Euro-American missionary model to better meet the needs of their non-Christian, non-Western, Japanese audience that led to the mission's closure.

COMPONENTS OF THE MORMON MISSIONARY MODEL

"The Elders have not only had to learn a very difficult language, but also come to an understanding of a people whose ideas, ideals, manners, customs and mode of worship are entirely foreign to their own. How to approach the Japanese has been a problem in missionary work, as they do not believe in God, in Jesus Christ, or the Bible," one missionary summarized.[4] As described in chapter 5, the Mormons were largely inflexible in adapting their traditional evangelistic practices to the Japanese. Moreover, their personal backgrounds, missionary training, financial arrangements, and human deployment played a major role in their struggles among the Japanese.

Homogeneity of Personal Backgrounds

Nearly all of the men and women assigned to the Japan Mission were young and lacked varied life and ecclesiastical experience: their homogeneous backgrounds hamstrung their ability to innovate in Japan. Just how similar were the eighty-eight missionaries called to Japan? Seventy-eight (89 percent) missionaries were born in Utah. Of the remaining ten, half were born in neighboring Idaho.[5] Moreover, almost all were baptized at the customary age of eight. This suggests that they were born into traditional Mormon homes with orthodox parents. Louis A. Kelsch, who was baptized in Germany, appears to be the only adult convert in the group.[6] Everyone else grew up as a second- or third-generation Mormon. In fact, seventy-nine (90 percent) were still living in Utah when they received their call to Japan; fifty-nine (67 percent) were still residing in the county of their birth. Only nine were living beyond the borders of Utah: eight in Idaho and one in Oregon. In other words, nearly all of the elders and sisters were born and reared as Latter-day Saints in the Mormon corridor.

Only five of the elders and sisters were born before the death of Brigham Young in 1877. Three of the missionaries were born during the 1850s, two during the 1870s, thirty-two during the 1880s, forty-two during the 1890s, and nine during the 1900s. In addition, only two elders walked across the plains as pioneers. And fifty-one (58 percent) were born during or after 1890, the year that Wilford Woodruff renounced the practice of polygamy.[7] Their mean and median ages were twenty-two and twenty-one years, respectively.[8] The married missionaries were generally older than their single counterparts. Their mean and median ages were twenty-five and twenty-seven years, respectively. Of the eighty-eight missionaries who served in Japan, twenty-four (27 percent) were married. Eleven couples

served together as evangelizing companions.[9] Two married missionaries, Louis A. Kelsch and Justus B. Seely, served their entire missions alone
while their wives remained in America. Young single males made up 70
percent of the mission staff. Twenty-three-year-old Lillian L. Broadbent
and thirteen-year-old Mary Grant were the only two unmarried female
missionaries. Of the mission's eight male mission presidents, six—Heber
J. Grant, Horace S. Ensign, Elbert D. Thomas, Joseph H. Stimpson, Lloyd
D. Ivie, and Hilton A. Robertson—were married. Only presidents Alma O.
Taylor and H. Grant Ivins were unmarried, as both were called to preside
when they were already serving in Japan as evangelizing bachelors.

In addition to hailing from remarkably similar geographic and social
backgrounds, the elders of the Japan Mission also shared almost the same
priesthood office and ecclesiastical training. Grant was the only apostle
to serve in Japan. Only three missionaries—Horace S. Ensign, Joseph
H. Stimpson, and Lloyd D. Ivie—were high priests (office holders of the
higher priesthood responsible for presiding) when they arrived in Asia.
And they all became mission presidents.[10] Of the remaining missionaries,
eleven (13 percent) were seventies (office holders of the higher priesthood
responsible for evangelism), sixty-one (69 percent) were elders (office
holders of the higher priesthood), and twelve (14 percent) were women
who held no priesthood offices. It was the elders' quorums, not the seventy's quorums, that staffed the church's only Asian mission.

The missionaries called to Japan were an incredibly homogeneous
bunch who seemed to suffer from "group think." Their lack of diverse
life experiences and unique perspectives hindered their ability to adapt
traditional missionary practices to the Japanese. Innovation requires the
cross-fertilization of ideas, born of divergent experiences and views. As
described in chapter 3, the Mormons generally imposed or translated their
message in Japan, with little adaptation or inculturation. Their lack of missionary experience and training, as we shall learn below, compounded the
problem. The elders' and sisters' only point of reference on how to evangelize was the current system in the mission when they arrived. As a result,
the missionaries in Japan in 1924 evangelized almost exactly as the missionaries had two decades earlier in 1904, and with the same depressing
results. While it is true that their group demographics mirrored that of
other contemporary LDS missions, innovation was not nearly as important in the North Atlantic world. The Euro-American missionary model
evolved through the experiences of thousands of Mormon elders in North
America and Western Europe during the nineteenth century. It was tailored to Christian Westerners. As a result, the elders in Great Britain and

Scandinavia were not required by circumstances to rethink their missionary approach, in contrast to their counterparts in Japan.

Lack of Missionary Training

The missionaries' lack of formal evangelistic training, including actual
missionary experience, was another reason why they struggled to evangelize in East Asia. Almost none of the eighty-eight missionaries called
to Japan had ever labored as a missionary. When called to open the Japan
Mission in 1901, Heber J. Grant was the only member of the Quorum of
the Twelve who had never served a mission.[11] Feeling overwhelmed by
his new responsibility, the middle-aged apostle selected seasoned companions to compensate for his lack of experience. He first called Horace S. Ensign, his former private secretary, to accompany him to Japan.
Ensign had previously served a lengthy mission in Colorado.[12] Grant next
received permission from the First Presidency to invite Louis A. Kelsch,
acting president of the Northern States Mission, to join him in Japan. Kelsch had earlier labored for two years in the Southern States Mission, one
year in the Northern States Mission, twenty-nine months in the European
Mission, and nearly another five years in the Northern States Mission.[13]
Grant selected eighteen-year-old Alma O. Taylor as the final member of
his cohort, despite the fact he had no missionary experience.[14]

Kelsch and Ensign were the *only* elders assigned to Japan during the
entire mission's history that had served as full-time missionaries elsewhere. After Ensign departed for Utah in July 1905, not another missionary or mission president (with the exception of Joseph H. Stimpson
and Lloyd D. Ivie, who *returned* as mission presidents) allocated to Japan
had evangelized full-time. Therefore, it was the inexperienced Taylor
who best represented the other seven dozen missionaries who labored
in Japan during the twenty-three-year period. As a result, the elders and
sisters learned their trade once they arrived in Japan from others who
had learned in similar fashion; they were amateurs training and leading
other novices. While a handful of elders attended preparatory classes at
LDS academies, their meager training was not specific to Japan. Most of
the Mormons lacked education beyond a high school diploma and none
had formal theological training or divinity school pedigrees. Instead
they were haphazardly trained as members of a lay clergy. Moreover,
unlike many of the Protestant, Catholic, Orthodox, and Anglican missionaries who dedicated their lives to serving the Japanese, none of the
Mormons planned to evangelize in Japan more than a few years. When

their missions were over they intended to go back to their Utah fields as farmers or Idaho stores as clerks.

The Mormons struggled to communicate with the Japanese in their own tongue. None of the Americans received formal language training before they arrived in Japan. Once they disembarked in Yokohama, they had to rely on more seasoned missionaries who helped them learn how to speak, read, and write Japanese. The female missionaries were at an even greater disadvantage because of their domestic responsibilities, including the care of young children, which limited their interaction with native Japanese speakers outside of the home. Alma O. Taylor may have been the only missionary to try to prepare linguistically for his sojourn among the Japanese. Unable to find Japanese textbooks in Salt Lake City, he contacted a former acquaintance, Paul Carus, a Buddhist sympathizer and founder of Open Court Publishing, whom he met in Chicago while studying to be a mortician at Harvey Medical College. Carus encouraged him to contact Nishijima Kakuryo, leader of the recently created Buddhist Mission of North America, living in San Francisco. Taylor wrote to Nishijima and related that he could not find any suitable Japanese language textbooks or primers in Utah and asked for suggestions. The Buddhist priest responded with a thoughtful letter of his own, apologizing that he would be unable to provide the requested study materials, given only a few weeks' notice.[15] The historical record is silent if any other elders or sisters even tried to start their language studies before arriving in Japan. The Japanese language proved to be a major stumbling block.[16]

Timely language acquisition became such an issue in the mission that Hilton A. Robertson, the mission's final president, suggested that much of the blame for the mission's travail and closure needed to be unloaded from the backs of the Japanese and placed on the shoulders of the non-fluent (in Japanese) American missionaries. Although missionary work in Japan was difficult, "many times the Japanese people have been condemned because they did not accept the gospel, but [he felt] that the missionaries were partly responsible for this" due to their lack of linguistic skills. "You heard many times President Grant make the expression that he learned the Japanese language but the people couldn't understand their own language when he spoke it. This, I think, was true of most of the missionaries," Robertson maintained in 1947.[17]

While there is no question that Grant toiled in vain to learn Japanese, Robertson seems to be downplaying some of his fellow missionaries' linguistic skills. Missionary journals, letters, and reports suggest that the majority of the missionaries eventually became sufficiently advanced in the language to evangelize the Japanese. In fact, business managers, government leaders, and military boards in the United States recruited returned missionaries specifically for their Japanese language skills. Perhaps Robertson was championing the cause of the abandoned Japanese church members who were again receiving missionaries in the wake of World War II and the reopening of missionary work in East Asia. Horace S. Ensign, the mission's second president, stated that his missionaries became relatively fluent in Japanese in several years.[18] Men and women called to Japan were generally expected to serve between three and five years, almost twice the time of their contemporaries in other missions. The mean mission length in Japan was 3.3 years, while the median length and mode length was 3.5 and 4.0 years, respectively. Of the eighty-eight missionaries who evangelized in Japan, sixty-four (72.7 percent) actually served between two and five years. Only fifteen missionaries (17.1 percent) served less than two years.[19]

Simply stated, most of the missionaries assigned to Japan eventually gained impressive fluency in Japanese. As fifty-three of the eighty-eight missionaries labored in Japan at least three years, nearly two-thirds of the elders and sisters lived in Japan long enough to gain sufficient oral fluency to fulfill their evangelistic responsibilities by the *end* of their missions. One might assume then that language acquisition was not a major stumbling block for the mission. However, and this is the key point, it took them most of their mission tenures to become *effective* Japanese-speaking evangelizers. By the time they gained sufficient language skills they had only a few months, a year at the most, to leverage their linguistic proficiency. Moreover, fluent American missionaries were expected to devote a good deal of their time to training newly arrived missionaries who lacked any language training. As a result, language acquisition played a major role in the mission's overall ineffectiveness.

Financial Burdens

Evangelism is a spiritual activity with a price tag. Although serving as a missionary without personal financial resources worked well for missionaries during the nineteenth century in North America and Western Europe, it proved disastrous for missionaries in Hong Kong. By the turn of the twentieth century this financial arrangement had been largely supplanted by a more organized and funded system in some mission fields. The families, friends, and congregations of the missionaries were expected to support their ecclesiastical representatives abroad.

When Heber J. Grant and his companions arrived in Japan, they stayed in reputable lodging to avoid the stigma of being leeches on Japanese society. The apostle also discouraged his missionaries from traveling without personal funds among the Japanese. Alma Taylor attributed Grant's progressive perspective on missionary finances to the fact that he had never been a missionary before. "He was without missionary experience. That is probably why the Lord chose him for Japan," he suggested. "The things President Grant did and directed his three companions to do were quite out of line with what first missionaries had done and current missionaries were doing in other missions." Taylor believed that if the missionaries had arrived in Japan expecting financial support from the locals, they would have been looked down upon by the Japanese. Had they not enjoyed their own financial support they may not have obtained the proper government permits to begin missionary work.[20] In brief, rejecting the traditional LDS missionary custom of traveling without purse or scrip was one of the few attempts by mission leaders to localize their practices to Japan. In this case, it was a positive adjustment with respect to Japanese public opinion. At the same time, however, it placed heavy financial burdens on the missionaries, as we shall see.

In subsequent years, after the Japan Mission and its missionaries were recognized by the local government officials, only one elder, Moroni S. Marriott, decided to try a variation of the financial arrangement. But he relied on the extensive telegraph system, which enabled him to wire the mission headquarters for money whenever it was needed.[21] His experience remained a rare exception in the Japan Mission.

One mission president had to explain to the father of one of his missionaries, who was overwhelmed by the cost of his son's mission to Japan, why the missionaries in Japan did not rely on the local Japanese for room and board. The leader saw two major problems, specific to Japan, with the alternative financial arrangement. First, as Taylor suggested, the Japanese would be repulsed by a Christian denomination whose representatives expected to be housed and fed on a regular basis. "I doubt if we would be allowed to stay in the country if we had no definite support, for I think that we would be treated as the missionaries are treated in Germany if we had no money, although of course we have never carried the point to a test here." (Vagrancy laws had led to their harassment and expulsion in Germany.) Second, it would not work logistically. The missionaries in Japan were necessarily confined to specific evangelizing areas where they attempted to build up small conferences. "Preaching without purse or scrip is only possible where missionaries are on the move. That is, you could hardly expect a missionary to stay at one place and be kept for, say, a year, could you?" President Taylor queried the father.[22]

As traveling without purse or scrip was not an option, the missionaries called to the Japan Mission were expected to fund their own evangelism. The heavy financial burden fell first on the shoulders of the missionary's family and then on the backs of friends. Contrary to popular belief, the early Japan Mission was not one of the church's most expensive missions. Between 1920 and 1923, the average missionary in Japan spent about $40 a month on living expenses. It was more expensive for elders and sisters to serve on a monthly basis in the Canadian ($52), California ($51), Eastern States ($49), Northwestern States ($45), Danish ($44), South African ($43), Northern States ($43), British ($42), and Western States ($41) missions.[23] But missionaries called to Japan often served twice as long as their peers in other missions. For that reason the personal cost of evangelizing in Japan exceeded that of any other mission in the world. As a result, many missionaries and their parents petitioned to have their Japanese missions shortened. Accepting a mission call to Japan meant great financial sacrifice, a price some were unable or unwilling to pay.

Human Deployment Neglect

The Japan Mission never received the institutional support it needed from church leaders in Utah. All of its understaffed mission presidents begged for more elders and sisters, especially during the last decade of the mission's existence. Some have suggested that World War I explains why church leaders sent so few elders and sisters to Japan during the second decade of the twentieth century. However, even before World War I, general authorities had allocated few resources to Japan. In the five years leading up to World War I (1910–1914), church leaders called 4,354 missionaries to serve throughout the world. More specifically, 2,312 (53 percent) served in the United States and Canada, 1,599 (37 percent) labored in Europe, 372 (9 percent) evangelized in Pacific-Asia (excluding Japan), 30 (0.7 percent) missionized in South Africa, 20 (0.5 percent) made their way to Latin America, while only 21 (0.5 percent) worked in Japan.[24]

In 1900 the estimated world population was 1,608,000,000: 915,000,000 in Asia (57 percent); 423,000,000 in Europe (26 percent); 120,000,000 in Africa (7 percent); 81,000,000 in North America (5 percent); 63,000,000 in Latin America (4 percent); and 6,000,000 in Oceania (less than 1 percent).[25] In brief, church leaders were allocating the majority of their resources to the minority populations of the world. By focusing on the final decade of the mission (1915–1924), one can truly appreciate how dire this staffing need was and how it affected the mission. In 1915, Amasa W. Clark shared his frustration about the number of missionaries in the Japan Mission. "There is one thing which greatly hinders the work in Japan, and that is the scarcity of missionaries. We have only eleven missionaries to preach the gospel to more than fifty-six millions of people. There are three of us laboring here in Tokyo; the fourth largest city in the world."[26] In 1922 mission president Lloyd D. Ivie likewise lamented the mission's numbers. "Our force of missionaries in Japan is small. If each missionary could meet and preach the gospel to 200 new people every day—100 each for the sisters, without resting for Sundays, these ten missionaries would finish their job in 105 ½ [years]. They are the representatives of truth to 77,000,000 people."[27]

Even during the Great War, when missionaries were called back from Europe, the numbers in Japan did not improve significantly. Nearly three thousand LDS missionaries served during the war years (1914–1918). This was a decrease of only 32 percent globally compared to the previous period (1910–1914). During this period, 2,252 (76 percent) men and women evangelized in the United States and Canada, 389 (13 percent) served in Europe, 294 (10 percent) labored in the Pacific basin (excluding Japan), 6 (0.2 percent) missionized in Latin America, and 20 (0.7 percent) worked in South Africa. This left only 18 (0.6 percent) to evangelize in Japan.[28] Clearly missionaries were available for assignment in Japan, but church leaders sent them elsewhere, despite the fact they had pulled out their missionaries from Europe by October 1914. Moreover, by 1917 the British government was withholding travel visas from Americans, including LDS missionaries, trying to enter Australia and New Zealand, as well as making it hard for elders and sisters to enter Great Britain after April 1917.[29] In contrast, Japan never closed its borders or limited its entry visas to LDS missionaries: there was no need.

The signing of the armistice in November 1918 marked the end of World War I. LDS mission presidents stationed around the world began to anticipate resurgence in missionary activity and personnel. Joseph H. Stimpson presided over the Japan Mission from 1915 until 1921. He was hopeful that more missionaries would be sent his way now that mission-aged men were no longer being drafted into the military. "We have hopes for some new missionaries but that is all," he wrote to Lafayette C. Lee serving in Sapporo. "As yet we have heard nothing that will indicate how soon they will be fulfilled. I hope they will transfer one of the Mormon regiments from France over here in a body. I do not suppose they will need their arms though. We need the numbers however."[30] He likewise pleaded to Harold G. Reynolds at church headquarters: "What we need worst of all is a few more missionaries.... we have not had any for over a year now." Laboring under the false assumption that the number of available missionaries had declined far below actual numbers, he continued: "I realize the unsettled condition of the world has made it impossible to send missionaries out but now peace is restored I hope you will do what you can to get our mission fitted up."[31] Unfortunately, Stimpson's plea for reinforcements went unheeded; authorities did not allocate a single missionary to Japan in 1919. What is more, between 1915 and 1919 the Japan Mission was assigned only fourteen new missionaries out of a total of 3,432 allocated worldwide.[32] While it was certainly possible for church leaders to send more missionaries to Japan, they continued to choose a different course before, during, and after World War I.

As described in chapter 5, the First Presidency eventually assigned David O. McKay to tour the Japan Mission and mainland China in 1920. The apostle's visit temporarily energized the mission. Stimpson felt that church leaders in Utah had finally turned their attention to Japan and anticipated that the apostle would become an advocate for the church's only Asian mission. Strengthened, Stimpson wrote several letters to former missionaries, updating them on the mission's future prospects. "The work here is getting along fine. I expect to see a big increase in the church in the near future," he penned to Val W. Palmer. "I expect that [McKay's] visit will result in more missionaries being sent to Japan and the work here will be pushed on in a more systematic and forceful way. One thing sure the mission will not be given up and will only be given a boost."[33] Stimpson noted to Alma O. Taylor that the apostle "seems to be well pleased with the people and says that the work ought to be pushed" by sending more missionaries from the United States.[34]

Shortly after McKay departed for Hawaii, Lloyd D. Ivie arrived in Japan and replaced Joseph H. Stimpson as mission president. That spring four unmarried elders—Ernest B. Woodward, William E. Davies, Aldo Stephens, and Orlando Fowler—arrived in Yokohama. Even more promising was the appearance of Hilton A. Robertson and his wife, Hazel, who arrived that June. And three more couples were supposedly on their way to Japan: F. Wallace and Louise M. Browning; William L. and Sylvia P. Glover; and Elwood L. and Arva B. Christensen. So it is not surprising that Ivie was optimistic about evangelism in Japan.[35] The following summer Ivie expressed his appreciation to the First Presidency for the influx of additional missionaries, the result of McKay's recommendations. "We are indeed grateful for the three couples which are being sent to this mission," Ivie wrote. "It seems that our prayers in behalf of this mission are beginning to be realized." He then offered unsolicited advice to the church's presiding officers: each stake in North America should be encouraged to supply at least one missionary to the Japan Mission.[36] The three promised couples did arrive in July 1922, and three unmarried elders—Rulon Esplin, Vinal G. Mauss, and Milton B. Taylor—arrived that December. Lewis H. Moore, the mission's final reinforcement, arrived in June 1923. Not every stake would send a representative to Japan, and the First Presidency would send only four more elders before closing the mission in 1924.

Nevertheless, Ivie and his missionaries were unable to sustain a brief period of growth in the mission. The number of missionaries dwindled to the point that Ivie had to close the Kofu conference in early 1922, after fourteen years of missionary work in the area.[37] Japan continued to be one of the least supported missions, in terms of human resources, into the early 1920s, averaging only 14.5 missionaries in residence annually. During the entire tenure of the mission, there were never more than twenty missionaries laboring simultaneously in Japan. In contrast, between 1920 and 1923, missions like the British, California, Central States, Eastern States, Northern States, Northwestern States, and Western States all annually averaged over one hundred missionaries in residence. Moreover, missions like the Canadian, Hawaiian, Mexican, and New Zealand all enjoyed at least fifty missionaries yearly. Only a handful of LDS missions around the world suffered more than the Japan Mission in terms of manpower during these years.[38] "It is like trying to run a sixty horsepower machine with a one horsepower motor and that out of repair," David O. McKay despaired after touring the Japan Mission in 1921.[39] Nevertheless, church authorities continued to understaff the mission, while focusing their resources on the North Atlantic world. Eventually the Japan Mission's motor burned out and the machine came to a grinding halt.

THE TURBULENT EARLY 1920S

During the final years of the Japan Mission, the Tokyo-Yokohama Earthquake and deteriorating international relations between the United States and Japan precipitated a sense of crisis. Yet neither event doomed the missionary field. The quake seems to have temporarily emboldened the millenarian missionaries; the rise of anti-American sentiment, as distracting as it was to the missionaries, did not reach its tipping point until the summer of 1924, after the First Presidency shuttered the mission because of its poor conversion results. Notwithstanding the mission's obvious flaws and struggles, some former missionaries sought to wring new meaning out of their old problems after World War II. With Japan smoldering in military defeat, they recast the closure of the mission in prophetic terms in the late 1940s: Heber Grant closed the mission, not because it was a failure, but because he anticipated the coming Pacific war and resulting destruction. But as I have argued, the Japan Mission seemed doomed from the start because of the missionaries' reliance on an anachronistic evangelistic approach.

Tokyo-Yokohama Earthquake Destruction

Previous scholars of the mission have suggested that the Tokyo-Yokohama Earthquake contributed to the mission's closure.[40] On September 1, 1923, a devastating earthquake rocked the Tokyo-Yokohama region. Flames then reduced the already crippled metropolitan area to heaps of charred rubble. Approximately 120,000 buildings were shaken to the ground and 450,000 were razed by fire. An estimated 140,000 people perished and another 250,000 found themselves out of work. Almost fifteen years earlier, Japan's national wealth had been projected at 86 billion yen. However, financial losses attributed to earthquake-related disasters were estimated at a staggering 10 billion yen.[41]

On the other side of the Pacific, Latter-day Saints learned of the natural disaster through newsprint. "YOKOHAMA IN FLAMES FOLLOWING EARTHQUAKE," the headlines read in Salt Lake City.[42] Mormons in Utah waited anxiously for news from the Japan Mission. "There are twenty one there from Utah including their wives and children," one article revealed.[43] By September 5, Utahns received word that at least five of the missionaries were safe.[44] The First Presidency had received a letter from Lloyd D. Ivie, dated August 17, that all of the missionaries were planning to gather in northern Japan for a mission conference. "Hopes are also entertained by Church officials that the remainder of the missionaries and their families had not left the conference at Sapporo in time to reach the disrupted area at the time the quakes began," another article noted. One returned missionary offered his own optimistic opinion on the missionaries' chances of survival if they were in Tokyo.[45] On September 11, ten days after the quake limited communication, Grant received a welcomed cablegram from Ivie which read, "Missionaries Safe."[46] Weeks later the church president reported on the safety of the Japan Mission personnel: "We are grateful indeed to the Lord that all of our missionaries in Japan were preserved during the awful calamity that came to that country."[47] As it turned out, only four elders—Ernest B. Woodward, Rulon C. Esplin, Milton B. Taylor, and Lewis H. Moore—were in Tokyo when the earthquake rattled the region.

The millenarian missionaries and their leaders saw the hand of providence in their safety and deliverance as well as the destruction of a nation that refused to heed their spiritual warning, an interpretation that only further alienated them from the local populations. "Of all the Saints in the city of Tokyo, only one lost her home," Woodward testified. "This has been a testimony to me, that God does look after his people."[48] Likewise, Hilton A. Robertson, who was returning from Sapporo to Osaka by train, recalled the safety he and his family enjoyed while tens of thousands of Japanese perished in the rubble and the flames. "Had we been one day slower in getting to our destination, no doubt we would have been in the earthquake." Like Woodward, Robertson believed God had watched over the church. "Our Church building in the city of Tokyo was still intact. Plaster and some of the tile from the roof had been shaken off, but other than this our mission property was safe and we were supplied with food. This to me was a great testimony. God will protect those who keep holy his law."[49]

Robertson's comments betray the prevailing dualistic worldview of Latter-day Saints in Japan: the righteous were protected while the wicked were destroyed.[50] Woodward concluded an *Improvement Era* article, for example, by evoking millenarian imagery. Quoting from LDS scripture, he declared that "the signs of the times predict that the advent of the Son of God is near at hand." For the revelations seemed to warn of such disasters as the Tokyo-Yokohama seismic activity, if the missionaries' testimonies were rejected: "For after your testimony cometh the testimony of earthquakes, that shall cause groanings in the midst of her, and men shall fall upon the ground and shall not be able to stand" (D&C 88:89). "Can we stand and doubt more?" he inquired of his LDS readers.[51] In Woodward's mind, a portion of this prophecy had been fulfilled before his very eyes in the destruction of Tokyo. Robertson used similar logic to make sense of the catastrophe. "We are told in the Doctrine and Covenants that after the testimony of the servants of God, earthquakes, pestilence, and disease, etc., will follow, and I bear testimony to you folks, to the brethren and sisters assembled here today, that those things have taken place in that land; I have seen them," he declared. "On the first day of September, at two minutes to 12 o'clock noon, it seemed that the gates of hell had swung open on the central part of the Island of Japan."[52]

The missionaries in Japan were not the only Latter-day Saints to link the quake to the destruction leading up to the Second Coming of Christ.

Apostle James E. Talmage, residing in the safety of faraway Utah, evoked similar sentiments, but he was more circumspect than Woodward and Robertson in attributing the hand of God to the recent Japanese tremors. "I have only to say that the occurrence of such earthquakes is in accordance with predictions," he stated. "The Lord forbid that I should assume to pass judgment upon those who are immediately affected, upon those who have lost their lives through such catastrophes." The apostle further cautioned his audience against drawing hasty conclusions: "It is beyond the wisdom of men to correctly deduce results by applying general laws or causes to individual cases; and whenever the judgments of the Lord are permitted to fall upon the earth and upon its inhabitants, there are many of the innocent who suffer with the guilty."[53]

Some missionaries anticipated that the earthquake would humble the Japanese and improve prospects for evangelism. "We must reap while the day lasts," Woodward declared. "God has spoken to us by the voice of earthquakes, thunderings, and by tidal waves!…The time is short, and there is much to do to prepare the nations for the advent of our Lord." Putting the best face on the circumstances, he exuded "great hope" for the future of LDS evangelism in Japan after the earthquake. He suggested the seismic devastation might prove to be a defining moment for his fledgling mission: a wakeup call to the Japanese people. "I feel the people of this nation can see wherein 'tis folly to trust in earthly things. I hope so, at least. I hope that through this it will be easier to reach the hearts of the people with the message of truth." He rationalized that according to "the great economy of the Lord, it was necessary that all of these should die, in order that the others might find themselves." But the missionaries must seize the providential teaching opportunity, he declared, "for if not, all these lives have been sacrificed in vain! Such can never be!"[54]

Although there is little doubt that the natural disaster worried leaders back in Utah, the upheaval seems to have spurred the efforts of the missionaries in Japan. The missionaries felt that they were running out of time to warn the Japanese. But they did not link the earthquake with the subsequent closing of the mission ten months later. Vinal G. Mauss, for instance, was serving in Japan during both the earthquake and the mission closing. When asked if the earthquake was a key factor in the mission's closing he replied: "No, I don't feel that it was a major thing at all.…I don't think it had any major effect as the closing of the mission was concerned."[55] Neither did the destruction suspend missionary work in Tokyo. While it is true that the missionaries in Tokyo did help with community rebuilding efforts and that some of the missionaries spent a few days surveying the situation, they were all back to evangelism as usual within a matter of weeks. The millenarian elders and sisters were emboldened, if anything, by the earthquake. They interpreted the seismic destruction, and their subsequent safety, as another sign that God was on their side in the winding-down scene of the end of the world.

Frayed International Relations

While frayed international relations between America and Japan may have contributed to a sense of crisis in the Japan Mission in the early 1920s, it was not responsible for its closure in 1924.[56] The issue of Asian immigration to America increasingly drove a wedge between the United States and Japan during the tenure of the early Japan Mission. Beginning in the 1850s, tens of thousands of Chinese laborers immigrated to America. Although Japan began to emerge from international seclusion in 1854, the Meiji government controlled the travel of its citizens abroad until 1885. The Chinese Exclusion Act of 1882 severely limited further Chinese immigration while opening the door for increased Japanese immigration. Soon Japanese laborers could be found working across the Hawaiian Islands and the length of California. However, American attitudes toward Japanese immigrants soon turned for the worse in the American West. By the early twentieth century, white American workers were clamoring for anti-Japanese immigration legislation. In 1906, Japanese students were segregated in San Francisco public schools. During 1907 and 1908, the U.S. and Japanese governments hammered out the Gentleman's Agreement that promised to limit future Japanese immigration.[57] Japanese citizens were justifiably outraged.

While the Japanese in the American West bore the brunt of the conflict, Americans in East Asia were occasional targets for reprisal. During the summer of 1907 the relationship between the two Pacific powers strained over the "Japanese Question" in California. The LDS missionaries in Japan felt the backlash. John L. Chadwick, stationed in Sendai, peppered his journal entries with short statements describing the unrest that June. "As the people feel very indignant over the affair in America we thought of not going out tracting but after thinking it over we decided to go out and see what we could do."[58] The following week he noted in three separate journal entries that the Japanese newspapers had printed numerous articles about the treatment of Japanese immigrants in California, and [they] were stirring up the Japanese against all Americans.[59] His companion, Daniel P. Woodland, wrote the following in a letter home: "We are making a few friends, and distributing our literature freely in all parts of the city. However, the people are somewhat indifferent towards Christianity, and we find it very hard to get into their homes. The Japanese question in America has caused some animosity here."[60] In 1913 the state of California passed the Alien Land Law, which prevented Japanese residents from owning property.[61] "Japanese all stirred up about Calif. Land Laws," Edwin J. Allen noted in his journal.[62]

During the early 1920s, relations between the United States and Japan continued to deteriorate. Alma O. Taylor sent Joseph H. Stimpson an ominous warning in October 1920. "You are perhaps anxious about the present agitation and ill feelings over the pending legislation in California against the Japanese," he alerted. "I can see no way out of the situation as the people of California have more support from the rest of the U.S. than ever before. Something should be done now to prevent the constant recurrence of the question. Before the settlement the feeling in Japan among the populous [sic] will perhaps run high against the Americans."[63] Some of the missionaries tried to soothe tensions back home. Stimpson wrote a revealing letter to A. Ray Olpin, another former missionary, disclosing that relations between Japan and the United States were at a boiling point. He was mortified that the Utah legislature and many of the citizens of Utah, a predominantly Mormon state, were expressing anti-Japanese sentiment. "It comes out in the papers here and sort of goes against what we have told the people about our state," Stimpson bemoaned. "Fight any such thing as that. It is all based on ignorance like the agitation against the Mormons."[64] Hilton A. Robertson wrote to the editor of one of the church's periodicals pleading that the Latter-day Saints show their Japanese neighbors respect. "We ask the readers of the *Era* to do all in their power to see that foreigners living among them get fair and just treatment, such as you would like yourself if in a strange land. Especially do we ask you not to participate in any unnecessary sentiment against the Japanese people."[65]

Moreover, Japanese nationalism had been on the rise for many years, a fact not lost on the American missionaries living in Japan. "After the Russo-Japan War Japan was the strongest power in Asia. In the next two decades it increased its stature and emerged as one of the five Great Powers, with a permanent seat on the Council of the League of Nations," historian Marius B. Jansen describes. "It was not long before this remarkable transformation had led to an equally remarkable change in world, and especially Asian, perception of Japan. Meiji Japan had projected the image of a young, vigorous country determined to free itself from restrictions imposed by imperialist powers, but it went on to impose its own colonialism on Taiwan, Korea, and South Manchuria."[66] During the interwar years, Japan emerged as the might of Asia.

Soon missionaries were noting the rise of Japanese nationalism in their journals and letters. After only three months in Japan as a missionary, Lewis H. Moore lamented the disturbing nationalistic pride of the Japanese in a letter dated August 31, 1923. "We certainly have a mighty big problem to solve over here. This people are certainly a stiff necked bunch. Something will have to happen to humble them before they will receive the Gospel as they should," he warned. But it wasn't just growing nationalism that worried him: the Japanese were becoming militaristic and aggressive. "Japan is getting about like Germany was. All they think of is military life. It is taught them from the ground up," Moore described. "All the girls are trained nurses and all the boys trained soldiers." He then cautioned his family and friends back in the United States against similar jingoism. "The boasting in America about how easy Japan could be licked would be hushed if they could just spend some time here and see that these people would be forces to be feared. They are marvelously skilled in hand to hand fighting. They are good shots, they are hardy, and coupled with this they have that utter disregard for life. They think it a great glory to die in a fight."[67]

Things came to a head with the passage of the Immigration Act of 1924 in the United States. At this point, the Japanese were barred from further immigration to America.[68] "Attendance at our meetings dropped and continued to do so until only a few of the faithful members ever showed up around the church," Woodward recalled. "Wherever we went we were greeted with either stony silence or with insults and arguments concerning international conditions. The talk of 'War' with the United States was heard on every hand. We missionaries used to talk of its possibilities and wonder what would happen to us if we were caught in Japan when it happened."[69] Vinal G. Mauss related one of the more extreme encounters between the Latter-day Saints and Japanese radicals during 1924. One day he and a couple of missionaries decided to go to downtown Tokyo by streetcar. As they rode into town they saw a man staring at them. "We noticed a Japanese that was dressed in high school clothes, which was sort of a military uniform. He was eyeing us up very, very carefully, and finally he jumped to his feet and he said, 'Come on, let's kill these people. They're killing our people in California,'" he described. "It happened that there was some news that came out in the newspapers over there that some of their Japanese people had been killed over there.... And he made an effort to come down there toward us." But as the man rushed the missionaries, Mauss knocked him off balance, preventing the attack. Concerned bystanders then alerted the police, who arrested the would-be-assailant.[70]

Nevertheless, these types of conflicts and experiences were sporadic and extreme, not the norm, at least until late spring of 1924. "Generally, people were very friendly and very nice to us," Mauss clarified in a later interview.[71] Hilton A. Robertson downplayed such events when he returned to America and instead complimented the Japanese for their kindness to his missionaries. "Those people are not bad at heart; we have friends there whom we hold just as dear as any we have in this land, educated people, men who are holding high positions, who care nothing for our gospel, yet were kind to us. In all our missionary work we were not mistreated," he stated in October 1924, and continued:

> If you went to the door of a Japanese home, if they did not want your tract they would politely tell you so. We received no persecution. We were allowed the privilege of standing on the street to explain the gospel—on street corners, where as high as one or two hundred people would gather to hear the message, but we were not molested in the least. If any one undertook to disturb the meeting, he was hissed out. And so the missionaries who are returning from that land, although the gospel is not being preached there now, hold many of the Saints and friends in high esteem.[72]

Heber J. Grant and his counselors alluded to the "existing conditions in Japan" (almost certainly the rise of Japanese nationalism and anti-American sentiment) when they announced the temporary closure of the Japan Mission in June 1924. But the timing of their announcement with events in Japan needs to be taken into consideration. The First Presidency wired Robertson a cablegram on Monday, June 9, 1924, informing him that they had decided to temporarily retreat from Japan. The next day they followed up with a detailed letter explaining what the missionaries should do with church property and other administrative matters. But, and this is the key point, they assured Robertson they were not alarmed "over the [political] situation in Japan" and trusted that the wave of anti-Americanism would soon dissipate.[73] Moreover, it is likely that they made their closure decision the previous Thursday, June 5, during the weekly meeting of the First Presidency and Quorum of the Twelve, as was custom for major issues.[74] It was not until June 28, three weeks *after* church leaders decided to close the mission, that angry Japanese posted signs on the mission home doors warning the Americans to leave Japan.[75] Therefore, deteriorating relations between the United States and Japan did not apparently lead to the closure of the mission or consistently contribute to its struggles during the previous twenty-three years.

Prophetic Warning

Latter-day Saints believe themselves to be a people led by a prophet. So it is not surprising that several returned missionaries from Japan and LDS scholars have interpreted Heber J. Grant's 1924 decision to close the Japanese mission as prophetic counsel.[76] Yet the Mormons in Japan admitted that they struggled to receive inspiration regarding their missionary labors. Even Grant, when president of the Japan Mission (1901–1903), was unsure how to proceed as the "way ahead was dark and uncharted." Alma O. Taylor described the apostle's frustration: "Divine inspiration was needed and diligently sought for by prayer, fasting, counsel, and work." Yet decades after laboring with Grant in Asia, Taylor still puzzled over the comparable "absence of tangible encouragement and manifestations of the spirit in the experience of the pioneer missionaries to Japan with the abundance of such blessings enjoyed by the first missionaries to England, Hawaii, and other countries." It remained an "unexplained thing" to him "that there should be so little response to the ardent pleadings of the Lord's servants in the midst of what, to them at least, seemed such justifiable need." He further confided that Grant told him "that he never once felt sure, with that sureness which the clear witness of the Spirit gives, that any given decision or plan was right" while serving in Japan.[77] Two decades after he opened the Japan Mission as an apostle, Grant contemplated closing the mission as church president. What to do with Mormonism's only Asian mission in the early 1920s seems to have been just as inchoate in his mind as it was in 1901.

By the time Grant called Hilton A. Robertson to succeed Lloyd D. Ivie as mission president, the mission was truly floundering. Robertson immediately conveyed the unflattering circumstances of the Japan Mission to Grant and his counselors. "Spent the day making out reports for the First Presidency and reporting the true conditions of the Mission," he noted on February 1, 1924. "I don't know what kind of reports have been going to them but I do know that the way some of the conferences, especially Tokyo, has been operating it is only a waste of time and money for missionaries to be here. And unless we can change the situation here it should be closed down at least in Tokyo and people in some other parts be given an opportunity."[78] Robertson's harsh assessment of the Japan Mission is supported by Vinal G. Mauss, who claimed that by 1924 "you could count on one hand the number of active members of the Church. There were many more than that who were baptized, and on record, but as far as attendance at a meeting, you could count them on one hand."[79] While reflecting on the precarious condition of each of the three surviving conferences of the mission—Tokyo, Osaka, and Sapporo—Robertson pointed out to the First Presidency that the mission was nearly out of publications, except for a number of copies of the Book of Mormon, hymnals, and miscellaneous proselyting tracts. He also logged the mission's "discouraging" finances, lamenting an overdraft balance of 1,368 yen caused by Ivie appropriating the Japanese saints' building fund monies to cover his own expenses.[80]

Grant and his counselors responded to Robertson's report weeks later. They revealed that they were contemplating shuttering the Japan Mission based on his on-the-ground evaluation. One historian notes their phrase "if the work continues" and highlighted that they "doubted as to the wisdom of continuing the mission." Reacting to Robertson's dismal claim— "We haven't over five or six real Saints in the mission who are willing and ready to help carry on the word"—the First Presidency decided something must be done. "When we stop to think that over twenty years of hard labor have been performed in Japan, it certainly looks as though the Lord would justify us if we saw fit to close that mission," they wrote in early 1924. "We do not wish to lose one soul in Japan, but if the same amount of labor in some other country was performed the chances are we would have many times as many converts."[81] The First Presidency felt compelled to shift evangelistic resources from Japan, as long as they had "done [their] duty in warning the Japanese nation."[82]

As millenarians, the elders and sisters of the Japan Mission determined to ensure that they had properly warned those in their ecclesiastical stewardship before they abandoned their posts. It was clear that the residents of Tokyo, Sapporo, and Osaka had little interest in joining Mormonism. But what about their Japanese converts who demonstrated widely varying devotion to the church? To answer this question, Robertson and another elder visited the Tokyo members to gauge their interest in the church. "We called on Brother Nakagawa the forenoon and Brother Yamada was visiting him at that time so we talked to them for about an hour and a half about their responsibility in helping to carry on the work," Robertson recorded. The missionaries warned the Japanese brethren "that unless the saint[s] took more of an interest in the work the mission might be closed as the First Presidency are not at all satisfied with the results here."[83] They continued their visits for the next several days and were discouraged.

That April, Grant updated his Utah general conference audience on the progress of the church's twenty-four missions based on conversion statistics. Japan had been the lowest baptizing mission in the world in terms of converts per mission and converts per missionary for several years.[84] "The reports from our Missions from all over the world are very satisfactory," Grant stated. Japan was the "only one real exception" to the progress of the church worldwide. "After twenty-odd years of labor in that country, we are convinced that not a dozen people have been thoroughly converted to the gospel of the Lord Jesus Christ. We have seriously considered the question of closing that mission, but have not yet arrived at any conclusion."[85] The elders and sisters in Japan learned of Grant's conference remarks in May 1924 when they read the text in the *Deseret News*.[86] They were discouraged by their prophet's assessment of their mission, but they had little quarrel with his claims. Grant closed the ailing mission before October general conference later that year. Yet the church president's frequent correspondence with Robertson, the final president of the early Japan Mission, makes no reference to specific moments of inspiration or spiritual promptings. Instead, he cites reports and mission statistics. Grant's closure decision, then, seems to have been one of pragmatism flavored by millenarianism.

In subsequent decades, as political events unfolded in Japan after the Second World War, some Mormons began to interpret Grant's closure of the mission as divinely inspired. Several missionaries suggested that he was inspired to withdraw the elders and sisters from Japan in 1924, thereby protecting them from subsequent harm during the war years.[87] Hilton A. Robertson suggested in 1947 that Grant closed the Japan Mission by inspiration. "I think that the mission was closed for a purpose in 1924....I feel that the Lord knew what was going to transpire and he called the missionaries home and ordered the mission closed temporarily. Later on we find that the other denominations throughout the world who were proselyting in Japan were forced to close their missions and return to America at great loss and sacrifice" as a result of World War II.[88] Ernest B. Woodward likewise claimed in 1949 that when he and the other missionaries returned to America, Grant welcomed them and said: "Thank God you are home because I know what is in store for the people of that land and we are glad you are safely home."[89] Both Woodward and Robertson made their statements two decades after Grant closed the mission and in the aftermath of World War II. Their memories were likely colored by what transpired during the war years or by a desire to save face for the closure of the mission.

TEMPORARY RETREAT

By the summer of 1924, church leaders were convinced that it was time to temporarily retreat from Japan. On June 9, the First Presidency wired a cablegram to Hilton A. Robertson: "Have decided to withdraw all missionaries from Japan temporarily. Cabling you twelve thousand yen for that purpose. If more needed cable us. Arrange return immediately. Grant."[90] They sent a detailed letter the following day and instructed Robertson to "dispose of all church property and close the mission."[91] But the president of the Japan Mission did not receive the missive until weeks later. Given the "tyranny of distance" between Tokyo and Salt Lake City and the resulting early twentieth-century communication limitations, it is not surprising that President Grant's official announcement of the Japan Mission's pending closure came as a partial shock to missionaries in Japan when it finally did arrive.

Believing that they had properly notified Robertson and his missionaries, the First Presidency broadcast their decision in LDS newspapers. On June 12, the *Deseret News* ran the following announcement titled "Japanese Mission Temporarily Closed" over the signatures of Heber J. Grant, Charles W. Penrose, and Anthony W. Ivins, the First Presidency. "In consideration of existing conditions in Japan and because of the almost negligible results of missionary effort in that country since the mission was opened in 1901 the matter of the temporary closing of the mission and the withdrawal of the missionaries who are laboring there, has long been under consideration by the Presidency and the Council of the Twelve," the notice read. "At a meeting recently held it was decided that this action should be taken without further delay. A cablegram has been sent to President Hilton A. Robertson, authorizing him to release all Elders laboring in Japan, and return them to their homes at once. Funds have been forwarded to meet the expense of the return trip."[92] The Latter-day Saints in Utah knew of the First Presidency's decision before their counterparts in Japan.

Still unaware of the First Presidency's action, Robertson was puzzled when he received a letter on June 13, from the Yokohama Specie Bank notifying him that church authorities had wired 12,000 yen (about $6,000) to the mission's account. "I was rather surprised at receiving this amount as I hadn't ask[ed] for such an amount at this time," he noted. Nevertheless, he speculated that it was likely for the "closing of the mission and sending the missionaries home."[93] Two days later American missionaries and Japanese members in Tokyo read in a local newspaper that church leaders in Utah had shuttered their mission.[94] But it was another two weeks until Robertson received the First Presidency's cablegram on June 26. In the meantime, the elders and sisters began shuttering the mission and arranging for steamer passage home.[95] On June 28 Robertson finally received the First Presidency's June 10 letter that confirmed their June 9 cablegram. "Some telegraph service!" he vented in his diary. That same day, the missionaries in Tokyo discovered two posters on their church door with a threatening message.[96]

Over the next few weeks the missionaries continued to dispose of church property and prepare for their temporary retreat to America. They said goodbye to church members and friends before gathering in Tokyo, where they distributed enormous numbers of tracts for the last time. (They sent the remaining mission literature in Japanese to Hawaii where it was later used to teach the Japanese immigrants living in the islands.) They were sad to sell the mission home's prized piano to a furniture dealer. "It begins to look like we are leaving for sure to see this go," Robertson conceded after pawning the musical instrument.[97] One of the banes of the mission, the lack of physical infrastructure, proved to be a mixed blessing in the end. As the church never purchased land or property in Japan, the missionaries were able to terminate their lodging leases and did not have to worry about disposing of real estate assets or providing for landlord caretakers. At the same time, the abandoned Japanese members had no real sense of place, in the absence of mission headquarters and rented assembly halls.

The *Deseret News* in Utah announced that the staff of the Japan Mission would sail for America in late July. It also notified the missionaries' families and the Utah Mormons that Robertson would sail from Yokohama on the steamer *President Cleveland* on Pioneer Day (July 24), exactly twenty-three years after the original quartet departed from Salt Lake City for Japan in 1901. "There are a number of faithful Saints there who regret to see the missionaries go," the short announcement also noted.[98] However, Robertson was unable to secure enough berths on one steamer for all of the American missionaries, so he arranged for the elders and sisters to trickle back to America during the months of July and August. The last group of missionaries departed from Japan on August 7, 1924.[99]

When Robertson spoke in October 1924 general conference in Utah, just months after returning from Japan, he stated: "The missionaries were united in feeling that the Japanese had had a fair chance of hearing the gospel, under the limited number of elders which we had present. The First Presidency felt that inasmuch as the people were anxious, in other parts of the world, that it might be more feasible to withdraw the missionaries from that land and take them to other parts, where the people were better prepared to receive the message of truth."[100] Two years later, former mission president Lloyd D. Ivie shared his feelings about the future of Mormonism among the Japanese: "It is my firm belief and opinion that there is the blood of Israel among that people. I believe that some day, although the time may not be fully ripe, that blood will show itself in greater good works in the land."[101]

Epilogue

Despite the dedicated efforts of nearly ninety committed LDS evangelists, the Japan Mission claimed only 166 converts before it was shuttered. For twenty-three years, the sons and grandsons of the original Mormon pioneers struggled to complete their evangelistic errand to Japan. From the beginning, diminuendo, not crescendo, seemingly characterized the church's only Asian mission. Because the number of Japanese conversions seemed to creep upward like molasses, LDS leaders in Utah and the missionaries in Japan "never had a chance to become elated with their success," one historian suggests. Both the American missionaries and the Japanese converts did not "feel that they were a part of a successful operation."[1] But did the missionaries themselves measure their success or failure solely in numerical terms?

Twenty-three years before his successor Heber J. Grant closed the church's efforts among the Japanese in June 1924, LDS Church president Lorenzo Snow hosted a reception for the first four men called to evangelize to the Japanese. On that June 1901 evening, South Temple Street in Salt Lake City was clogged with buggies and streetcars filled with men returning to their homes after a long day's work. The local merchants, too, were packing up their wares and buttoning up their street-front shops. The Beehive House, the residence of the Mormon prophet, buzzed with preparations. This particular evening held much promise for the quartet called to Asia. While general authorities crowded the main room, it was the missionaries—Heber J. Grant, Louis A. Kelsch, Horace S. Ensign, and Alma O. Taylor—who commanded the crowd's affection. After several rounds of singing and speeches, Snow finally rose from his seat to make his address. After surveying his audience, he began his short, yet disquieting, remarks on the immediate prospects of Mormonism in Japan: "As to these brethren who will shortly leave for Japan, the Lord has not revealed to me that they will succeed, but He has shown me that it is their duty to go."[2]

The Mormon prophet couched his eyebrow-raising remarks in the context of the previous missionary experiences of men such as latter-day apostle Orson Pratt and Old Testament prophets Noah and Moses. While these leaders "failed in some respects," Snow noted they fulfilled their duty. Pratt and a companion tried to evangelize in Austria in 1864, for example. Yet because of religious persecution they were unsuccessful. "Nevertheless, they did their duty and were blessed," he clarified. Snow next referred to the missionary labors of Noah. Although Noah preached repentance for 120 years, no one but his wife, three sons, and their wives—only seven souls—ultimately accepted his testimony. While Noah "failed" because he was rejected by the people, Snow argued that he "was a grand man and did his duty" and "secured to himself exaltation and glory." Similarly, Moses was unable to lead the children of Israel to the Promised Land because of their disobedience. Therefore he "failed to accomplish what the Lord wanted." Regardless, the LDS leader assured his listeners that Moses had likewise attained his heavenly reward.[3] Not surprisingly, Snow's remarks sobered the festivities that evening.[4]

So how did the elders and sisters in Japan, who, like Pratt, Noah, and Moses, enjoyed little numerical success, view their evangelistic sojourns in Japan? Based on my reading of their letters, journals, and reports, most of the elders and sisters (with the notable exception of Heber J. Grant) viewed their missionary efforts among the Japanese as successful because of their premillennarian orientation.[5] Recall that historian Grant Underwood suggests that "the Mormons did not expect to convert the world, only to warn it."[6] One could argue that the very fact that they were there in Japan, holding out the possibility of salvation for those they encountered, made them successful. It was the Japanese who had failed to accept the gospel—not the elders who were offering it, in the missionaries' minds.

The American elders and sisters generally understood their success in the proffered warning. "We are working earnestly, with perhaps more hope than success, but we feel unable to rightly judge the good which we are doing. We know one thing, however, which gives us much satisfaction—we know that we are carrying the first news of the teachings of our Savior to many of Japan's people," H. Grant Ivins reported. "We are doing our best to spread that light, and feel in a way satisfied with our labors here."[7] Alma O. Taylor also argued that his mission was a success. "Is the Japan mission a failure? Is it premature? The shortest answer to both these questions is an emphatic 'No,'" he declared.

> It is the mission of "Mormonism" to preach the gospel to all the world for a witness before the end shall come. Therefore, counting its success or failure by the number of converts made, is a gross mistake. The aim of the Japanese mission is to preach the everlasting gospel and bear witness of Jesus Christ, that the people of this land, like those of all other lands, may be left without excuse. Our success or failure, then, must be determined by the answer to the question, "What has the Japan mission done, and what is it doing, for the spread of truth?"[8]

Taylor then rehearsed all that he and his fellow missionaries were doing to evangelize the Japanese, including the number of miles walked and ridden, as well as the number of homes visited, tracts distributed, and books sold. He then challenged his readers to refute the success of missionary work in Japan. "Compare the work with the number and ability of the workers, take into consideration the language and what has had to be learned about the people and the country, and, no doubt, the reader will agree with me that the work of laying a foundation in this mission has progressed," he affirmed.[9]

Elwood Christensen, moreover, arrived in Japan in summer 1922 with his wife and was distraught when the mission closed two years later. He later dismissed the idea that he and his fellow missionaries viewed their evangelism a fiasco. "The spirit of the missionaries at the time the mission was closed was excellent," he exclaimed. "Everyone loved President Robertson who had just been put in charge. We just felt that things were beginning, even though the work was very difficult. Just like any missionaries, we were thrilled with the work and thrilled with the Saints we had." Christensen continued: "I know a lot of people felt, 'Oh, the mission was a failure and all the missionaries thought it was a failure and thought it ought to be closed.' That's all wrong. Missionaries who are sincere in the gospel just don't react that way."[10] For most of the missionaries, the closing of the mission was "like attending a funeral, where you kind of weep over the remains."[11] As these examples suggest, the missionaries' personal writings do not betray a sense of failure.

Although the First Presidency officially suspended missionary work in Japan in 1924, several committed Japanese Latter-day Saints scattered throughout Honshu and Hokkaidō attempted to preserve their faith community. Nara Fujiya, for example, oversaw the Mutual Improvement Association activities in Japan, and even produced an LDS newsletter titled *Shuro* (The Palm) to keep in touch with his fellow Japanese saints between 1925 and 1929. During these years the First Presidency called Nara as the presiding LDS priesthood leader for all of Japan, which enabled sacred ordinances to be again performed, despite the absence of personnel from the United States. Alma O. Taylor, one of the original missionaries called to Japan in 1901, also corresponded with some Japanese Mormons for a time, encouraging them to remain faithful until the Japan Mission reopened at some future date. Franklin S. Harris, then president of the LDS Church-sponsored Brigham Young University in Provo, Utah, visited Japan in 1926 and also offered hope to abandoned Japanese church members. During his visit Harris became acquainted with Fujiwara Takeo, whom he invited to study in Utah. Fujiwara became BYU's first Japanese graduate and returned to Japan in 1934 to replace Nara as the presiding elder, as Nara had relocated to Manchuria the previous year. Fujiwara did his best to shepherd Mormonism's dwindling flock of converts in Japan until his death in 1936. Nara characterized this trying period of Mormonism in Japan as the "absolute dark ages."[12]

In the meantime, President Heber J. Grant determined to evangelize the growing number of Japanese living in the Hawaiian Islands, especially after meeting a number of Japanese converts while organizing the Oahu Stake in 1935. For years, Japanese and Chinese residents had joined the church and been given their own LDS Sunday schools in Hawaii. A former elder of the Japan Mission, Elwood Christensen, was leading a fledgling Japanese congregation in Honolulu, and President Grant was impressed. "It would seem not improbable that Hawaii is the most favorable place for the Church to make its next effort to preach the Gospel to the Japanese people; and it would further appear that a strong colony of Japanese Saints in Hawaii could operate from there into their homeland in a way that might bring many Japanese to a knowledge not only of Christianity, but of the restored Gospel," Grant's counselor J. Reuben Clark suggested. A year later President Grant appointed Hilton A. Robertson, former president of the early Japan Mission, to open the Japanese Mission in Honolulu, which would become known in time as the Japanese–Central Pacific Mission. In 1937, when the Hawaii-based mission was formed, there were five missionaries, four convert baptisms, and a total membership of seventeen Latter-day Saints in the entire mission. By 1948, the mission's numbers had grown to eighty-nine missionaries, fifty-two convert baptisms, and a total membership of 604 Latter-day Saints. The evangelism success enjoyed by Mormon missionaries in Hawaii during these years is all the more remarkable given the struggles of the early Japan Mission.[13]

The Japan Mission (in Asia) remained closed until 1948, when Edward L. Clissold reopened the mission under the direction of church president George Albert Smith, Grant's successor. In the year since Japan's World War II surrender, a number of Mormon servicemen helping with the Allied occupation of Japan had begun meeting as LDS groups. When Clissold arrived in Japan there were already dozens of American and Japanese Latter-day Saints and prospective converts gathering for church services on Sundays. The LDS Church has had a constant presence in Japan ever since.[14] While Mormonism, like other Christian faiths moving into Asia, still has its share of challenges, it is more firmly established in twenty-first-century Japan. By the beginning of 2007 there were over 121,000 members,

29 stakes and 14 districts (ecclesiastical units similar to Catholic dioceses), 165 wards and 133 branches (parishes) in the island nation. The church has built two temples, a sign of ecclesiastical maturity, for the Japanese saints in Tokyo and Fukuoka.[15] Church leaders have subdivided the early Japan Mission, which originally encompassed the entire nation, into seven geographically smaller missions: Fukuoka, Hiroshima, Nagoya, Sapporo, Sendai, Tokyo North, and Tokyo South.[16] Currently, nearly a thousand missionaries labor between the northern peninsula of Wakanai and the southern archipelago of Okinawa, with greater success than their earlier counterparts who arrived in and departed from Japan as strangers in a strange land.

LDS authorities have since expended great effort and resources to try to overcome many of the inadequacies of their earlier Euro-American missionary approach to the Japanese, with more favorable results. Asian converts, as well as returned missionaries and mission presidents from Asia, have contributed to Mormonism's institutional memory and have helped localize the church's evangelistic practices, although there is still much to be done to truly internationalize Mormonism in Japan.[17] All non-Japanese elders and sisters now arrive in Japan with months of language and cultural training. They are able to communicate effectively after being in the field for less than a year and are heavily recruited for their language skills upon their return to North America.[18] The church's missionary training centers have received international acclaim for their language pedagogical practices and ability to prepare young people for global service.[19] The missionaries' volunteer stints are now partially subsidized by church funds, easing the financial burden on families. All missions have been standardized at twenty-four months for young men and eighteen months for young women. The church also has instituted a financial equalization program which mandates that all elders and sisters pay the same monthly costs regardless of where they are called to serve. Human deployment to East Asia is now less of an issue. Since the end of World War II, Japan, Korea, Hong Kong, and Taiwan have become focal points of Mormon evangelism; there are thousands of missionaries currently serving in over a dozen missionary fields throughout East Asia.

Notes

PREFACE

1. Japan Mission Manuscript History and Historical Reports, Church History Library, The Church of Jesus Christ of Latter-day Saints, Salt Lake City, Utah.

2. See Grant Wacker, "Second Thoughts on the Great Commission: Liberal Protestants and Foreign Missions, 1890–1940," in *Earthen Vessels: American Evangelicals and Foreign Missions, 1880–1980*, ed. Joel A. Carpenter and Wilbert R. Shenk (Grand Rapids, Mich.: William B. Eerdmans, 1990), 281–300.

3. L. Tom Perry Special Collections, Harold B. Lee Library, Brigham Young University, Provo, Utah (hereafter cited as Perry Special Collections).

4. See Alma O. Taylor, Journal, Perry Special Collections. See also Reid L. Neilson, "The Japanese Missionary Journals of Elder Alma O. Taylor, 1901–10" (Master's thesis, Brigham Young University, 2001; *BYU Studies*, 2002).

5. Taylor, Journal, August 12 and October 13, 1901; Louis A. Kelsch, in *Seventy-third Semi-annual Conference of The Church of Jesus Christ of Latter-day Saints* (Salt Lake City: The Church of Jesus Christ of Latter-day Saints, 1902), 35.

6. Gary Shepherd and Gordon Shepherd, *Mormon Passage: A Missionary Chronicle* (Urbana: University of Illinois Press, 1998), 9. Note the differences between the Mormon and Protestant missionary systems in chapter two.

7. See Dana L. Robert, "From Missions to Mission to Beyond Missions: The Historiography of American Protestant Foreign Missions since World War II," in *New Directions in American Religious History*, ed. Harry S. Stout and D. G. Hart (New York: Oxford University Press, 1997), 362–93.

8. Some conservative Protestants, who are also responsible for most mission-related publications, would argue that the LDS Church is not a Christian tradition; therefore, its missionaries have no place in Christian missiology. To better understand this theological debate, which I will not review in this book, see Robert L. Millet, *A Different Jesus? The Christ of the Latter-day Saints* (Grand Rapids, Mich.: William B. Eerdmans, 2005); and Jan Shipps, "'Is Mormonism Christian?' Reflections on a Complicated Question," *BYU Studies* 33, no. 3 (1993): 438–65.

9. Noted mission historian Kenneth Scott Latourette writes only of nineteenth-century Mormon evangelistic efforts in India: "We hear of Mormon missionaries, but they seem not to have attracted an extensive following." Regarding contemporaneous LDS missions in Southeast Asia, he notes: "We hear, too, of Mormon missionaries, but they seem not to have founded a continuing mission." While early LDS evangelism in South and Southeast Asia was abandoned after several years in the 1850s, Latourette makes no mention of Mormon missionary work in Japan during the first quarter of the twentieth century. Kenneth Scott Latourette, *A History of the Expansion of Christianity, Vol. 6: The Great Century: North America and Asia, A.D. 1800–A.D. 1914* (Grand Rapids, Mich.: Zondervan, 1970), 6:178, 245. Historian Charles W. Iglehart

spills no ink on the early Japan Mission, making scant reference to its existence in 1958. Charles W. Iglehart, *A Century of Protestant Christianity in Japan* (Rutland, Vt.: Charles E. Tuttle, 1959), 341. Historian Otis Cary devotes one long paragraph to the early Japan Mission. Otis Cary, *A History of Christianity in Japan: Roman Catholic, Greek Orthodox, and Protestant Missions* (New York: Fleming H. Revell, 1909), 2:309–10. I have been unable to find additional treatments of Mormonism in Japan in traditional survey histories.

10.	See David J. Whittaker, "Mormon Missiology: An Introduction and Guide to the Sources," in *Disciple as Witness: Essays on Latter-day Saint History and Doctrine in Honor of Richard Lloyd Anderson*, ed. Stephen D. Ricks, Donald W. Parry, and Andrew H. Hedges (Provo, Utah: Foundation for Ancient Research and Mormon Studies, Brigham Young University, 2000), 507–17.

11.	Whittaker, *Mormon Missiology*, 466.

12.	See Reid L. Neilson, "Mormonism and the Japanese: A Guide to the Sources," in *Taking the Gospel to the Japanese, 1901–2001*, ed. Reid L. Neilson and Van C. Gessel (Provo, Utah: Brigham Young University Press, 2006), 435–44.

13.	"A Visitor from Japan," *Millennial Star* 84 (February 16, 1922): 101.

Chapter One
Mormon Mappings of Asian Religions

1.	Thomas A. Tweed and Stephen Prothero, *Asian Religions in America: A Documentary History* (New York: Oxford University Press, 1999), 51. See also East-India Marine Society of Salem, *By-laws and regulations of the East India Marine Society, Massachusetts: An association of masters and commanders of vessels, and of such persons as may be hereafter described, who have been, or are, engaged in the East India trade from the town of Salem* (Salem, Mass.: Thomas C. Cushing, 1800).

2.	Dan Vogel, ed., *Early Mormon Documents* (Salt Lake City: Signature Books, 1996), 1:243–47; and Richard L. Bushman, *Joseph Smith and the Beginnings of Mormonism* (Urbana: University of Illinois Press, 1984), 1:30.

3.	Daniel Finamore, "Displaying the Sea and Defining America: Early Exhibitions at the Salem East India Marine Society," *Journal for Maritime Research* (May 2002). http://www.jmr.nmm.ac.uk/server/show/conJmrArticle.4 (accessed November 16, 2009).

4.	David R. Proper, "Joseph Smith and Salem," *Essex Institute Historical Collections* 100 (April 1964): 94. See also Donald Q. Cannon, "Joseph Smith in Salem (D&C 111)," in *Studies in Scripture, Vol. 1: The Doctrine and Covenants*, ed. Kent P. Jackson and Robert L. Millet (Salt Lake City: Deseret Book, 1989), 432–36.

5.	For an overview of the concepts of contacts, exchanges, and encounters, see Thomas A. Tweed, "Introduction: Narrating U.S. Religious History"; and Laurie F. Maffly-Kipp, "Eastward Ho! American Religion from the Perspective of the Pacific Rim," in *Retelling U.S. Religious History*, ed. Thomas A. Tweed (Berkeley: University of California Press, 1997), 17–19, 127–48.

6.	Tweed and Prothero, *Asian Religions in America*, 5–6.

7. Thomas A. Tweed, "Introduction: Hannah Adams's Survey of the Religious Landscape," in Hannah Adams, *A Dictionary of All Religions and Religious Denominations: Jewish, Heathen, Mahometan, Christian, Ancient and Modern* (Atlanta: Scholars Press, 1992), vii–ix.

8. Tweed, "Introduction," xxiv–xxv.

9. Ibid., xiv–xv, xxv.

10. See Sydney E. Ahlstrom, *The American Protestant Encounter with World Religions* (Beloit, Wis.: Beloit College, 1962); Thomas A. Tweed, *The American Encounter with Buddhism, 1844–1912: Victorian Culture and the Limits of Dissent* (Chapel Hill: University of North Carolina Press, 2000); Robert S. Ellwood, *Alternative Altars: Unconventional and Eastern Spirituality in America* (Chicago: University of Chicago Press, 1979); Carl T. Jackson, *The Oriental Religions and American Thought: Nineteenth-Century Explorations* (Westport, Conn.: Greenwood Press, 1981); and George Hunston Williams, "The Attitude of Liberals in New England toward Non-Christian Religions, 1784–1885," *Crane Review* 9 (Winter 1967): 59–89.

11. Grant Wacker, "A Plural World: The Protestant Awakening to World Religions," in *Between the Times: The Travail of the Protestant Establishment in America, 1900–1960,* ed. William R. Hutchison (Cambridge: Cambridge University Press, 1989), 256.

12. Tweed, *American Encounter with Buddhism,* 2.

13. Tweed, *American Encounter with Buddhism*; Wacker, "A Plural World," 253–56.

14. Wacker, "A Plural World," 257.

15. Alan Race, *Christians and Religious Pluralism: Patterns in the Christian Theology of Religions* (London: SCM Press, 1983), 1.

16. Wacker, "A Plural World," 253–57; Race, *Christians and Religious Pluralism,* 1–3.

17. Gavin D'Costa, *Theology and Religious Pluralism: The Challenge of Other Religions* (New York: Basil Blackwell, 1986), 22, 52.

18. William C. Wilkinson, "The Attitude of Christianity to Other Religions," in *The World's Parliament of Religions,* ed. John H. Barrows (Chicago: Parliament Publishing Company, 1893), 2:1249; and Richard Hughes Seager, ed., *The Dawn of Religious Pluralism: Voices from the World's Parliament of Religions, 1893* (La Salle, Ill.: Open Court, 1993), 70–74.

19. Thomas Wentworth Higginson, "The Sympathy of Religions," in Barrows, *The World's Parliament of Religions,* 1:780–84; Seager, *The Dawn of Religious Pluralism,* 321–22.

20. D'Costa, *Theology and Religious Pluralism,* 80.

21. John Henry Barrows, "Words of Welcome," in *The World's Parliament of Religions,* 1:72–79; Seager, *The Dawn of Religious Pluralism,* 23–31.

22. Dianna L. Eck, *Encountering God: A Spiritual Journey from Bozeman to Banaras* (Boston: Beacon Press, 1993), 179.

23. Some eighteenth-century deists advanced their own version of "primitive monotheism" or "original monotheism" although it differed from the later Christ-centered LDS theological position. See Samuel Shuckford, *The Sacred and the Profane History of the World Connected,* vols. 1 and 2, 3d ed. (London: Pr. for J. and R. Tonson, 1743).

Peter Harrison describes primitive monotheism in his book *"Religion" and the Religions in the English Enlightenment* (Cambridge: Cambridge University Press, 1990), 139–46. Wilhelm Schmidt, a non-LDS critic of evolutionism, argued a similar original monotheism theory, but not until the first decades of the twentieth century. According to Eric Sharpe, Schmidt's "overriding concern was to demonstrate that the older the stratum of human culture, the more clearly can one discern in it clear evidence of the worship of a Supreme Being." Eric J. Sharpe, *Comparative Religion: A History* (New York: Charles Scribner's Sons, 1975), 182–84. See also W. Schmidt, *The Origin and Growth of Religion: Facts and Theories* (London: Methuen and Company, 1930).

24. Spencer J. Palmer, *Religions of the World: A Latter-day Saint View* (Provo, Utah: Brigham Young University, 1988), 191–96. His *primordial images theory* posits that "human predispositions of thought and feeling may be viewed as 'echoes of eternity,' since all men lived together under common conditions with God in a premortal spirit world." His *devil invention theory* speculates that "the devil has exerted a powerful influence upon men in counterfeiting the true principles and ordinances of the gospel ... in an effort to lull mankind into satisfaction with partial truths and to weaken the appeal of divinely appointed teachers." His *common human predicament theory* argues "certain experiences are fundamental to all human beings." Therefore, "common beliefs and practices arise from the common predicaments faced by man."

25. Palmer, *Religions of the World*, 197.

26. Joseph Smith, "Baptism for the Dead," *Times and Seasons* (Nauvoo, Illinois) 3 (April 15, 1842): 759. Smith writes in this same editorial: "To say that the heathens would be damned because they did not believe the Gospel would be preposterous, and to say that the Jews would all be damned that do not believe in Jesus would be equally absurd; for 'how can they believe on him of whom they have not heard and how can they hear without a preacher, and how can he preach except he be sent.'" See David L. Paulsen, "The Redemption of the Dead: A Latter-day Saint Perspective on the Fate of the Unevangelized," in *Salvation in Christ: Comparative Christian Views*, ed. Roger R. Keller and Robert L. Millet (Provo, Utah: Religious Studies Center, Brigham Young University, 2005), 263–97.

27. For an overview of Mormon evangelistic history in the Pacific world see Laurie F. Maffly-Kipp and Reid L. Neilson, eds., *Proclamation to the People: Nineteenth-Century Mormonism and the Pacific Basin Frontier* (Salt Lake City: University of Utah Press, 2008).

28. David J. Whittaker, "Parley P. Pratt and the Pacific Mission: Mormon Publishing in 'That Very Questionable Part of the Civilized World,'" in *Mormons, Scripture, and the Ancient World: Studies in Honor of John L. Sorenson*, ed. Davis Bitton (Provo, Utah: Foundation for Ancient Research and Mormon Studies, 1998), 51, 55; *The Essential Parley P. Pratt* (Salt Lake City: Signature Books, 1990), 152, 156.

29. Tweed, *American Encounter with Buddhism*, xxix–xxx; *The Essential Parley P. Pratt*, 161.

30. George D. Watt, et al., eds., *Journal of Discourses*, 26 vols. (Liverpool, England: F. D.

Richards, et al., 1854–1886): 1:155, June 12, 1853.

31. Brigham Young, December 3, 1854, *Journal of Discourses*, 2:140.

32. Moses Thatcher, "Chinese Classics," *Contributor* 8 (June 1887): 301.

33. Brian H. Stuy, ed., *Collected Discourses Delivered by Wilford Woodruff, His Two Counselors, the Twelve Apostles, and Others* (Burbank, Calif.: B. H. S. Publishing, 1987–1992): 1:162, June 24, 1888.

34. George Q. Cannon, *Journal of Discourses*, 14:54–55, August 15, 1869.

35. George Q. Cannon, *Juvenile Instructor* 12 (February 1, 1877): 30; George Q. Cannon, *Journal of Discourses*, 21:74–75, October 5, 1879. Cannon later taught that Mohammad, "whom the Christians deride and call a false prophet and stigmatize with a great many epithets, was a man raised up by the Almighty and inspired to a certain extent by Him." George Q. Cannon, *Journal of Discourses*, 24:371, September 2, 1883.

36. George Q. Cannon, "Editorial Thoughts," *Juvenile Instructor* 21 (August 15, 1886): 248. See also George Q. Cannon, "Topics of the Times," *Juvenile Instructor* 22 (October 1, 1887): 291.

37. I am currently writing a monograph on the Mormon representation at the 1893 Chicago World's Fair, including the Parliament of Religions. See also Davis Bitton, "B. H. Roberts at the World Parliament of Religion, 1893," *Sunstone* 7 (January/February 1982): 46–51; and Richard Hughes Seager, *The World's Parliament of Religions: The East/West Encounter, Chicago, 1893* (Bloomington: Indiana University Press, 1995).

38. See Judith Snodgrass, *Presenting Japanese Buddhism to the West: Orientalism, Occidentalism, and the Columbian Exposition* (Chapel Hill: University of North Carolina Press, 2003).

39. Stuy, *Collected Discourses*, 3:356–59.

40. Palmer, *Religions of the World*, 194.

41. Stuy, *Collected Discourses*, 3:356–59.

42. George Q. Cannon, *Juvenile Instructor* 28 (November 1, 1893): 675–76.

43. Stuy, *Collected Discourses*, 5:155.

Chapter Two
Mormon Encounters with Asians

1. See Arrell Morgan Gibson, *Yankees in Paradise: The Pacific Basin Frontier* (Albuquerque: University of New Mexico Press, 1993), 263–68.

2. Gibson, *Yankees in Paradise*, 266–84, 292–95.

3. Ibid., 266–84. See also Laurie F. Maffly-Kipp, "Assembling Bodies and Souls: Missionary Practices on the Pacific Frontier," in *Practicing Protestants: Histories of Christian Life in America, 1630–1965*, ed. Laurie F. Maffly-Kipp, Leigh E. Schmidt, and Mark Valeri (Baltimore: Johns Hopkins University Press, 2006); and Neil Gunson, *Messengers of Grace: Evangelical Missionaries in the South Seas, 1797–1860* (New York: Oxford University Press, 1978).

4. William R. Hutchison, *Errand to the World: American Protestant Thought and Foreign Missions* (Chicago: University of Chicago Press, 1987), 1.

5. Wacker, "A Plural World," 256.

6. Tweed and Prothero, *Asian Religions in America*, 1–12.

7. Jan Shipps, *Sojourner in the Promised Land: Forty Years among the Mormons* (Urbana: University of Illinois Press, 2000), 258–60.

8. See Maffly-Kipp and Neilson, *Proclamation to the People*; Laurie F. Maffly-Kipp, "Looking West: Mormonism and the Pacific World," *Journal of Mormon History* 26 (Spring 2000): 41–63; R. Lanier Britsch, *Unto the Islands of the Sea: A History of the Latter-day Saints in the Pacific* (Salt Lake City: Deseret Book, 1986).

9. Parley P. Pratt and Franklin D. Richards, "An Epistle of the Twelve to President Orson Pratt, and The Church of Jesus Christ of Latter-day Saints in the British Isles," *Millennial Star* 11 (August 15, 1849): 247; and LDS Journal History, May 6, 1849.

10. See A. Delbert Palmer and Mark L. Grover, "Hoping to Establish a Presence: Parley P. Pratt's 1851 Mission to Chile," *BYU Studies* 38, no. 4 (1999): 115–38; and Matthew J. Grow, "A Providential Means of Agitating Mormonism: Parley P. Pratt and the San Francisco Press in the 1850s," *Journal of Mormon Studies* 29 (Fall 2003): 158–85.

11. See Craig Livingston, "Eyes on 'The Whole European World': Mormon Observers of the 1848 Revolutions," *Journal of Mormon History* 32 (Fall 2005): 78–112.

12. "Sixth General Epistle of the Presidency of The Church of Jesus Christ of Latter-day Saints," *Millennial Star* 14 (January 15, 1852): 17–18, 25.

13. "Seventh General Epistle of the Presidency of The Church of Jesus Christ of Latter-day Saints," *Millennial Star* 14 (July 17, 1852): 325.

14. LDS Journal History, August 28, 1852; and Eugene E. Campbell, *Establishing Zion: The Mormon Church in the American West, 1847–1869* (Salt Lake City: Signature Books, 1988), 174.

15. R. Lanier Britsch, *From the East: The History of the Latter-day Saints in Asia, 1851–1996* (Salt Lake City: Deseret Book, 1998), 8–42.

16. Jonathan D. Spence, *The Search for Modern China* (New York: W. W. Norton, 1999), 171–80. See also Thomas H. Reilly, *The Taiping Heavenly Kingdom: Rebellion and the Blasphemy of Empire* (Seattle: University of Washington Press, 2004).

17. Stout to Young, May 16, 1853, as quoted in Stout, *Hosea Stout*, 172.

18. James Lewis, *Deseret News*, January 4, 1854; and R. Lanier Britsch, "Church Beginnings in China," *BYU Studies* 10 (Winter 1970): 169.

19. "Eleventh General Epistle of the Presidency of The Church of Jesus Christ of Latter-day Saints," *Millennial Star* 16 (July 8, 1854): 417.

20. Marius B. Jansen, *The Making of Modern Japan* (Cambridge, Mass.: Belknap Press of Harvard University Press, 2000), 257–93; and Kenneth B. Pyle, *The Making of Modern Japan* (Lexington, Mass: D. C. Heath and Company, 1996), 57–60.

21. "Opening of Japan," *Millennial Star* 35 (September 2, 1854): 552.

22. Wilford Woodruff, Journal, November 18, 1856, and March 22, 1857.

23. "William Wood—Pioneer," *Our Pioneer Heritage*, comp. Kate B. Carter, 20 vols. (Salt Lake City: Daughters of Utah Pioneers, 1958–77), 13:264. See also William G. Hartley, "Adventures of a Young British Seaman, 1852–1862," *New Era* 10 (March 1980): 38–47.

24. "William Wood—Pioneer," 13:264.

25. William Willes, Journal, June 17, 1884, reprinted in *The Life of William Willes: From His Own Personal Journals and Writings*, ed. Charleen Cutler (Provo, Utah: Family Footprints, 2000).

26. William Willes, "Tidings from Japan and China," *Juvenile Instructor* 19 (October 1, 1884): 291–92; and Willes, Journal, July 1, 1884.

27. Willes, "Tidings from Japan and China," 292.

28. See Wendy Butler, "The Iwakura Mission and Its Stay in Salt Lake City," *Utah Historical Quarterly* 66 (Winter 1998): 26–47.

29. See Kume Kunitake, comp., *The Iwakura Embassy, 1871–1873: A True Account of the Ambassador Extraordinary and Plenipotentiary's Journal of Observation Through the United States of America and Europe*, trans. Martin Collcutt (Princeton, N.J.: Princeton University Press, 2002), 1:133–41, for a Japanese account of the unexpected stay in Utah.

30. "Opening of a Mission in Japan," *Deseret Evening News*, April 6, 1901, 9.

31. George Q. Cannon, "Editorial Thoughts," *Juvenile Instructor* 8 (February 17, 1872): 28.

32. "Opening of a Mission in Japan," 9.

33. Niijima Jo to Alphaeus Hardy, October 29, 1874, as quoted in Arthur Sherburne Hardy, *Life and Letters of Joseph Hardy Neesima* (Boston: Houghton, Mifflin and Company, 1891), 174–75.

34. John E. Van Sant, *Pacific Pioneers: Japanese Journeys to America and Hawaii, 1850–80* (Urbana: University of Illinois Press, 2000), 76.

35. R. David Arkush and Leo O. Lee, eds. and trans., *Land Without Ghosts: Chinese Impressions of America from the Mid-Nineteenth Century to the Present* (Berkeley: University of California Press, 1989), 51.

36. See Edward Leo Lyman, "From the City of Angeles to the City of Saints: The Struggle to Build a Railroad from Los Angeles to Salt Lake City," *California History* 70 (Spring 1991): 76–93; and Brian D. Corcoran, "'My Father's Business': Thomas Taylor and Mormon Frontier Economic Enterprise," *Dialogue: A Journal of Mormon Thought* 28 (Spring 1995): 105–41.

37. Dwight L. Smith, "The Engineer and the Canyon," *Utah Historical Quarterly* 28 (July 1960): 273; and Dwight L. Smith, "Robert B. Stanton's Plan for the Far Southwest," *Arizona and the West* 4 (Winter 1962): 369–72.

38. Heber J. Grant, Diary Excerpts, August 8, 1895. See also Leonard J. Arrington, *Great Basin Kingdom: An Economic History of the Latter-day Saints, 1830–1900* (1958; reprint, Salt Lake City: University of Utah Press and Tanner Trust Fund, 1993), 399–400.

39. Abraham H. Cannon, Journal, August 19, 1895, Perry Special Collections.

40. Cannon, Journal, August 19, 1895.

41. Ibid., September 1 and 5–8, 1895, October 3, 1895. See also Abraham H. Cannon, "A Future Mission Field," *Contributor* 16 (October 1895): 764–65.

42. Heber J. Grant, Diary Excerpts, August 8, 1895.

43. Michael P. Malone, *James J. Hill: Empire Builder of the Northwest* (Norman, Okla-

homa: University of Oklahoma Press, 1996), 164. See also Albro Martin, *James J. Hill and the Opening of the Northwest* (New York: Oxford University Press, 1976), 471–74; E. Mowbray Tate, *Transpacific Steam: The Story of Steam Navigation from the Pacific Coast of North America to the Far East and the Antipodes, 1867–1941* (New York: Cornwall Books, 1986), 121.

44. Church president Wilford Woodruff retained his interest in Japan. On April 22, 1896, he attended a lecture on Japan by Frank G. Carpenter in Salt Lake City. The following year he allowed Senator Frank J. Cannon to speak on his recent trip to Japan and China to a large crowd in the church's Tabernacle. See Woodruff, Journal, April 22, 1896; "Some People of the Far East," *Deseret News,* November 29, 1897.

45. "A Japanese Idol," *Juvenile Instructor* 8 (May 10, 1872): 73–74; "A Country Scene in Japan," *Juvenile Instructor* 8 (October 25, 1873): 169–70; "Festival of the Idol Tengou in Japan," *Juvenile Instructor* 9 (February 28, 1874): 49; "Japanese Peasant in Winter Costume," *Juvenile Instructor* 9 (March 23, 1874): 81; "Japanese Amusements," *Juvenile Instructor* 10 (August 21, 1875): 193–94; "Japanese Customs," *Juvenile Instructor* 11 (January 15, 1876): 18–20; "A Japan Shoe Store," *Juvenile Instructor* 13 (June 15, 1878): 133–34; "Japanese Children," *Juvenile Instructor* 13 (November 1, 1878): 245; "Japanese Temple," *Juvenile Instructor* 11 (June 1, 1876): 127–28.

46. "Japanese Soldiers," *Juvenile Instructor* 17 (May 1, 1882): 138–39; George Q. Cannon, "Editorial Thoughts," *Juvenile Instructor* 18 (January 15, 1883): 24; "A Japanese Tea-House," *Juvenile Instructor* 18 (March 15, 1883): 81–82; George Q. Cannon, "Editorial Thoughts," *Juvenile Instructor* 18 (June 1, 1883): 168; "A Japanese Meal," *Juvenile Instructor* 19 (March 15, 1884): 81–82; "A Japanese Execution," *Juvenile Instructor* 19 (April 15, 1884): 126–27; "Varieties: A Word for the Japanese," *Juvenile Instructor* 19 (May 15, 1884): 149; "The City of Yokohama, Japan," *Juvenile Instructor* 20 (June 15, 1885): 177–78; "The Metropolis of Japan," *Juvenile Instructor* 22 (November 15, 1887): 337–38; and "A Japanese Traveling Equipage," *Juvenile Instructor* 23 (April 15, 1888): 113; George Q. Cannon, "Editorial Thoughts," *Juvenile Instructor* 18 (June 1, 1883): 168. Articles from the 1890s include: Vidi, "A Progressive People," *Juvenile Instructor* 28 (October 1, 1893): 595–97; "The Parliament of Religions," *Juvenile Instructor* 28 (October 1, 1893): 605–8; "A Commercial City of Japan," *Juvenile Instructor* 30 (January 15, 1895): 41–42; Editor, "Strength in Unity, Not in Numbers," *Juvenile Instructor* 30 (June 1, 1895): 341–43; "Japan," *Juvenile Instructor* 31 (January 1, 1896): 9–12; Editor, "Japanese Progress," *Juvenile Instructor* 32 (June 1, 1897): 354–55; and "In the Land of the Mikado," *Juvenile Instructor* 33 (December 15, 1898): 809–11.

47. Vidi, "A Progressive People," *Juvenile Instructor* 28 (October 1, 1893): 597.

48. Maffly-Kipp, "Eastward Ho!" 128–30.

49. Tweed and Prothero, *Asian Religions in America,* 8–10.

50. Robert McClellan, *The Heathen Chinee: A Study of American Attitudes toward China, 1890–1905* (Columbus: Ohio State University Press, 1971), passim. See also Roger Daniels, *Asian America: Chinese and Japanese in the United States since 1850* (Seattle: University of Washington Press, 1988), 29–66.

51. Bill Ong Hing, *Making and Remaking Asian America through Immigration Policy,*

1850–1990 (Stanford, Calif.: Stanford University Press, 1993), 44–47. See also Daniels, *Asian America*, 9–28; and Bruce B. Lawrence, *New Faiths, Old Fears: Muslims and Other Asian Immigrants in American Religious Life* (New York: Columbia University Press, 2002).

52. Hing, *Making and Remaking Asian America*, 53–59. See also Daniels, *Asian America*, 100–54; and Tsurutani Hisashi, *American-Bound: The Japanese and the Opening of the American West* (Tokyo: Japan Times, 1989), 13–35.

53. Daniels, *Asian America*, passim. See also Gary Y. Okihiro, *Margins and Mainstreams: Asians in American History and Culture* (Seattle: University of Washington Press, 1994).

54. Latourette, *A History of the Expansion of Christianity*, 6:300–69. See also John K. Fairbank, ed., *The Missionary Enterprise in China and America* (Cambridge, Mass.: Harvard University Press, 1974).

55. Latourette, *A History of the Expansion of Christianity*, 6:382–411. See also Winburn T. Thomas, *Protestant Beginnings in Japan: The First Three Decades, 1859–1889* (Rutland, Vt.: Charles E. Tuttle, 1959).

56. Laurie F. Maffly-Kipp, *Religion and Society in Frontier California* (New Haven, Conn.: Yale University Press, 1994), 48.

57. Wesley Stephen Woo, "Protestant Work among the Chinese in the San Francisco Bay Area, 1850–1920 (California)" (Ph.D. diss., Graduate Theological Union, 1984), 30–153.

58. Daniel Liestman, "'To Win Redeemed Souls from Heathen Darkness': Protestant Response to the Chinese of the Pacific Northwest in the Late Nineteenth Century," *Western Historical Quarterly* 24 (May 1993): 179–201.

59. R. Lanier Britsch, *Moramona: The Mormons in Hawaii* (Laie, Hawaii: Institute for Polynesian Studies, 1989), 90.

60. Will Bagley, ed., *"Cities of the Wicked": Alexander Badlam Reports on Mormon Prospects in California and China in the 1850s* (Spokane, Wash.: Arthur H. Clark, 1999), 12–22.

61. Brigham Young to John R. Young, March 1, 1857.

62. Bagley, *"Cities of the Wicked,"* 14.

63. As both Katsunuma and Sato were Asian American immigrants, I have used the westernized spelling and order of their names.

64. Shinji Takagi, "Tomizo and Tokujiro: The First Japanese Mormons," *BYU Studies* 39, no. 2 (2000): 73–106.

65. See Russell T. Clement and Sheng-Luen Tsai, "East Wind to Hawai'i: Contributions and History of Chinese and Japanese Mormons in Hawaii," in *Voyages of Faith: Explorations in Mormon Pacific History*, ed. Grant Underwood (Provo, Utah: Brigham Young University Press, 2000), 89–106; and Britsch, *Moramona*, 141–44.

66. Shipps, *Sojourner in the Promised Land*, 258–60.

67. *Deseret Morning News 2004 Church Almanac* (Salt Lake City: Deseret News, 2004), 234.

68. Pamela S. Perlich, *Utah Minorities: The Story Told by 150 Years of Census Data* (Salt Lake City: Bureau of Economic and Business Research, David S. Eccles School of Business, University of Utah, 2002), 1–19. "Hispanic" was not a separate category

until the 1970 census.

69. Chung-Myun Lee, "Korean," in *Asian Americans in Utah: A Living History*, comp. John H. Yang (Salt Lake City: State of Utah Office of Asian Affairs, Asian American Advisory Council, 1999), 145–77.

70. Dong Sull Choi, "A History of The Church of Jesus Christ of Latter-day Saints in Korea, 1950–1985" (Ph.D. diss., Brigham Young University, 1990), 80–92; and Spencer J. Palmer, *The Korean Saints: Personal Stories of Trial and Triumph, 1950–1980* (Provo, Utah: Religious Education, Brigham Young University, 1995).

71. Don C. Conley, "The Chinese in Utah," in *Utah History Encyclopedia*, ed. Allan Kent Powell (Salt Lake City: University of Utah Press, 1994), 85–86; Perlich, *Utah Minorities*, 13; Daniel Liestman, "Utah's Chinatowns: The Development and Decline of Extinct Ethnic Enclaves," in *Chinese on the American Frontier*, ed. Arif Kirlik (New York: Rowman and Littlefield Publishers, 2001), 269–89; Don C. Conley, "The Pioneer Chinese of Utah," in *The Peoples of Utah*, ed. Helen Z. Papanikolas (Salt Lake City: Utah State Historical Society, 1976), 251–77.

72. Liestman, "Utah's Chinatowns," 269.

73. Ibid., 269–80. See also Michael Lansing, "Race, Space, and Chinese Life in Late-Nineteenth-Century Salt Lake City," *Utah Historical Quarterly* 72 (Summer 2004): 219–38.

74. Liestman, "Utah's Chinatowns," 281–82. Lansing, "Race, Space, and Chinese Life," 236–37.

75. See Wendy Butler, "Strategies, Conditions, and Meanings of Early Japanese Labor in Salt Lake City, Utah, 1890–1920" (Master's thesis, Brigham Young University, 2002). I have used the westernized spelling and order of their names.

76. Helen Z. Papanikolas and Alice Kasai, "Japanese Life in Utah," in *The Peoples of Utah*, ed. Helen Z. Papanikolas (Salt Lake City: Utah State Historical Society, 1976), 333–39; Robert A. Wilson and Bill Hosokawa, *East to America: A History of the Japanese in the United States* (New York: William Morrow and Company, 1980), 76–93; Nancy J. Taniguchi, "Japanese Immigrants in Utah," in *Utah History Encyclopedia*, 281–83.

77. Perlich, *Utah Minorities*, 8, 13–14.

78. For a preliminary history of twentieth-century race relations between the residents of Utah and the Japanese, see Elmer R. Smith, "The 'Japanese' in Utah," *Utah Humanities Review* 2 (June 1948): 129–44, and "The 'Japanese' in Utah: Part II," *Utah Humanities Review* 2 (July 1948): 208–30.

79. To study twentieth-century race relations between the Mormons and Japanese in Canada, see David B. Iwaasa, "The Mormons and Their Japanese Neighbours," *Alberta History* 53 (Winter 2005): 7–22.

80. Eric Walz, "Japanese Immigrants and the Mormons," paper presented at "A Centennial Celebration: The History of The Church of Jesus Christ of Latter-day Saints in Japan 1901–2001," Brigham Young University, Provo, Utah, October 2001, pp. 1–11. See also Wendy Butler, "Eyes Only for the Orient: Early Twentieth-Century Mormon Neglect of Salt Lake City Japanese," paper presented at "A Centennial

Celebration: The History of The Church of Jesus Christ of Latter-day Saints in Japan 1901–2001," Brigham Young University, Provo, Utah, October 2001.

81. Leonard J. Arrington, "Utah's Ambiguous Reception: The Relocated Japanese Americans," in *Japanese Americans: From Relocation to Redress*, ed. Roger Daniels, Sandra C. Taylor, and Harry H. L. Kitano (Salt Lake City: University of Utah Press, 1986): 92–97; Leonard J. Arrington, *The Price of Prejudice: The Japanese-American Relocation Center in Utah during World War II* (Logan: The Faculty Organization, Utah State University, 1962); and Sandra C. Taylor, "Leaving the Concentration Camps: Japanese American Resettlement in Utah and the Intermountain West," *Pacific Historical Review* 60 (May 1991): 169–94.

82. Armand L. Mauss, *All Abraham's Children: Changing Mormon Conceptions of Race and Lineage* (Urbana: University of Illinois Press, 2003), 1–2. See also Armand L. Mauss, "In Search of Ephraim: Traditional Mormon Conceptions of Lineage and Race," *Journal of Mormon History* 25 (Spring 1999): 131–73; and Norman Douglas, "The Sons of Lehi and the Seed of Cain: Racial Myths in Mormon Scripture and their Relevance to the Pacific Islands," *Journal of Religious History* 8 (June 1974): 90–104.

83. Mauss, *All Abraham's Children*, 32–33.

84. See Douglas, "The Sons of Lehi and the Seed of Cain."

85. Britsch, "Church Beginnings in China"; and Britsch, "The East India Mission of 1851–56: Crossing the Boundaries of Culture, Religion, and Law," *Journal of Mormon History* 27 (Fall 2001): 150–76.

86. Gordon Irving, *Numerical Strength and Geographical Distribution of the LDS Missionary Force, 1830–1974* (Salt Lake City: Historical Department of The Church of Jesus Christ of Latter-day Saints, 1975), 11.

87. Alma O. Taylor to the Rev. Nishijima Kakuryo, June 14, 1901, as found in Taylor, Journal, July 28, 1901, Perry Special Collections.

88. Don C. Conley, "The Pioneer Chinese of Utah" (Master's thesis, Brigham Young University, 1976), 114. See also Shi Xu, "The Images of the Chinese in the Rocky Mountain Region: 1855–1882" (Ph.D. diss., Brigham Young University, 1996), 289.

CHAPTER THREE
EURO-AMERICAN MORMON MISSIONARY MODEL

1. I use the term "pagan" consciously to describe how the Western Mormons viewed the inhabitants of Asia during the nineteenth and early twentieth centuries. For example, see Alma O. Taylor, "Japan, the Ideal Mission Field," *Improvement Era* 13 (July 1910): 779–85.

2. *Deseret Morning News 2004 Church Almanac* (Salt Lake City: Deseret News, 2004), 580–81.

3. A few scholars have been careful to delineate between the different meanings of these and other terms. For example, see Dana L. Robert, "The First Globalization: The Internationalization of the Protestant Missionary Movement between the

World Wars," *International Bulletin of Missionary Research* 26 (April 2002): 50–66; and John F. Gorski, "Christology, Inculturation, and Their Missiological Implications: A Latin American Perspective," *International Bulletin of Missionary Research* 28 (April 2004): 60–63.

4.   See Gorski, "Christology, Inculturation, and Their Missiological Implications"; and Ruy O. Costa, "Introduction: Inculturation, Indigenization, and Contextualization," in *One Faith, Many Cultures: Inculturation, Indigenization, and Contextualization*, ed. Ruy O. Costa (Maryknoll, NY: Orbis Books, 1988), ix–xvii.

5.   Peter Schineller, *A Handbook on Inculturation* (New York: Paulist Press, 1990), 14–17. See also Louis J. Luzbetak, "Two Centuries of Cultural Adaptation in American Church Action: Praise, Censure, or Challenge?" in *American Missions in Bicentennial Perspective*, ed. R. Pierce Beaver and Catherine Albanese, 332–53 (South Pasadena, Calif.: William Carey Library, 1977).

6.   Schineller, *A Handbook on Inculturation*, 18–24.

7.   See Ronald E. Poelman, "The Gospel and the Church," *Ensign* 14 (November 1984): 64–65; Spencer J. Palmer, *The Expanding Church* (Salt Lake City: Deseret Book, 1978); and James R. Moss, et al., eds., *The International Church* (Provo, Utah: Brigham Young University Publications, 1982).

8.   For example, see Levi S. Peterson, "Thinking Globally: Explorations into a Truly International, Multi-Cultural Church," *Dialogue: A Journal of Mormon Thought* 38 (Winter 2005): 1–2; Jiro Numano, "How International Is the Church in Japan?" *Dialogue* 13 (Spring 1980): 85–91; Garth N. Jones, "Spreading the Gospel in Indonesia: Organizational Obstacles and Opportunities," *Dialogue* 15 (Winter 1982): 79–90; Thomas W. Murphy, "Reinventing Mormonism: Guatemala as Harbinger of the Future?" *Dialogue* 29 (Spring 1996): 177–92; and Jennifer Huss Basquiat, "Embodied Mormonism: Performance, Vodou, and the LDS Faith in Haiti," *Dialogue* 37 (Winter 2004): 1–34.

9.   Patricia R. Hill, "The Missionary Enterprise," in *Encyclopedia of the American Religious Experience: Studies of Traditions and Movements*, ed. Peter Williams and Charles Lippy (New York: Scribner, 1988): 1683.

10.   Ibid.; and Hutchison, *Errand to the World*, 15–42.

11.   Hill, "The Missionary Enterprise," 1683–84; and Hutchison, *Errand to the World*, 43–61. See also David W. Kling, "The New Divinity and the Origins of the American Board of Commissioners for Foreign Missions," in *North American Foreign Mission, 1810–1914: Theology, Theory, and Policy*, ed. Wilbert R. Shenk (Grand Rapids, Mich.: William B. Eerdmans, 2004), 11–38; and Clifton J. Phillips, *Protestant America and the Pagan World: The First Half Century of the American Board of Commissioners for Foreign Missions, 1810–1860* (Cambridge, Mass.: Harvard University Press, 1969).

12.   Shipps, *Sojourner in the Promised Land*, 258–60.

13.   Jan Shipps, *Mormonism: The Story of a New Religious Tradition* (Urbana: University of Illinois Press, 1985), 54–58.

14.   Richard Lee Rogers, "'A Bright and New Constellation': Millennial Narratives and the Origins of American Foreign Missions," in Shenk, *North American Foreign Mission*, 39–60.

15. Grant Underwood, *The Millenarian World of Early Mormonism* (Urbana: University of Illinois Press, 1993), 2.

16. As quoted in Underwood, *Millenarian World*, 7.

17. Gary Shepherd and Gordon Shepherd, *A Kingdom Transformed: Themes in the Development of Mormonism* (Salt Lake City: University of Utah Press, 1984), 45.

18. William E. Hughes, "A Profile of the Missionaries of The Church of Jesus Christ of Latter-day Saints, 1849–1900" (Master's thesis, Brigham Young University, 1986), 1–2. See also Rex Thomas Price Jr., "The Mormon Missionary of the Nineteenth Century" (Ph.D. diss., University of Wisconsin-Madison, 1991).

19. Hughes, "Profile of the Missionaries," 2–3; and Rodney Stark, "The Basis of Mormon Success: A Theoretical Application," in *Mormons and Mormonism: An Introduction to an American World Religion*, ed. Eric A. Eliason, 215–20 (Urbana: University of Illinois Press, 2001). See also S. George Ellsworth, "A History of Mormon Missions in the United States and Canada, 1830–1860" (Ph.D. diss., University of California at Berkeley, 1951), chapter five; and James B. Allen, Ronald K. Esplin, and David J. Whittaker, *Men with a Mission: The Quorum of the Twelve Apostles in the British Isles, 1837–1841* (Salt Lake City: Deseret Book, 1992).

20. Hughes, "Profile of the Missionaries," 5–7.

21. See Nicholas Griffiths and Fernando Cervantes, eds., *Spiritual Encounters: Interactions Between Christianity and Native Religions in Colonial America* (Lincoln: University of Nebraska Press, 1999); Susan M. Yohn, *A Contest of Faiths: Missionary Women and Pluralism in the American Southwest* (Ithaca: Cornell University Press, 1995); Liestman, "'To Win Redeemed Souls from Heathen Darkness,'" 179–201; and Jana K. Riess, "Heathen in our Fair Land: Anti-Polygamy and Protestant Women's Missions to Utah, 1869–1910" (Ph.D. diss., Columbia University, 2000). For an overview of the home missionary movement see Robert T. Handy, *We Witness Together: A History of Cooperative Home Missions* (New York: Friendship Press, 1957).

22. Hutchison, *Errand to the World*, 138–45.

23. Hill, "The Missionary Enterprise," 1685; Shepherd and Shepherd, *Mormon Passage*, 7; and Hutchison, *Errand to the World*, 102–11. See also Lian Xi, *The Conversion of Missionaries: Liberalism in American Protestant Missions in China, 1907–1932* (University Park: Pennsylvania State University Press, 1997); and Grant Wacker, "Second Thoughts on the Great Commission," 281–300.

24. Laurie Maffly-Kipp, "Looking West: Mormonism and the Pacific World," *Journal of Mormon History* 26 (Spring 2000): 47–51. See also M. Guy Bishop, "Waging Holy War: Mormon-Congregationalist Conflict in Mid-Nineteenth-Century Hawaii," *Journal of Mormon History* 17 (1991): 110–19.

25. Hughes, "Profile of the Missionaries," 88–99. See also David J. Whittaker, "Early Mormon Pamphleteering" (Ph.D. diss., Brigham Young University, 1982).

26. An important exception to this occurred in the Pacific world, where the Mormons organized schools and helped improve agricultural techniques among the Polynesians. See Britsch, *Moramona*, 29–31. In these isolated cases, the LDS civilizing impulse seems to have stemmed from two Mormon beliefs. First, they felt it necessary

to provide a non-Protestant educational alternative for the children of their converts for retention purposes. Second, they believed that many of the Pacific Islanders were actually the descendents of Book of Mormon peoples to whom they had a theological obligation to both spiritually and temporally uplift. See Douglas, "The Sons of Lehi and the Seed of Cain," 90–104; and Maffly-Kipp, "Looking West," 57–61.

27. Valentin H. Rabe, "Evangelical Logistics: Mission Support and Resources to 1920," in Fairbank, *The Missionary Enterprise in China and America*, 75, 77–79.

28. Rabe, "Evangelical Logistics," 75–77. See also Patricia Grimshaw, *Paths of Duty: American Missionary Wives in 19th Century Hawaii* (Honolulu: University of Hawaii Press, 1989); and Jane Hunter, *The Gospel of Gentility: American Women Missionaries in Turn-of-the-Century China* (New Haven, Conn.: Yale University Press, 1984).

29. Barbara Welter, "'She Hath Done What She Could': Protestant Women's Missionary Careers in Nineteenth-Century America," *American Quarterly* 30 (Winter 1978): 638.

30. Hughes, "Profile of the Missionaries," 7–8, 176–78.

31. Ibid., 179–81. For a history of LDS women missionaries, see Calvin S. Kunz, "A History of Female Missionary Activity in The Church of Jesus Christ of Latter-day Saints, 1830–1898" (Master's thesis, Brigham Young University, 1976); and Carol Cornwall Madsen, "Mormon Missionary Wives in Nineteenth Century Polynesia," *Journal of Mormon History* 13 (1986/87): 61–85.

32. Rabe, "Evangelical Logistics," 74–75.

33. Hughes, "Profile of the Missionaries," 37–41.

34. Reid L. Neilson, "Introduction: Laboring in the Old Country," in *Legacy of Sacrifice: Missionaries to Scandinavia, 1872–1894*, ed. Susan Easton Black, Shauna C. Anderson, and Ruth Ellen Maness (Provo, Utah: Religious Studies Center at Brigham Young University, 2007), xiii–xix; and Hughes, "Profile of the Missionaries," 41–46.

35. Rabe, "Evangelical Logistics," 81–89; and David G. Dawson, "Funding Mission in the Early Twentieth Century," *International Bulletin of Missionary Research* 24 (October 2000): 155–58. See also Richard S. Wierenga, "The Financial Support of Foreign Missions," in *Lengthened Cords: A Book about World Missions in Honor of Henry J. Evenhouse*, ed. Roger S. Greenway (Grand Rapids, Mich.: Baker Book House, 1975), 343–46. For a study on how foreign missions and fundraising impacted Protestant congregations back in America, see Lawrence D. Kessler, "'Hands across the Sea': Foreign Missions and Home Support," in *United States Attitudes and Policies Toward China: The Impact of American Missionaries*, ed. Patricia Neils (Armonk, N.Y.: M. E. Sharpe, 1990), 78–96.

36. Alvyn Austin, "No Solicitation: The China Inland Mission and Money," in *More Money, More Ministry: Money and Evangelicals in Recent North American History*, ed. Larry Eskridge and Mark A. Noll (Grand Rapids, Mich.: W. B. Eerdmans, 2000), 207–34. See also Alvyn Austin, "'Hotbed of missions': The China Inland Mission, Toronto Bible College, and the Faith Missions–Bible School Connection," in *The Foreign Missionary Enterprise at Home: Explorations in North American Cultural History*, ed. Daniel H. Bays and Grant Wacker (Tuscaloosa: University of Alabama Press, 2003), 134–51.

37. Hughes, "Profile of the Missionaries," 49–56.
38. Ibid., 57–70. See also Richard L. Jensen, "Without Purse or Scrip? Financing Latter-day Saint Missionary Work in Europe in the Nineteenth Century," *Journal of Mormon History* 12 (1985): 3–14; and Jessie L. Embry, "Without Purse or Scrip," *Dialogue* 29 (Fall 1996): 77–93.
39. Henry Otis Dwight, H. Allen Tupper, and Edwin Munsell Bliss, *The Encyclopedia of Missions*, 2d ed. (New York: Funk and Wagnalls, 1904), 835, 838–45.
40. James A. Field Jr., "Near East Notes and Far East Queries," in Fairbank, *The Missionary Enterprise in China and America*, 31–33.
41. Ibid., 33–37.
42. W. Richie Hogg, "The Role of American Protestantism in World Mission," in *American Missions in Bicentennial Perspective*, ed. R. Pierce Beaver (South Pasadena, Calif.: William Carey Library, 1977), 376–77.
43. Leonard J. Arrington, "Historical Development of International Mormonism," *Religious Studies and Theology* 7 (January 1987): 9.
44. Mauss, *All Abraham's Children*, 1–2. See also Mauss, "In Search of Ephraim," 131–73; and Douglas, "The Sons of Lehi and the Seed of Cain," 90–104.
45. Irving, *Numerical Strength and Geographical Distribution*, 9–15.
46. Hosea Stout, Diary, August 28 1852, as reprinted in *On the Mormon Frontier: The Diary of Hosea Stout*, ed. Juanita Brooks, 2 vols. (Salt Lake City: University of Utah Press, 1964).
47. James Lewis, Autobiography, 3, Perry Special Collections.
48. Hosea Stout to Brigham Young, May 16, 1853, as quoted in Wayne Stout, *Hosea Stout: Utah's Pioneer Statesman* (Salt Lake City: n.p., 1953), 170–71.
49. Britsch, *Moramona*, 90.
50. Stout to Young, May 16, 1853, as quoted in Stout, *Hosea Stout*, 172.
51. Britsch, *Moramona*, 13–17. See also Donald R. Shaffer, "Hiram Clark and the First LDS Hawaiian Mission: A Reappraisal," *Journal of Mormon History* 17 (1991): 94–109.
52. "Chinese in California," *Deseret Evening News*, June 22, 1854.
53. *Deseret Weekly News*, December 14, 1854, 2.
54. Lewis, Autobiography, 3.
55. Stout to Young, May 16, 1853, as quoted in Stout, *Hosea Stout*, 172.
56. LDS Journal History, February 16, 1855.
57. Stout, Diary, May 6, 1853.
58. See Orson Pratt, "Celestial Marriage," in *Journal of Discourses*, 26 vols. (Liverpool: F. D. Richards, 1855–86), 1:53–66, August 29, 1852. See also David J. Whittaker, "The Bone in the Throat: Orson Pratt and the Public Announcement of Plural Marriage," *Western Historical Quarterly* 18 (July 1987): 293–314.
59. James Lewis, *Deseret Evening News*, January 4, 1854.
60. Hosea Stout, James Lewis, and Chapman Duncan to Brigham Young, August 27, 1853, as quoted in Stout, *Hosea Stout*, 179.
61. Stout, Diary, June 7, 1853.
62. Ibid., June 9, 1853.

63. Spence, *The Search for Modern China*, 172–76; and Latourette, *A History of the Expansion of Christianity*, 6:361–63. See also Jonathan D. Spence, *The Taiping Vision of a Christian China, 1836–1864* (Waco, Tex.: Baylor University Press, 1998).
64. Maffly-Kipp, "Looking West," 48–56. See also Laurie F. Maffly-Kipp, "Assembling Bodies and Souls: Missionary Practices on the Pacific Frontier," in *Practicing Protestants: Histories of Christian Life in America, 1630–1965*, ed. Laurie F. Maffly-Kipp, Leigh E. Schmidt, and Mark Valeri (Baltimore, Md.: Johns Hopkins University Press, 2006). See also R. Laurence Moore, *Religious Outsiders and the Making of Americans* (New York: Oxford University Press, 1986).
65. Historian William R. Hutchison framed missionary history in terms of these two goals. See Hutchison, *Errand to the World*, chapter three, "Christ, Not Culture," 62–90.
66. *Deseret Morning News 2004 Church Almanac*, 580–81.

CHAPTER FOUR
OPENING THE JAPAN MISSION

1. See Cyrus Augustus Bartol, "The Puritan and the Mormon," *Unitarian Review and Religious Magazine* 23 (February 1885): 155–63; David Brion Davis, "The New England Origins of Mormonism," *New England Quarterly* 26 (June 1953): 147–68; Gustav H. Blanke with Karen Lynn, "'God's Base of Operations': Mormon Variations on the American Sense of Mission," *BYU Studies* 20 (Fall 1979): 83–92; and Rex Cooper, "The Promises Made to the Fathers: A Diacritical Analysis of Mormon Covenant Organization with Reference to Puritan Federal Theology" (Ph.D. diss., University of Chicago, 1985).
2. William Mulder and A. Russell Mortensen, eds., *Among the Mormons: Historical Accounts by Contemporary Observers* (New York: Alfred A. Knopf, 1958), 382–84.
3. Klaus J. Hansen, *Mormonism and the American Experience* (Chicago: University of Chicago Press, 1981), 207–11.
4. Perry Miller, *Errand into the Wilderness* (Cambridge, Mass.: The Belknap Press of Harvard University Press, 1984), 14–15. See also Samuel Danforth, *A brief recognition of New-England's errand into the wilderness* (Cambridge, Mass.: printed by Samuel Green and Marmaduke Johnson, 1671). For an alternative view see Theodore Dwight Bozeman, "The Puritans' 'Errand into the Wilderness' Reconsidered," *New England Quarterly* 59 (June 1986): 231–51.
5. Hutchison, *Errand to the World*, 8.
6. See Wendy J. Deichmann Edwards, "Forging an Ideology for American Missions: Josiah Strong and Manifest Destiny," in Shenk, *North American Foreign Mission*, 163–91.
7. Miyazaki Kentarō, "Roman Catholic Mission in Pre-Modern Japan," in *Handbook of Christianity in Japan*, ed. Mark R. Mullins (Leiden: Brill, 2003), 1–7. See also Neil S. Fujita, *Japan's Encounter with Christianity: The Catholic Mission in Pre-Modern Japan* (New York: Paulist Press, 1991); Cary, *A History of Christianity in Japan*, vol. 2; and Michael Cooper, *They Came to Japan: An Anthology of European Reports on Japan,*

1543–1640 (London: Thames and Hudson, 1965).

8. Miyazaki, "Roman Catholic Mission in Pre-Modern Japan," 9–17. See also Charles Ralph Boxer, *The Christian Century in Japan, 1549–1650* (Berkeley: University of California Press, 1951); and Higashibaba Ikuo, *Christianity in Early Modern Japan: Kirishitan Belief and Practice* (Leiden: Brill, 2001).

9. Pyle, *The Making of Modern Japan*, 57–59; and Jansen, *The Making of Modern Japan*, 257–93.

10. Pyle, *The Making of Modern Japan*, 59–60; and Jansen, *The Making of Modern Japan*, 274–79.

11. Pyle, *The Making of Modern Japan*, 65; and Jansen, *The Making of Modern Japan*, 283–85.

12. Miyazaki Kentarō, "The Kakure Kirishitan Tradition," in Mullins, *Handbook of Christianity in Japan*, 19–34. See also Ann M. Harrington, *Japan's Hidden Christians* (Chicago: Loyola University Press, 1993).

13. Helen J. Ballhatchet, "The Modern Missionary Movement in Japan: Roman Catholic, Protestant, Orthodox," in Mullins, *Handbook of Christianity in Japan*, 39–42. See also Cary, *A History of Christianity in Japan*, vol. 2.

14. Ballhatchet, "The Modern Missionary Movement in Japan," 52–57. See also Cary, *A History of Christianity in Japan*, vol. 2.

15. Ballhatchet, "The Modern Missionary Movement in Japan," 42–52. See also David R. Ambaras, "Social Knowledge, Cultural Capital, and the New Middle Class in Japan, 1895–1912," *Journal of Japanese Studies* 24 (1998): 1–33; and Richard H. Drummond, *A History of Christianity in Japan* (Grand Rapids, Mich.: William B. Eerdmans, 1971).

16. Mauss, *All Abraham's Children*, 2–3.

17. Douglas, "The Sons of Lehi and the Seed of Cain," 100. See also Norman Douglas, "'Unto the Islands of the Sea': The Erratic Beginnings of Mormon Missions in Polynesia, 1844–1900," in *Vision and Reality in Pacific Religion*, ed. Phyllis Herda, Michael Reilly, and David Hilliard (New Zealand: Macmillan Brown Centre for Pacific Studies, University of Canterbury, 2005), 249–51.

18. Mauss, *All Abraham's Children*, 32–33.

19. G. Stanford Jarvis, "The Far East: Footprints and Fulfillments," unpublished manuscript in author's possession, 1–2.

20. N. [Nicholas] McLeod, *Epitome of the Ancient History of Japan* (Nagasaki: printed at the Rising Sun Office, 1875); *Illustrations to the Epitome of the Ancient History of Japan* (Kyoto: 1878); *Album and Guide Book of Japan, from Satsuporo [sic] in the North to Kagoshima in the South, with historical and statistical notes compiled by N. McLeod* (Yokohama: published for the author at the Seishi Bunsha Co., 1879); and *Korea and the Ten Lost Tribes of Isreal [sic], with Korean, Japanese and Isrealitish [sic] illustrations* (Yokohama: published for the author at C. Levy and the Seishi Bunsha Co., 1879). See Joseph Rogala, comp., *A Collector's Guide to Books on Japan in English* (Surrey, England: Japan Library, 2001), 142.

21. "Are They of Israel?" *Millennial Star* 49, no. 3 (January 17, 1887): 33–36.

22. "Are They of Israel?" *Millennial Star* 58, no. 31 (August 2, 1906): 479–80.

23. C. H. Kang and Ethel R. Nelson, *The Discovery of Genesis: How the Truths of Genesis were Found Hidden in the Chinese Language* (St. Louis, Mo.: Concordia Publishing House, 1979); Joseph Eidelberg, *The Biblical Hebrew Origin of the Japanese People* (Jerusalem: Gefen Publishing House, 2005); and Sidney Shapiro, ed., *Jews in Old China: Studies by Chinese Scholars* (New York: Hippocrene Books, 1984).

24. Davis Bitton, *George Q. Cannon: A Biography* (Salt Lake City: Deseret Book, 1999), 423; and Maureen Ursenbach Beecher and Paul Thomas Smith, "Lorenzo Snow," in *Encyclopedia of Mormonism*, ed. Daniel H. Ludlow (New York: Macmillan, 1992), 3:1369–70. See also Thomas G. Alexander, *Mormonism in Transition: A History of the Latter-day Saints, 1890–1930* (Urbana: University of Illinois Press, 1986), 3–6; and Boyd Payne, ed., "Rudger Clawson's Report on LDS Church Finances at the Turn of the Twentieth Century," *Dialogue: A Journal of Mormon Thought* 31 (Winter 1998): 165–79.

25. *Our Heritage: A Brief History of The Church of Jesus Christ of Latter-day Saints* (Salt Lake City: The Church of Jesus Christ of Latter-day Saints, 1996), 104; Irving, *Numerical Strength and Geographical Distribution*, 14–15.

26. Rudger Clawson, Diary, June 26, 1901; "A Farewell Reception," *Improvement Era* 4 (August 1901): 796.

27. Joseph F. Smith, "The Last Days of President Snow," *Juvenile Instructor* 36 (November 15, 1901): 689–90; and B. H. Roberts, *A Comprehensive History of The Church of Jesus Christ of Latter-day Saints, Century One* (Provo, Utah: Corporation of the President, The Church of Jesus Christ of Latter-day Saints, 1965), 6:375.

28. Apostle Erastus Snow, for instance, led the first band of LDS missionaries to Scandinavia in 1850. That same year Apostle John Taylor opened the French Mission and Apostle Lorenzo Snow began preaching Mormonism in Italy. Moreover, during ensuing decades, Apostle Lorenzo Snow started the East Indian Mission (1851) and the Malta Mission (1852), Taylor reopened the Eastern States Mission (1854), Apostle Franklin D. Richards led the European Mission (1854), Apostle Joseph F. Smith reopened the Sandwich Islands Mission (1864), and Apostle Moses Thatcher organized the Mexican Mission (1879). Other apostles served as missionaries in these and other mission fields during these same years. *Deseret Morning News 2006 Church Almanac* (Salt Lake City: Deseret News, 2005), 484–87.

29. George Q. Cannon, Journal, July 12, 1900, as quoted in Bitton, *George Q. Cannon*, 436.

30. Mauss, *All Abraham's Children*, 32–34. See also Bruce R. McConkie, *Mormon Doctrine* (Salt Lake City: Bookcraft, 1966), 81, "Believing Blood."

31. George Q. Cannon, in *Seventy-first Semi-annual Conference of The Church of Jesus Christ of Latter-day Saints* (Salt Lake City: The Church of Jesus Christ of Latter-day Saints, 1900), 63–64, 66–68. See also Cannon, Journal, September 6, 1900, as quoted in Bitton, *George Q. Cannon*, 436–37.

32. Heber J. Grant, Japanese Journal, February 14 and June 26, 1901; Rudger Clawson, Diary, February 14, 1901.

33. Arrington, "Utah's Ambiguous Reception," 92.

34. "Opening of a Mission in Japan," *Deseret Evening News*, April 6, 1901, 9.
35. Rudger Clawson, Diary, April 25, 1901; "The Japanese Mission Benefit," *Deseret Evening News*, May 30, 1901.
36. "American and Japanese Flags," *Deseret Evening News*, June 19, 1901.
37. For positive appraisals during April 1901 general conference, see Reed Smoot, in *Seventy-first Annual Conference of The Church of Jesus Christ of Latter-day Saints* (Salt Lake City: The Church of Jesus Christ of Latter-day Saints, 1901), 6; Matthias F. Cowley, in *Seventy-first Annual Conference*, 16.
38. Rudger Clawson, in *Seventy-first Annual Conference*, 8.
39. John W. Taylor, in *Seventy-first Annual Conference*, 29.
40. Matthias F. Cowley, in *Seventy-second Semi-annual Conference of The Church of Jesus Christ of Latter-day Saints* (Salt Lake City: The Church of Jesus Christ of Latter-day Saints, 1901), 18. See also Seymour B. Young, in *Seventy-second Semi-annual Conference*, 40.
41. *Buddhist Churches of America* (Chicago: Nobart, 1974), 1:43–48. Tweed and Prothero, *Asian Religions in America*, 78–82; Rick Fields, *How the Swans Came to the Lake: A Narrative History of Buddhism in America* (Boston: Shambhala, 1986), 143–45.
42. Alma O. Taylor to the Reverend Nishijima Kakuryo, June 14, 1901, as found in Alma O. Taylor, Journal, July 28, 1901. Perry Special Collections.
43. The Reverend Nishijima Kakuryo to Alma O. Taylor, June 27, 1901, as found in Taylor, Journal, July 28, 1901.
44. Alma O. Taylor to Nishijima Kakuryo, June 28, 1901, as found in Taylor, Journal, July 28, 1901.
45. See Shinji Takagi, "Mormons in the Press: Reactions to the 1901 Opening of the Japan Mission," *BYU Studies* 40, no. 1 (2000): 141–75.
46. Taylor, Journal, July 24, 1901.
47. Ibid.
48. Grant, Japanese Journal, July 25, 1901.
49. Tate, *Transpacific Steam*, 141–51; and Takagi, "Mormons in the Press," 141.
50. Taylor, Journal, August 12, 1901.
51. Louis A. Kelsch, in *Seventy-third Semi-annual Conference of The Church of Jesus Christ of Latter-day Saints* (Salt Lake City: The Church of Jesus Christ of Latter-day Saints, 1902), 35.
52. Taylor, Journal, September 6, 1901.
53. Ibid., August 25, 1901.
54. Sarah Cox Smith, "Translator or Translated? The Portrayal of The Church of Jesus Christ of Latter-day Saints in Print in Meiji Japan," in *Taking the Gospel to the Japanese, 1901–2001*, ed. Reid L. Neilson and Van C. Gessel (Provo, Utah: Brigham Young University Press, 2006), 127–45.
55. Takagi, "Mormons in the Press," 141–75.
56. Taylor, Journal, September 1, 1901.
57. Victor L. Ludow, *Principles and Practices of the Restored Gospel* (Salt Lake City: Deseret Book, 1992), 346–56. See Gregory A. Prince, *Power from on High: The Devel-*

opment of Mormon Priesthood (Salt Lake City: Signature Books, 1995), 80, for an alternative list of priesthood ordinances, including when each was first performed during Joseph Smith's lifetime.

58. Tad Callister, "Dedication," in *Encyclopedia of Mormonism*, 1:367.

59. See Samuel Brown, "A Sacred Code: Mormon Temple Dedication Prayers, 1836–2000," *Journal of Mormon History* 32, no. 2 (Summer 2006): 173–96, who points out that "[a]lthough no saving power is attributed to the prayers per se, they clearly transform temples into holy spaces where salvation may be bestowed; without such transformation, these temples would not be capable of supplying salvation to the Latter-day Saints" (p. 175). It is unclear if lands actually *need* to be dedicated for the successful preaching of the gospel, as many have not been to the present.

60. Callister, "Dedication," 1:367. See LaMar C. Berrett and Blair G. Van Dyke, *Holy Lands: A History of the Latter-day Saints in the Near East* (American Fork, Utah: Covenant Communications, 2005), Appendix E, "Dedications of the Holy Land: Ten by Apostles and One by Ferdinand Hintze, Pastor of the Turkish Mission," 427–28.

61. Smith, *History of the Church*, 2:200. Emphasis mine.

62. Ibid., 2:417. Emphasis mine.

63. Taylor, Journal, September 1, 1901.

64. Mauss, *All Abraham's Children*, 33.

65. Ibid., 34.

66. Taylor, Journal, December 11, 1901.

67. Ibid., December 15, 1901.

68. Ibid., February 13, 1902.

69. Ibid., March 2, 1902.

70. Ibid.

Chapter Five
Mormon Missionary Practices in Japan

1. See Hosea Stout to Brigham Young, May 16, 1853, as quoted in Stout, *Hosea Stout*, 170–71.

2. First Presidency to Alma O. Taylor, March 4, 1907, Japan Mission Incoming Letters.

3. Anthon H. Lund, in *Seventy-sixth Semi-annual Conference of The Church of Jesus Christ of Latter-day Saints* (Salt Lake City: The Church of Jesus Christ of Latter-day Saints, 1905), 6–7.

4. Hutchison, *Errand to the World*, 1.

5. While personal backgrounds, missionary training, financial arrangements, and human deployment are also components of the Euro-American Mormon missionary model, I would argue that evangelistic practices, what missionaries actually do, is the most important component and therefore the theme of this chapter.

6. Cyril H. Powles, "Foreign Missionaries and Japanese Culture in the Late Nineteenth Century: Four Patterns of Approach," *North East Asia Journal of Theology* (1969): 17–27.

7. Thomas, *Protestant Beginnings in Japan*, 96.

8. Ibid., 96–110. See also Junias V. Venugopal, "Prolegomena to a Historical Perspective: The Use of Education as a Mission Strategy in Asia," in *Asian Church and God's Mission*, ed. Wonsuk Ma and Julie C. Ma (Manila, Philippines: OMF Literature, 2003), 233–56; and Jon T. Davidann, *A World of Crisis and Progress: The American YMCA in Japan, 1890–1930* (Bethlehem, Pa.: Lehigh University Press, 1998).

9. Thomas, *Protestant Beginnings in Japan*, 110–16. See also Thomas John Hastings, "Japan's Protestant Schools and Churches in Light of Early Mission Theory and History," in Mullins, *Handbook of Christianity in Japan*, 101–23; *Christian Education in Japan: A Study* (New York: International Missionary Council, 1932); and Robert E. Lewis, *The Educational Conquest of the Far East* (New York: Revell, 1903).

10. Thomas, *Protestant Beginnings in Japan*, 128–31; and Iglehart, *A Century of Protestant Christianity in Japan*, 48, 59, 84, and 91.

11. Thomas, *Protestant Beginnings in Japan*, 131–35; Iglehart, *A Century of Protestant Christianity in Japan*, 84, 91, 106–7, 129, 156, 158, and 184; and Cary, *A History of Christianity in Japan*, 2:72, 134–136, 205–8.

12. Thomas, *Protestant Beginnings in Japan*, 117–21; and Iglehart, *A Century of Protestant Christianity in Japan*, 34, 36, 43, 83, and 162. See also Bernardin Schneider, "Bible Translations," in Mullins, *Handbook of Christianity*, 205–25.

13. Thomas, *Protestant Beginnings in Japan*, 121–27; and Iglehart, *A Century of Protestant Christianity in Japan*, 41, 44, 59, 61, 132, 147, and 151.

14. "Opening of a Mission in Japan," *Deseret Evening News*, April 6, 1901, 9.

15. A. Ray Olpin, "The Art of Tracting in Japan," *Improvement Era* 21 (November 1917): 41–44.

16. John L. Chadwick, Journal, July 25, 1905.

17. Ibid., November 20, 1905.

18. Sanford Wells Hedges, "Scenery and Customs of Japan," *Improvement Era* 6 (September 1903): 818–19.

19. Alma O. Taylor, Journal, June 14, 1904.

20. Chadwick, Journal, December 23, 1907.

21. Murray L. Nichols, "History of the Japan Mission of The Church of Jesus Christ of Latter-day Saints, 1901–1924" (Master's thesis, Brigham Young University, 1957), 140.

22. Taylor, Journal, September 30, 1907.

23. James A. Miller, "Messages from the Missions," *Improvement Era* 17 (January 1914): 388.

24. Taylor, Journal, December 10, 1903.

25. Ibid., March 25, 1904.

26. Ibid., June 5, 1904.

27. Ibid., February 5, 1907.

28. David O. McKay, Diary, January 2, 1920.

29. Jay Jensen, "Proselyting Techniques of Mormon Missionaries" (Master's thesis, Brigham Young University, 1974), 9.

30. Taylor, Journal, July 26, 1901.

31. Chadwick, Journal, August 15, 1905.

32. Taylor, Journal, October 6, 1907.

33. Ibid., November 24, 1907.

34. Elbert D. Thomas, "The Gospel Preached for the First Time to the Ainu," *Improvement Era* 14 (February 1911): 289.

35. Thomas, "The Gospel Preached for the First Time to the Ainu," 293.

36. Joseph H. Stimpson to David O. McKay, July 8, 1920, Japan Mission Outgoing Letters. See also Joseph H. Stimpson to Heber J. Grant and Counselors, September 30, 1920, Japan Mission Outgoing Letters.

37. Pearl M. Lee, "The Latter-day Saints in Japan," *Improvement Era* 22 (October 1919): 1089.

38. A. Ray Olpin, "Japan Church Membership Doubled in Five Months," *Improvement Era* 23 (October 1920): 1102.

39. Lee, "The Latter-day Saints in Japan," 1090.

40. Julius Pfragner, *The Motion Picture: From Magic Lantern to Sound Film* (Great Britain: Bailey Brothers and Swinfen Limited, 1974), 12–13, 226.

41. Britsch, *Unto the Islands of the Sea*, 284.

42. Ibid., 368.

43. Marjorie Newton, *Southern Cross Saints: The Mormons in Australia* (Laie, Hawaii: Institute for Polynesian Studies, Brigham Young University–Hawaii, 1991), 64–65.

44. Thomas, "The Gospel Preached for the First Time to the Ainu," 291.

45. Ibid., 292.

46. Edwin J. Allen Jr., Diary, February 12 and 22, 1913, and March 27, 1913. The missionaries sometimes called them moving picture shows.

47. Chadwick, Journal, February 4, 1906.

48. Ibid., July 17, 1905. Seely was very tall, even for a Westerner.

49. Ibid., July 18, 1905, and January 17, 1908.

50. "O Ye Mountains High," *Hymns of The Church of Jesus Christ of Latter-day Saints* (Salt Lake City: The Church of Jesus Christ of Latter-day Saints, 1985), no. 34. See Isaiah 2:2–3 and D&C 64:41–43.

51. Sanford W. Hedges, "Life in Japan," *Improvement Era* 6 (June 1903): 600.

52. J. Ray Stoddard, "Elders before a Y. M. A. in Japan," *Improvement Era* 21 (July 1918): 829–31.

53. Britsch, *From the East*, 59.

54. Elbert D. Thomas, "The Tokyo-American Baseball Team," *Improvement Era* 15 (May 1912): 663–64.

55. Thomas, "The Tokyo-American Baseball Team," 663–64.

56. Smith, "Translator or Translated?" 127–45.

57. See Philip L. Barlow, *Mormons and the Bible: The Place of the Latter-day Saints in American Religion* (New York: Oxford University Press, 1991).

58. Frederick R. Brady, "A Study of the Translations of the Four Standard Works of the L.D.S. Church into Japanese," (University Scholar Project, Brigham Young University, 1976), 58–64. See also William Elliot Griffis, *Hepburn of Japan* (Philadelphia: Westminster Press, 1913).

59. *Deseret Morning News 2006 Church Almanac* (Salt Lake City: Deseret News, 2005), 656.

60. *Morumon Kei* [Book of Mormon] (Nihon: Matsu Jitsu Seio Iesu Kirisuto Kyōkai, Shūeisha Daiichi Kōba, 1909). See Jiro Numano, "The Japanese Translation of the Book of Mormon: A Study in the Theory and Practice of Translation" (Master's thesis, Brigham Young University, 1976); Frederick R. Brady, "The Japanese Reaction to Mormonism and the Translation of Mormon Scripture into Japanese" (Master's thesis, Sophia University, International College, Tokyo, 1979), 187–207; Van C. Gessel, "'Strange characters and expressions': Three Japanese Translations of the Book of Mormon," *Journal of Book of Mormon Studies* 14, no. 1 (2005): 32–47.

61. Terryl Givens, *By the Hand of Mormon: The American Scripture that Launched a New World Religion* (New York: Oxford University Press, 2002), 84–85.

62. Olpin, "Japan Church Membership Doubled in Five Months," 1101.

63. Aldo Stephens, "Placing Books of Mormon in Japan," *Improvement Era* 25 (August 1922): 938–39.

64. Nichols, "History of the Japan Mission," 40; Brady, "Japanese Reaction to Mormonism," 209.

65. Brady, "Japanese Reaction to Mormonism," 209.

66. Taylor, Journal, February 9 to March 19, 1903.

67. Heber J. Grant, *An announcement concerning the Church of Jesus Christ of Latter-day Saints* (Tokyo: Matsu Jitsu Seio Iesu Kirisuto Kyōkai Nihon Dendōbu, 1903). For an English translation of this tract, see Heber J. Grant, "Introducing the Gospel in Japan," *Improvement Era* 6 (July 1903): 710–14. See Taylor, Journal, March 20 to April 8, 1903, and April 9 to 22, 1903.

68. Heber J. Grant, *Matsu Jitsu Seito Iesu Kirisuto Kyōkai ni kansuru kinkyū rinkoku* [The Church of Jesus Christ of Latter-day Saints: An Urgent Message] (Tokyo: Matsu Jitsu Seito Iesu Kirisuto Kyōkai Nihon Dendōbu, 1903).

69. Alma O. Taylor, *Ikeru shin no Kami* [The True and Living God] (Tokyo: Matsu Jitsu Seito Iesu Kirisuto Kyōkai Nihon Dendōbu, 1904). See Taylor, Journal, June 8 to July 10, 1903.

70. Alma O. Taylor, *Kami wa imasu ka?* [Is There a God?] (Tokyo: Matsu Jitsu Seito Iesu Kirisuto Kyōkai Nihon Dendōbu, 1905); and Alma O. Taylor, *Matsu Jitsu* [Latter-day Saints] (Tokyo: Matsu Jitsu Seito Iesu Kirisuto Kyōkai Nihon Dendōbu, 1906).

71. Alma O. Taylor, *Morumon Kyōkai to ippu ta sai* [The Mormon Church and Polygamy] (Tokyo: Nihon Dendōbu, 1907); and Alma O. Taylor, *Tasai shugi no osore nashi* [Have No Fear of Polygamy] (Tokyo: Matsu Jitsu Seito Iesu Kirisuto Kyōkai Nihon Dendōbu, 1907).

72. Robert M. B. Thomas, *Waga Eikoku Kyōkai wo sarite, Matsu Jitsu Seito Iesu Kirisuto Kyōkai ni haireru riyū* [My Reasons for Leaving the Church of England and Joining the Church of Jesus Christ of Latter-day Saints] (Tokyo: Matsu Jitsu Seito Iesu Kirisuto Kyōkai Nihon Dendōbu, 1905). See Taylor, Journal, March 6, 1905.

73. R. Lanier Britsch, "Early Latter-day Saint Mission to South and East Asia" (Ph.D. diss., Claremont Graduate School, 1968), 337–38. See also First Presidency to Horace

S. Ensign, August 6, 1904, Japan Mission Incoming Letters.

74. See Stark, "The Basis of Mormon Success," 215–20.

75. John W. Stoker, *Shinkō* [Faith] (Tokyo: Matsu Jitsu Seito Iesu Kirisuto Kyōkai Nihon Dendōbu, 1907); Sanford W. Hedges, *Kitō no hitsuyō* [The Necessity of Prayer] (Matsu Jitsu Seito Iesu Kirisuto Kyōkai Nihon Dendōbu, 1905). For an English translation of the latter, see Sanford Wells Hedges, "Necessity of Prayer," *Improvement Era* 8 (June 1905): 603–12; and Sanford W. Hedges, *Matsu Jitsu Seito* [Latter-day Saints] (Tokyo: Matsu Jitsu Seito Iesu Kirisuto Kyōkai Nihon Dendōbu, 1905).

76. James E. Talmage, *Hito wa Kami no keitō wo yūsu* [Man in the Lineage of God] (Tokyo: Matsu Jitsu Seito Iesu Kirisuto Kyōkai Nihon Dendōbu, 1907). For a preliminary English translation of this tract, see James E. Talmage, "In the Lineage of the Gods," *Improvement Era* 8 (August 1905): 721–28.

77. Joseph F. Featherstone, *Iesu Kirisuto no ryakuden oyobi shimei* [The Brief Life of Christ and His Mission] (Tokyo: Matsu Jitsu Seito Iesu Kirisuto Kyōkai Nihon Dendōbu, 1906).

78. Frederick A. Caine, *Mormon Kyō to wa nanzo ya?* [What Is Mormonism?] (Tokyo: Matsu Jitsu Seito Iesu Kirisuto Kyōkai Nihon Dendōbu, 1909); and *Kami no shinshōsha naru dai shoseki: suguru hyakunen no chūsei ni arawaretaru shoseki no* [A Great Book that Is a New Witness for God: Greatest Book to Come Forth during the Nineteenth Century] (Tokyo: Matsu Jitsu Seito Iesu Kirisuto Kyōkai Nihon Dendōbu, 1909).

79. Nephi Jensen, *Jinmin no tokuchō* [Characteristics of the Citizens of God] (Tokyo: Matsu Jitsu Seito Iesu Kirisuto Kyōkai Dendōbu, 1920).

80. Joseph F. Featherstone, *Iesu Kirisuto no ryakuden oyobi shimei* [The Brief Life of Christ and His Mission] (Tokyo: Matsu Jitsu Seito Iesu Kirisuto Kyōkai Nihon Dendōbu, 1906).

81. Takahashi Gorō, *Morumon Kyō to Morumon Kyōto* [Mormonism and Mormons] (Tokyo: published by the author, 1902). See also Frederick R. Brady, "Two Meiji Scholars Introduce the Mormons to Japan," in *Taking the Gospel to the Japanese*, 221–32.

82. Takagi, "Mormons in the Press," 141–75; Smith, "Translator or Translated?" 127–45.

83. George Q. Cannon, *The Latter-day Prophet: History of Joseph Smith, Written for Young People* (Salt Lake City: Juvenile Instructor Office, 1900). Taylor, Journal, July 16, 1904.

84. Edward H. Anderson, *Matsu Jitsu Seito Iesu Kirisuto Kyōkai ryaku shi* [A Brief History of the Church of Jesus Christ of Latter-day Saints] (Tokyo: Matsu Jitsu Seito Iesu Kirisuto Kyōkai Nihon Dendōbu, 1907). Taylor, Journal, August 30 and 31, 1907.

85. Barney C. Taylor, *Kirisutokyō ni okeru daisekkei* [The Great Plan: The Christian Way] (Nihon: Matsu Jitsu Seito Iesu Kirisuto Kyōkai Nihon Dendōbu, 1910); and Elbert D. Thomas, *To shi sekkyo shu* [Mr. To's Preaching Book] (Tokyo: Matsu Jitsu Seito Iesu Kirisuto Kyōkai Nihon Dendōbu, [1912?]).

86. Ernest B. Woodward, "Missionaries in Japan Striving to Live and Teach the Gospel," *Improvement Era* 26 (October 1923): 1152.

87. William A. Morton, *From Plowboy to Prophet: Being a Short History of Joseph Smith,*

for Children (Salt Lake City: Deseret Sunday School Union, 1912). The mission reprinted the volume in Japan in 1920. Nichols, "History of the Japan Mission," 41.

88. Taylor, Journal, October 21 to 29, 1903.

89. Ibid., November 2 and 16, 1903; December 8, 1903; January 23, 1904; February 19, 1904; August 21 to 23, 1904.

90. Horace S. Ensign and Frederick A. Caine, *Matsu Jitsu Seito sanbika* [Psalmody of the Japan Mission of The Church of Jesus Christ of Latter-day Saints] (Tokyo: Matsu Jitsu Seito Iesu Kirisuto Kyōkai Nihon Dendōbu, 1905).

91. Taylor, Journal, May 29, 1905.

92. Ibid., June 27, 1905.

93. Maffly-Kipp, "Looking West," 48–56.

94. Mauss, *All Abraham's Children*, 1–2; and Douglas, "The Sons of Lehi and the Seed of Cain," 90–104.

95. "Our First Sunday School in Japan," *Juvenile Instructor* 37 (October 1, 1902): 624–25.

96. Horace S. Ensign, "News from Japan," *Juvenile Instructor* 38 (December 1, 1903): 727.

97. "Some of Our Sunday Schools: The Tokyo, Japan, Sunday School," *Juvenile Instructor* 39 (February 15, 1904): 119–21.

98. Justus B. Seely, "A Mormon Sunday School in Sapporo, Japan," *Juvenile Instructor* 43 (April 1, 1908): 154–55.

99. Horace S. Ensign, "The Japanese Mission," *Millennial Star* 22 (June 2, 1904): 340. See also Horace S. Ensign to George Reynolds, October 19, 1903, Japan Mission Outgoing Letters.

100. "'Mormon' Music and Literature in Japan," *Improvement Era* 8 (June 1905): 626. See also Horace S. Ensign, in *Seventy-sixth Semi-annual Conference of The Church of Jesus Christ of Latter-day Saints* (Salt Lake City: The Church of Jesus Christ of Latter-day Saints, 1905), 97.

101. First Presidency to Alma O. Taylor, March 4, 1907, Japan Mission Incoming Letters.

102. Elbert D. Thomas to George D. Pyper, December 20, 1910, Japan Mission Outgoing Letters.

103. Ibid.

104. Joseph H. Stimpson to the Missionaries in Osaka, Kōfu, and Sapporo, January 18, 1919, Japan Mission Outgoing Letters.

105. Joseph H. Stimpson to Val W. Palmer, May 20, 1919, Japan Mission Outgoing Letters.

106. David O. McKay, "Christmas in Tokyo," *Juvenile Instructor* 56 (March 1921): 114–15.

107. Taylor, Journal, June 22, 1904.

108. Ibid., November 10, 1906, and April 20, 1907.

109. Ibid., June 22, 1904.

110. Ibid., September 4, 1907.

111. Chadwick, Journal, October 26, 1905.

112. Heber J. Grant to Matthias F. Cowley, May 12, 1903, Japan Mission Outgoing Letters.

113. Taylor, Journal, July 16, 1904.

114. Ibid., June 28, 1906.

115. Alma O. Taylor to Joseph P. Cutler, January 3, 1908, Japan Mission Outgoing Letters.

116. Taylor, Journal, June 12, 1909.
117. Ibid., September 3, 1906.
118. Ibid., April 5, 1907.
119. See J. Christopher Conkling, "Members without a Church: Japanese Mormons in Japan from 1924 to 1948," *BYU Studies* 15 (Winter 1975): 199–207.
120. Amasa W. Clark, "Teaching English and the Gospel," *Improvement Era* 18 (June 1915): 741.
121. Taylor, Journal, October 17, 1906.
122. In contrast, see Janet F. Fishburn, "The Social Gospel as Missionary Ideology," in Shenk, *North American Foreign Mission*, 218–42.
123. Taylor, Journal, September 16, 1905.
124. Ibid., September 30, 1905.
125. I am unaware of any LDS medical missionaries until after World War II.
126. Taylor, Journal, February 12, 13, and 16, 1906.
127. Ibid., February 18, 1906.
128. Ibid., February 27, 1906.
129. Ibid.
130. Ibid., March 1, 1906.
131. Months later Taylor learned that Hedges had secretly spent the church's famine donation on himself and he had also engaged in sexual relations with a Japanese woman. Although excommunicated and sent back to America, Hedges's immoral conduct undermined the church's public relations campaign in Sendai. Taylor, Journal, April 25, 1906. The mission continued to donate a portion of its fast-offering collections to poor families living near the Tokyo mission home in subsequent years and the First Presidency also donated funds after the Tokyo Earthquake in 1923.
132. "Presiding Bishop's Office Bulletin #60," Anthony W. Ivins Papers.
133. "Presiding Bishop's Office Bulletin #63," Anthony W. Ivins Papers.
134. Britsch, *From the East*, 63. See also Britsch, "Early Latter-day Saint Missions to South and East Asia," 344–45. For comparable mission statistics see Tetsunao Yamamori, *Church Growth in Japan: A Study in the Development of Eight Denominations, 1859–1939* (South Pasadena, Calif.: William Carey Library, 1974).
135. Compare with Britsch, "Early Latter-day Saint Missions to South and East Asia," 344n1.
136. Yamamori, *Church Growth in Japan*, 155–61.
137. Ibid., 49.
138. Ibid., 86–108.
139. Nichols, "History of the Japan Mission," 133.
140. Yamamori, *Church Growth in Japan*, 155–61; Japan Mission Manuscript History and Historical Reports.
141. Yamamori, *Church Growth in Japan*, 105; Japan Mission Manuscript History and Historical Reports.
142. See Mauss, *All Abraham's Children*, 212–66, for an explanation of why the Latter-day Saints traditionally avoided black Africa. The LDS Church did have missionaries

teaching in white South Africa during the 1850s and 1860s. See Farrell R. Monson, "History of the South African Mission of The Church of Jesus Christ of Latter-day Saints, 1853–1970" (Master's thesis, Brigham Young University, 1971).

Chapter Six
Temporary Retreat from Japan

1. Heber J. Grant, in *Seventy-fourth Semi-annual Conference of The Church of Jesus Christ of Latter-day Saints* (Salt Lake City: The Church of Jesus Christ of Latter-day Saints, 1903), 97.
2. R. Lanier Britsch, "The Closing of the Early Japan Mission," *BYU Studies* 15 (Winter 1975): 171–90. See also Britsch, "Early Latter-day Saint Missions to South and East Asia," 303–46.
3. Andrew Jenson, *Conference Report*, April 1913, 80.
4. "A Visitor from Japan," *Millennial Star* 84 (February 16, 1922): 101.
5. More specifically, 17 were born in Salt Lake County; 13 in Weber County; 11 in Utah County; 8 in Cache County; 5 each in Box Elder County, Davis County, and Sevier County; 3 each in Summit County and Washington County; 2 each in Kane County and Uintah County; and 1 each in Garfield, Piute, Sanpete, and Wasatch counties. Arthur Cutler was born in Oakland, California; Arthur F. Crowther in Sanford, Colorado; John W. Stoker in Doncaster, England; Louis A. Kelsch in Vinningen, Germany; Elwood L. Christensen in Oakley, Idaho; Daniel P. Woodland in Oneida, Idaho; George A. Turner in Lago, Idaho; Lillian L. Broadbent in Franklin, Idaho; Myrl L. Bodily in Fairview, Idaho; and Pearl M. Lee in Dublan, Mexico.
6. John W. Stoker was born in Doncaster, England, but immigrated with his family to Utah and was baptized as a young boy.
7. Only two polygamists missionized in Japan: Heber J. Grant and Louis A. Kelsch. But Grant only had one of his wives with him in Asia and Kelsch served alone. As a result, no LDS missionary ever had more than one wife in Japan.
8. The oldest missionary was Augusta W. Grant at forty-six. Her husband, Heber, was the oldest male missionary at forty-four, just six days older than Louis A. Kelsch. Seventeen-year-old Sanford W. Hedges was the youngest male missionary, while thirteen-year-old Mary Grant was the youngest female missionary.
9. The missionary couples were Heber J. and Augusta W. Grant; Horace S. and Mary W. Ensign; Joseph F. and Marie S. Featherstone; Elbert D. and Edna H. Thomas; Joseph H. and Mary E. Stimpson; LaFayette C. and Pearl M. Lee; Lloyd O. and Nora B. Ivie; Hilton A. and Hazel M. Robertson; F. Wallace and Louise M. Browning; William L. and Sylvia P. Glover; and Elwood L. and Arva B. Christensen.
10. Alma O. Taylor, Elbert D. Thomas, H. Grant Ivins, and Hilton A. Robertson were already in Japan when they were called as mission presidents.
11. Alma O. Taylor, "Memories of Far-Off Japan: President Grant's First Foreign Mission 1901 to 1903," *Improvement Era* 39 (November 1936): 690.
12. Grant, Japanese Journal, February 21, 1901; "Opening of a Mission in Japan," *Deseret*

Evening News, April 6, 1901, 9; and Andrew Jenson, *Latter-day Saint Biographical Encyclopedia: A Compilation of Biographical Sketches of Prominent Men and Women in The Church of Jesus Christ of Latter-day Saints* (Salt Lake City: Andrew Jenson History, 1901–1936), 4:236.

13. "Opening of a Mission in Japan," 9; Grant, Japanese Journal, March 18, 1901.
14. Grant, Japanese Journal, May 9, 1901; "Alma O. Taylor Going to Japan: Young Man Called to Accompany Apostle Heber J. Grant and Elders Louis A. Kelsch and Horace S. Ensign to the Orient," *Deseret Evening News*, May 11, 1901.
15. Alma O. Taylor, Journal, July 28, 1901; Tweed and Prothero, *Asian Religions in America*, 78–82; Fields, *How the Swans Came to the Lake*, 143–45; Alma O. Taylor to the Rev. Nishijima Kakuryo, June 14, 1901, as found in Taylor, Journal, July 28, 1901; and the Rev. Nishijima Kakuryo to Alma O. Taylor, June 27, 1901, as found in Taylor, Journal, July 28, 1901.
16. Britsch, "Closing of the Early Japan Mission," 174.
17. Hilton A. Robertson, in *One Hundred Seventeenth Annual Conference of The Church of Jesus Christ of Latter-day Saints* (Salt Lake City: The Church of Jesus Christ of Latter-day Saints, 1947), 53.
18. Horace S. Ensign, in *Seventy-sixth Semi-annual Conference of The Church of Jesus Christ of Latter-day Saints* (Salt Lake City: The Church of Jesus Christ of Latter-day Saints, 1905), 97.
19. Japan Mission Manuscript History and Historical Reports.
20. Alma O. Taylor, "Memories of Far-Off Japan, 1901–1903," *Improvement Era* 39 (November 1936): 690.
21. Elbert D. Thomas, "The Gospel Preached for the First Time to the Ainu," *Improvement Era* 14 (February 1911): 291–92.
22. Elbert D. Thomas to Joseph J. Anderson, March 2, 1911, Japan Mission Outgoing Letters.
23. "Presiding Bishop's Office Bulletin #70," Anthony W. Ivins Papers.
24. Irving, *Numerical Strength and Geographical Distribution*, 16–18.
25. Charles Hirschman, "Population and Society: Historical Trends and Future Prospects," in *The Sage Handbook of Sociology*, ed. Craig Calhoun, Chris Rojek, and Bryan S. Turner (London: Sage Publications, 2005), 386.
26. "Teaching English and the Gospel," *Improvement Era* 18 (June 1915): 741.
27. "Messages from the Missions: Placing Books of Mormon in Japan," *Improvement Era* 25 (August 1922): 939.
28. Irving, *Numerical Strength and Geographical Distribution*, 16–18.
29. Alexander, *Mormonism in Transition*, 232.
30. Joseph H. Stimpson to Lafayette C. Lee, February 18, 1919, Japan Mission Outgoing Letters.
31. Joseph H. Stimpson to Harold G. Reynolds, January 31, 1919, Japan Mission Outgoing Letters.
32. Irving, *Numerical Strength and Geographical Distribution*, 16–18.
33. Joseph H. Stimpson to Val W. Palmer, January 18, 1921, Japan Mission Outgoing Letters.

34. Joseph H. Stimpson to Alma O. Taylor, January 19, 1921, Japan Mission Outgoing Letters.

35. Lloyd D. Ivie to Louring A. Whittaker, June 14, 1922, Japan Mission Outgoing Letters.

36. Lloyd D. Ivie to First Presidency, June 21, 1922, Japan Mission Outgoing Letters.

37. Japan Mission Manuscript History and Historical Reports.

38. "Presiding Bishop's Office Bulletin #62," Anthony W. Ivins Papers.

39. Quoted in Britsch, "Closing of the Early Japan Mission," 182.

40. Britsch, "Closing of the Early Japan Mission," 186. This may be partially true as the millenarian Latter-day Saints anticipated an escalation in end of the world cataclysms. But the claim of concern for the physical wellbeing of the missionaries does not come through in the journals, correspondence, or mission histories.

41. Jansen, *The Making of Modern Japan*, 533.

42. "Yokohama in Flames Following Earthquake," *Deseret News*, September 1, 1923, 1.

43. "Anxiety is Felt for Utah Missionaries," *Deseret News*, September 3, 1923.

44. *Deseret News*, September 5, 1923, 1.

45. A. Ray Olpin, "Description of Devastation in Quake Area Given by Returned Missionary from Japan," *Deseret News*, September 6, 1923, 8.

46. "All Mormon Church Workers in Japan Escape Holocaust," *Deseret News*, September 11, 1923, 1.

47. Heber J. Grant, in *Ninety-fourth Semi-annual Conference of The Church of Jesus Christ of Latter-day Saints* (Salt Lake City: The Church of Jesus Christ of Latter-day Saints, 1923), 7.

48. Ernest B. Woodward, "Thrilling Experience of Four 'Mormon' Missionaries in the Tokyo Disaster," *Improvement Era* 27 (December 1923): 131.

49. Hilton A. Robertson, in *Ninety-fifth Semi-annual Conference of The Church of Jesus Christ of Latter-day Saints* (Salt Lake City: The Church of Jesus Christ of Latter-day Saints, 1924), 124.

50. On Mormon dualism see Underwood, *Millenarian World*, 8–9, 44.

51. Woodward, "Thrilling Experience," 132.

52. Robertson, in *Ninety-fifth Semi-annual Conference*, 123.

53. Talmage, in *Ninety-fourth Semi-annual Conference*, 52.

54. Woodward, "Thrilling Experience," 127.

55. Vinal G. Mauss, Oral History [1975], 10.

56. In contrast, there is no question that the Taiping Rebellion in China played a major factor in Hosea Stout and his companions' decision to abandon their Asian mission in 1853. See "Eleventh General Epistle of the Presidency of The Church of Jesus Christ of Latter-day Saints," *Millennial Star* 16 (July 8, 1854): 417.

57. Hing, *Making and Remaking Asian America*, 26–29.

58. John L. Chadwick, Journal, June 10, 1907.

59. Chadwick, Journal, June 14, 16, and 17, 1907.

60. "Messages from the Missions," *Improvement Era* 10 (October 1907): 996.

61. Hing, *Making and Remaking Asian America*, 30.

62. Edwin J. Allen Jr., Diary, April 17, 1913.

63. Alma O. Taylor to Joseph H. Stimpson, October 17, 1920, Stimpson Letter Book.

64. Joseph H. Stimpson to A. Ray Olpin, January 20, 1921, Japan Mission Outgoing Letters.

65. "Japanese Natives Preaching the Gospel," *Improvement Era* 25 (October 1922): 1133.

66. Jansen, *The Making of Modern Japan*, 511–12.

67. Quoted in Spencer J. Palmer, *The Church Encounters Asia* (Salt Lake City: Deseret Book, 1970), 59–60.

68. Hing, *Making and Remaking Asian America*, 32–33.

69. Japan Mission Manuscript History and Historical Reports, August 22, 1924. Ernest B. Woodward wrote the memo in question on July 26, 1949, after the Japan Mission had been reopened.

70. Mauss, Oral History [1975], 11.

71. Mauss, Oral History [1989], 3.

72. Robertson, in *Ninety-fifth Semi-annual Conference*, 125.

73. Heber J. Grant to Hilton A. Robertson, June 10, 1924, as quoted in Britsch, "Closing of the Early Japan Mission," 188.

74. Due to current restrictions, researchers no longer have access to the records of the First Presidency and other church general authorities.

75. Hilton A. Robertson, Diary, June 28, 1924.

76. See Britsch, "Closing of the Early Japan Mission," 174.

77. Taylor, "Memories of Far-Off Japan," 691.

78. Robertson, Diary, February 1, 1924.

79. Vinal G. Mauss, Oral History [1989], 3.

80. Robertson, Diary, February 3, 1924.

81. First Presidency to Hilton A. Robertson, February 22, 1924, as quoted in Britsch, "Closing of the Early Japan Mission," 172. Britsch also notes, "In the same letter the First Presidency mentioned that Lloyd D. Ivie, the previous mission president, estimated that there were 'only five or six real converts to the Gospel in that mission.'"

82. Britsch, "Closing of the Early Japan Mission," 172.

83. Robertson, Diary, February 25, 1924.

84. "Presiding Bishop's Office Bulletin #60" and "Presiding Bishop's Office Bulletin #63," Anthony W. Ivins Papers.

85. Heber J. Grant, in *Ninety-fourth Annual Conference*, 3.

86. Robertson, Diary, May 5 to 9, 1924.

87. For a history of Christianity in Japan during the Pacific War years (1937–1945), see Iglehart, *A Century of Protestant Christianity in Japan*, 213–39.

88. Robertson, in *One Hundred Seventeenth Annual Conference*, 53.

89. Japan Mission Manuscript History and Historical Reports, August 22, 1924. Ernest B. Woodward wrote the memo in question on July 26, 1949, after the Japan Mission had been reopened.

90. Japan Mission Manuscript History and Historical Reports.

91. Robertson, Diary, June 28, 1924.

92. "Japanese Mission Temporarily Closed," *Deseret News*, June 12, 1924, 4. The same

notification ran in the British *Millennial Star* on July 10, 1924.

93. Robertson, Diary, June 13, 1924.

94. Japan Mission Manuscript History and Historical Reports; Britsch, "The Closing of the Early Japan Mission," 173.

95. Robertson, Diary, June 26, 1924.

96. Ibid., June 28, 1924.

97. Ibid.

98. "Missionaries in Japan Will Sail on July 24," *Deseret News*, July 19, 1924, 5.

99. Japan Mission Manuscript History and Historical Reports.

100. Robertson, in *Ninety-fifth Semi-annual Conference*, 123. See Conkling, "Members without a Church," 199–207.

101. Lloyd D. Ivie, *Conference Report*, April 1926, 96. In 1962, Apostle Joseph Fielding Smith spoke at a banquet on Asia at Brigham Young University, Provo, Utah, and addressed this lingering question of whether or not Latter-day Saints should evangelize in Asia. "Now I have been asked the question a score of times since I returned [from Asia] if I thought there was any of the blood of Israel in those Oriental countries. And some of the people who ask me that question, ask it with sort of a feeling, it seemed to me, that the blood of Israel just could not have penetrated there." He then related the story of the coming forth of the Abrahamic covenant in the Old Testament (Genesis) and the parable of the Olive Tree as found in the Book of Mormon (Jacob), which describes how branches of the olive tree have been scattered and planted all over the Lord's vineyard, understood to be the world. Smith concluded his remarks by stating: "Now there is your answer. That is the answer to these people who approach me with the question, what's the use of going out among the Chinese, the Japanese, the Koreans, and the people of the Far East to preach the gospel to them? The answer: because they are branches of the tree, they are of the house of Israel. The Lord took the branches of the tree, grafted them into the wild olives, the Gentiles, and is bringing the Gentiles into the gospel of Jesus Christ." Joseph Fielding Smith, *Answers to Gospel Questions* (Salt Lake City: Deseret Book, 1963), 4:201–7.

EPILOGUE

1. Britsch, "The Closing of the Early Japan Mission," 181.

2. Rudger Clawson, Diary, June 26, 1901; "A Farewell Reception," *Improvement Era* 4 (August 1901): 796.

3. Clawson, Diary, June 26, 1901.

4. "A Farewell Reception," 797.

5. See Ronald W. Walker, "Strangers in a Strange Land: Heber J. Grant and the Opening of the Japanese Mission," *Journal of Mormon History* 13 (1986/87): 20–43, to better understand Grant's sense of failure.

6. Underwood, *Millenarian World*, 8.

7. "Messages from the Missions," *Improvement Era* 15 (March 1912).

8. Alma O. Taylor, "About Japan and the Japan Mission," *Improvement Era* 10 (Novem-

ber 1906): 6.

9.   Taylor, "About Japan and the Japan Mission," 8–9.

10. Elwood L. Christensen, Oral History, 14–15.

11. Ibid., 15.

12. Britsch, *From the East*, 71–72. See also Conkling, "Members without a Church," 191–214.

13. Britsch, *From the East*, 72–79.

14. Ibid., 80–91. See also Shinji Takagi, "The Eagle and the Scattered Flock: Church Beginnings in Occupied Japan, 1945–48," *Journal of Mormon History* 28 (Fall 2002): 104–38; and Shinji Takagi, "Riding on the Eagle's Wings: The Japanese Mission under American Occupation, 1948–52," *Journal of Mormon History* 29 (Spring 2003): 200–32.

15. *Deseret Morning News 2008 Church Almanac* (Salt Lake City: Deseret News, 2008).

16. See Britsch, *From the East*, 602–3, for a chart diagramming how the missions have been subsequently subdivided.

17. See Numano, "How International Is the Church in Japan?" 85–91; and Jiro Numano, "Mormonism in Modern Japan," *Dialogue: A Journal of Mormon Thought* 29 (Spring 1996): 223–35.

18. James M. Fallows, "The World beyond Salt Lake City: Mormons in Japan May Lose the Battle for Converts—But They Are Helping to Win the War for American Competitiveness," *U.S. News and World Report* 104 (2 May 1988): 67. See also Cynthia Leah Hallen, "LDS Language Teaching and Learning: Highlights from 1830 to 1982" (Master's thesis, Brigham Young University, 1982).

19. S. Kent Brown, *Historical Atlas of Mormonism* (New York: Simon and Schuster, 1994), 136–37; Jay E. Jensen, "The Effect of the Initial Mission Field Training on Missionary Proselyting Skills" (Ph.D. diss., Brigham Young University, 1988); Richard O. Cowan, *Every Man Shall Hear the Gospel in His Own Language: A History of the Missionary Training Center and Its Predecessors* (Provo, Utah: Missionary Training Center, 1984).

Bibliography

ABBREVIATIONS

Church History Library, The Church of Jesus Christ of Latter-day Saints, Salt Lake City
(hereafter cited as Church History Library).

L. Tom Perry Special Collections, Harold B. Lee Library, Brigham Young University,
Provo, Utah (hereafter cited as Perry Special Collections).

Research Library and Collections, Utah State Historical Society, Salt Lake City (hereafter
cited as USHS Research Library).

Special Collections, J. Willard Marriott Library, University of Utah, Salt Lake City (hereafter cited as U of U Special Collections).

PRIMARY SOURCES (ENGLISH)

Allen, Edwin J., Jr. Diary. Edwin John Allen Jr. Collection. Perry Special Collections.

———. Letterbook. Edwin John Allen Jr. Collection. Perry Special Collections.

———. Letters and Miscellaneous Papers. Edwin John Allen Jr. Collection. Perry Special
Collections.

Caine, Fredrick A. Correspondence. Jesse W. Smith Papers. Church History Library.

Cannon, Abraham H. Journal. Abraham H. Cannon Collection. Perry Special Collections.

Chadwick, John L. Journal. Perry Special Collections.

China Mission. Manuscript History and Historical Reports. Church History Library.

Christensen, Elwood L. Oral History. Interview by R. Lanier Britsch, 9 June 1978, Honolulu, Hawaii. Church History Library.

Clawson, Rudger. Diary. *A Ministry of Meetings: The Apostolic Diaries of Rudger Clawson*.
Edited by Stan Larson. Salt Lake City: Signature Books in association with Smith
Research Associates, 1993.

Clawson, Thomas A. Diary Excepts. *New Mormon Studies CD-ROM*. Salt Lake City:
Smith Research Associates, 1998.

Cowley, Varsall. Journal. Church History Library.

———. Missionary Papers. Church History Library.

Cutler, Arthur. Diary. Arthur Cutler Collection. Perry Special Collections.

———. Papers. Arthur Cutler Collection. Perry Special Collections.

Davies, William E. Journal. William E. Davies Papers. Church History Library.

———. Scrapbooks. William E. Davies Papers. Church History Library.

Duncan, Chapman. Biography. Perry Special Collections.

Featherstone, Joseph F. Journal. Church History Library.

Featherstone, Joseph F., and Anna Marie Snow. Diary. Perry Special Collections.

Grant, Heber J. Diary. Scott G. Kenny Research Collection. Perry Special Collections.

———. Diary Excerpts. *New Mormon Studies CD-ROM*. Salt Lake City: Smith Research

Associates, 1998.

———. *A Japanese Journal*. Compiled by Gordon A. Madsen. Perry Special Collections.

Hatch, James L. Oral History. Interview by A. Wiley Huntington, April 1976. Church History Library.

Ivie, Lloyd O. Correspondence. William Elbert Ivie Papers. Perry Special Collections.

———. Diary. Perry Special Collections.

Ivins, H. Grant. Correspondence. H. Grant Ivins Papers. U of U Special Collections.

———. Diary. H. Grant Ivins Papers. U of U Special Collections.

———. Memoir. H. Grant Ivins Papers. U of U Special Collections.

Japan Mission. Annual Financial, Statistical and Historical Reports. Church History Library.

———. Articles from Japanese Newspapers. Church History Library.

———. Incoming Letters. Church History Library.

———. Kōfu Sunday School Minutes. Church History Library.

———. Outgoing Letters. Church History Library.

———. Manuscript History and Historical Reports. Church History Library.

———. Missionary Area Journals. Church History Library.

———. Record of Japan Mission Members. Church History Library.

Jarvis, G. Stanford. Jarvis Family in Japan. Church History Library.

Journal History of The Church of Jesus Christ of Latter-day Saints. Church History Library.

Judd, Mary Grant. Diary. Church History Library.

Lee, Lafayette C., and Pearl M. Lee. Journal. Lafayette C. Lee and Pearl M. Lee Collection. Perry Special Collections.

Lewis, James. Autobiography. Perry Special Collections.

Mauss, Vinal G. Oral History [1975]. Interview by R. Lanier Britsch, 6 October 1975, Provo, Utah. Church History Library.

———. Oral History [1989]. Interview by Matthew K. Heiss, September 13, 1989, Walnut Creek, California. Church History Library.

McKay, David O. Diary. David O. McKay Papers. U of U Special Collections.

Morton, William A. *From Plowboy to Prophet: Being a Short History of Joseph Smith*. Tokyo: The Church of Jesus Christ of Latter-day Saints, 1920.

Presiding Bishop's Office. Missionary Bulletins. Anthony W. Ivins Papers. USHS Research Library.

Robertson, Hilton A. Autobiography. Hilton A. Robertson Collection. Church History Library.

———. Diary. Hilton A. Robertson Collection. Church History Library.

Stimpson, Joseph H. Journal. Joseph Henry Stimpson Collection. Church History Library.

———. Letterbook. Church History Library.

———. Letterbooks. Joseph Henry Stimpson Collection. Church History Library.

———. Mission Journal. Joseph Henry Stimpson Collection. Church History Library.

———. Mission Letterbooks. Joseph Henry Stimpson Collection. Church History Library.

———. Record Books. Church History Library.

Stimpson, Mary E. Diary. Joseph Henry Stimpson Collection. Church History Library.

Stoker, John W. Journal. John W. Stoker Papers. Church History Library.

———. Papers. John W. Stoker Papers. Church History Library.

Stout, Hosea. Diary. *On the Mormon Frontier: The Diary of Hosea Stout.* 2 vols. Edited by Juanita Brooks. Salt Lake City: University of Utah Press, 1964.

Taylor, Alma O. Journal. Alma O. Taylor Papers. Perry Special Collections.

———. Papers. Alma O. Taylor Papers. Perry Special Collections.

Thomas, Edna H. Diary. Elbert D. Thomas Papers. USHS Research Library.

Thomas, Elbert D. Journal. Elbert D. Thomas Papers. USHS Research Library.

———. Letterbooks. Elbert D. Thomas Papers. USHS Research Library.

Willes, William. Journal. *The Life of William Willes: From His Own Personal Journals and Writings.* Edited by Charleen Cutler. Provo, Utah: Family Footprints, 2000.

Woodland, Daniel P. Journal. Church History Library.

Woodruff, Wilford. *Wilford Woodruff's Journals.* 9 vols. Edited by Scott G. Kenney. Midvale, Utah: Signature Books, 1985.

Young, Brigham. Letter [1857]. Perry Special Collections.

———. Office Journals. *New Mormon Studies CD-ROM.* Salt Lake City: Smith Research Associates, 1998.

Primary Sources (Japanese)

Anderson, Edward H. *Matsu Jitsu Seito Iesu Kirisuto Kyōkai ryaku shi* [A brief history of The Church of Jesus Christ of Latter-day Saints]. Tokyo: Matsu Jitsu Seito Iesu Kirisuto Kyōkai Nihon Dendōbu, 1907.

Caine, Frederick Augustus. *Morumon Kyō to wa nanzo ya?* [What Is Mormonism?]. Tokyo: Matsu Jitsu Seito Iesu Kirisuto Kyōkai Nihon Dendōbu, 1909.

Ensign, Horace S., and Frederick A. Caine. *Matsu Jitsu Seito sanbika* [Psalmody of the Japan Mission of The Church of Jesus Christ of Latter-day Saints]. Tokyo: Matsu Jitsu Seito Iesu Kirisuto Kyōkai Nihon Dendōbu, 1905.

Featherstone, Joseph F. *Iesu Kirisuto no ryakuden oyobi shimei* [The Brief Life of Christ and His Mission]. Tokyo: Matsu Jitsu Seito Iesu Kirisuto Kyōkai Nihon Dendōbu 1906.

Grant, Heber J. An Announcement Concerning The Church of Jesus Christ of Latter-day Saints. Tokyo: Matsu Jitsu Seito Iesu Kirisuto Kyōkai Nihon Dendōbu, 1903.

———. *Matsu Jitsu Seito Iesu Kirisuto Kyōkai ni kansuru kinkyū rinkoku* [The Church of Jesus Christ of Latter-day Saints: An Urgent Message]. Tokyo: Matsu Jitsu Seito Iesu Kirisuto Kyōkai Nihon Dendōbu, 1903.

Hedges, Sanford W. *Kitō no hitsuyō* [The Necessity of Prayer]. Tokyo: Matsu Jitsu Seito Iesu Kirisuto Kyōkai Nihon Dendōbu, 1906.

———. *Matsu Jitsu Seito* [Latter-day Saints]. Tokyo: Matsu Jitsu Seito Iesu Kirisuto Kyōkai Nihon Dendōbu, 1905.

Jensen, Nephi. *Jinmin no tokuchō* [Characteristics of the Citizens of God]. Tokyo: Matsu Jitsu Seito Iesu Kirisuto Kyōkai Nihon Dendōbu, 1920.

Kami no shinshōsha naru dai shoseki: suguru hyakunen no chusei ni arawaretaru shoseki no [A Great Book that Is a New Witness for God: Greatest Book to Come Forth during the Nineteenth Century]. Tokyo: Matsu Jitsu Seito Iesu Kirisuto Kyōkai Nihon Dendōbu, 1909.

Morumon Kei [Book of Mormon]. Nihon: Matsu Jitsu Seito Iesu Kirisuto Kyōkai, Shūeisha Daiichi Kōba, 1909.

Stoker, John W. *Shinkō* [Faith]. Tokyo: Matsu Jitsu Seito Iesu Kirisuto Kyōkai Nihon Dendōbu, 1907.

Takahashi, Gorō. *Morumon Kyō to Morumon Kyōto* [Mormonism and Mormons]. Tokyo: published by the author, 1902.

Talmage, James E. *Hito wa Kami no keitō wo yūsu* [Man in the Lineage of God]. Tokyo: Matsu Jitsu Seito Iesu Kirisuto Kyōkai Nihon Dendōbu, 1907.

Taylor, Alma O. *Ikeru shin no Kami* [The True and Living God]. Tokyo: Matsu Jitsu Seito Iesu Kirisuto Kyōkai Nihon Dendōbu, 1904.

———. *Kami wa imasu ka?* [Is There a God?]. Tokyo: Matsu Jitsu Seito Iesu Kirisuto Kyōkai Nihon Dendōbu, 1905.

———. *Matsu Jitsu* [Latter-day Saints]. Tokyo: Matsu Jitsu Seito Iesu Kirisuto Kyōkai Nihon Dendōbu, 1906.

———. *Morumon Kyōkai to ippu ta sai* [The Mormon Church and Polygamy]. Tokyo: Matsu Jitsu Seito Iesu Kirisuto Kyōkai Nihon Dendōbu, 1907.

———. *Tasai shugi no osore nashi* [Have No Fear of Polygamy]. Tokyo: Matsu Jitsu Seito Iesu Kirisuto Kyōkai Nihon Dendōbu, 1907.

Taylor, Barney C. *Kirisutokyō ni okeru daisekkei* [The Great Plan: The Christian Way]. Nihon: Matsu Jitsu Seito Iesu Kirisuto Kyōkai Nihon Dendōbu, 1910.

Thomas, Elbert D. *To shi sekkyō shū* [Mr. To's Preaching Book]. Tokyo: Matsu Jitsu Seito Iesu Kirisuto Kyōkai Nihon Dendōbu, 1912.

Thomas, Robert M. B. *Waga Eikoku Kyōkai wo sarite Matsu Jitsu Seito Iesu Kirisuto Kyōkai ni haireru riyū* [My Reasons for Leaving the Church of England and Joining The Church of Jesus Christ of Latter-day Saints]. Translated by Fred A. Caine. Tokyo: Matsu Jitsu Seito Iesu Kirisuto Kyōkai Nihon Dendōbu, 1905.

Newspapers and Popular Periodicals

Conference Reports. Salt Lake City, Utah

Contributor. Salt Lake City, Utah

Deseret Evening News. Salt Lake City, Utah

Deseret News. Salt Lake City, Utah

Deseret Weekly News. Salt Lake City, Utah

Elder's Journal. Atlanta, Ga., and Chattanooga, Tenn.

Ensign. Salt Lake City, Utah

Evening and Morning Star. Kirtland, Ohio

Improvement Era. Salt Lake City, Utah

Journal of Discourses. Liverpool, England

Juvenile Instructor. Salt Lake City, Utah

Messenger and Advocate. Kirtland, Ohio
Millennial Star. Manchester, England
Missionary Review of the World. New York, N.Y.
New Era. Salt Lake City, Utah
Relief Society Magazine. Salt Lake City, Utah
Salt Lake Tribune. Salt Lake City, Utah
Times and Seasons. Nauvoo, Ill.

SECONDARY SOURCES

Abe, Yoshiya. "From Prohibition to Toleration: Japanese Government Views Regarding
    Christianity, 1854–1973." *Japanese Journal of Religious Studies* 5 (June–September
    1978): 107–38.
Adams, Hannah. *A Dictionary of All Religions and Religious Denominations: Jewish, Hea-
    then, Mahometan, Christian, Ancient and Modern*. Atlanta, Ga.: Scholars Press, 1992.
Adler, Jacob, and Gwynn Barrett, eds. *The Diaries of Walter Murray Gibson, 1886, 1887*.
    Honolulu: The University Press of Hawaii, 1973.
Adler, Jacob, and Robert M. Kamins. *The Fantastic Life of Walter Murray Gibson: Hawaii's
    Minister of Everything*. Honolulu: University of Hawaii Press, 1986.
Ahlstrom, Sydney E. *The American Protestant Encounter with World Religions*. Beloit,
    Wis.: Beloit College, 1962.
———. *A Religious History of the American People*. New Haven: Yale University Press,
    1972.
Aizawa, Tomoko. "The LDS Church as a New Religious Movement in Japan." Master's
    thesis, Brigham Young University, 1995.
Alexander, Thomas G. *Mormonism in Transition: A History of the Latter-day Saints,
    1890–1930*. Urbana: University of Illinois Press, 1986.
Allen, James B., Ronald K. Esplin, and David J. Whittaker. *Men with a Mission: The
    Quorum of the Twelve Apostles in the British Isles, 1837–1841*. Salt Lake City: Deseret
    Book, 1992.
Ambaras, David R. "Social Knowledge, Cultural Capital, and the New Middle Class in
    Japan, 1895–1912." *Journal of Japanese Studies* 24 (1998): 1–33.
Andrew, John A. *Rebuilding the Christian Commonwealth: New England Congregational-
    ists and Foreign Missions, 1800–1830*. Lexington: University Press of Kentucky, 1976.
Arkush, R. David, and Leo O. Lee, eds. and trans. *Land without Ghosts: Chinese Impres-
    sions of America from the Mid-Nineteenth Century to the Present*. Berkeley: Univer-
    sity of California Press, 1989.
Arrington, Leonard J. *Great Basin Kingdom: An Economic History of the Latter-day Saints,
    1830–1900*. 1958. Reprint. Salt Lake City: University of Utah Press and Tanner Trust
    Fund, 1993.
———. "Historical Development of International Mormonism." *Religious Studies and
    Theology* 7 (January 1987): 9–22.
———. *The Price of Prejudice: The Japanese-American Relocation Center in Utah during*

World War II. Logan: The Faculty Organization, Utah State University, 1962.

———. "Utah's Ambiguous Reception: The Relocated Japanese Americans." In *Japanese Americans: From Relocation to Redress*, edited by Roger Daniels, Sandra C. Taylor, and Harry H. L. Kitano. Salt Lake City: University of Utah Press, 1986, 92–97.

Austin, Alvyn. "'Hotbed of missions': The China Inland Mission, Toronto Bible College, and the Faith Missions–Bible School Connection." In *The Foreign Missionary Enterprise at Home: Explorations in North American Cultural History*, edited by Daniel H. Bays and Grant Wacker, 134–51. Tuscaloosa: University of Alabama Press, 2003.

———. "No Solicitation: The China Inland Mission and Money." In *More Money, More Ministry: Money and Evangelicals in Recent North American History*, edited by Larry Eskridge and Mark A. Noll, 207–34. Grand Rapids, Mich.: W. B. Eerdmans, 2000.

Axtell, James. *The Invasion Within: The Contest of Cultures in Colonial North America*. New York: Oxford University Press, 1985.

Bagley, Will, ed. *"Cities of the Wicked": Alexander Badlam Reports on Mormon Prospects in California and China in the 1850s*. Spokane, Wash.: Arthur H. Clark Company, 1999.

Ballhatchet, Helen J. "The Modern Missionary Movement in Japan: Roman Catholic, Protestant, Orthodox." In Mullins, *Handbook of Christianity in Japan*, 35–68.

Barlow, Philip L. *Mormons and the Bible: The Place of the Latter-day Saints in American Religion*. New York: Oxford University Press, 1991.

Barrows, John H. *The World's Parliament of Religions*, 2 vols. Chicago: Parliament Publishing Company, 1893.

Bartol, Cyrus Augustus. "The Puritan and the Mormon." *Unitarian Review and Religious Magazine* 23 (February 1885): 155–63.

Basquiat, Jennifer Huss. "Embodied Mormonism: Performance, Vodou, and the LDS Faith in Haiti." *Dialogue* 37 (Winter 2004): 1–34.

Berrett, LaMar C., and Blair G. Van Dyke. *Holy Lands: A History of the Latter-day Saints in the Near East*. American Fork, Utah: Covenant Communications, 2005.

Bishop, M. Guy. "Waging Holy War: Mormon-Congregationalist Conflict in Mid-Nineteenth-Century Hawaii." *Journal of Mormon History* 17 (1991): 110–19.

Bitton, Davis. "B. H. Roberts at the World Parliament of Religion, 1893." *Sunstone* 7 (January/February 1982): 46–51.

———. *George Q. Cannon: A Biography*. Salt Lake City: Deseret Book, 1999.

———. "Zion's Rowdies: Growing Up on the Mormon Frontier." *Utah Historical Quarterly* 50 (Spring 1982): 182–95.

Blanke, Gustav, with Karen Lynn. "'God's Base of Operations': Mormon Variations on the American Sense of Mission." *BYU Studies* 20 (Fall 1979): 83–92.

Boxer, Charles R. *The Christian Century in Japan: 1549–1650*. Berkeley: University of California Press, 1951.

Boyle, Timothy D. "Jehovah's Witnesses, Mormons, and Moonies: A Critical Look at Christian Heterodoxy in Japan." *Japan Christian Quarterly* 57 (Winter 1991): 29–35.

Bozeman, Theodore Dwight. "The Puritans' 'Errand into the Wilderness' Reconsidered." *New England Quarterly* 59 (June 1986): 231–51.

Brady, Frederick R. "The Japanese Reaction to Mormonism and the Translation of

Mormon Scripture into Japanese." Master's thesis, Sophia University, International College, Tokyo, 1979.

———. "A Study of the Translations of the Four Standard Works of the L.D.S. Church into Japanese." University Scholar Project, Brigham Young University, Provo, Utah, 1976.

———. "Two Meiji Scholars Introduce the Mormons to Japan." *BYU Studies* 23 (Spring 1983): 167–78.

Breen, John, and Mark Williams, eds. *Japan and Christianity: Impacts and Reponses.* New York: St. Martins Press, 1996.

Britsch, R. Lanier. "Church Beginnings in China." *BYU Studies* 10 (Winter 1970): 161–72.

———. "The Closing of the Early Japan Mission." *BYU Studies* 15 (Winter 1975): 171–90.

———. "Early Latter-day Saint Missions to South and East Asia." Ph.D. diss., Claremont Graduate School, 1968.

———. "The Early Missions to Burma and Siam." *Improvement Era* 73 (March 1970): 35–44.

———. "The East India Mission of 1851–56: Crossing the Boundaries of Culture, Religion, and Law." *Journal of Mormon History* 27 (Fall 2001): 150–76.

———. "The Expansion of Mormonism in the South Pacific." *Dialogue* 13 (Spring 1980): 53–62.

———. *From the East: The History of the Latter-day Saints in Asia, 1851–1996.* Salt Lake City: Deseret Book, 1998.

———. *Moramona: The Mormons in Hawaii.* Laie, Hawaii: Institute for Polynesian Studies, 1989.

———. "Mormon Intruders in Tonga: The Passport Act of 1922." In *Mormons, Scripture, and the Ancient World: Studies in Honor of John L. Sorenson,* edited by Davis Bitton, 121–48. Provo, Utah: Foundation for Ancient Research and Mormon Studies, 1998.

———. "Mormon Missions: An Introduction to the LDS Missionary System." *Occasional Bulletin of Missionary Research* 3 (January 1979): 22–27.

———. "The Nobility of Failure." *Brigham Young University 1998–99 Speeches.* Provo, Utah: Brigham Young University, 1999, 253–59.

———. *Nothing More Heroic: The Compelling Story of the First Latter-day Saint Missionaries in India.* Salt Lake City: Deseret Book, 1999.

———. "The Refounding of the LDS Mission in French Polynesia, 1892." *Pacific Studies* 3 (Fall 1979): 68–80.

———. *Unto the Islands of the Sea: A History of the Latter-day Saints in the Pacific.* Salt Lake City: Deseret Book, 1986.

Britsch, R. Lanier, Paul S. Rose, H. Grant Heaton, Adney Y. Komatsu, and Spencer J. Palmer. "Problems and Opportunities of Missionary Work in Asia (A Symposium of Former Mission Presidents)." *BYU Studies* 12 (Autumn 1971): 85–106.

Brooks, Karl. "The Life of Amos Milton Musser." Master's thesis, Brigham Young University, 1961.

Brown, Kent S. *Historical Atlas of Mormonism.* New York: Simon and Schuster, 1994.

Brown, Samuel. "A Sacred Code: Mormon Temple Dedication Prayers, 1836–2000," *Journal of Mormon History* 32, no. 2 (Summer 2006): 173–96.

Buddhist Churches of America, 2 vols. Chicago: Nobart, 1974.

Bushman, Richard L. *Joseph Smith and the Beginnings of Mormonism*. Urbana: University of Illinois Press, 1984.

Butler, Wendy. "Eyes Only for the Orient: Early Twentieth-Century Mormon Neglect of Salt Lake City Japanese." Paper presented at "A Centennial Celebration: The History of The Church of Jesus Christ of Latter-day Saints in Japan 1901–2001." Brigham Young University, Provo, Utah, October 2001.

———. "The Iwakura Mission and Its Stay in Salt Lake City." *Utah Historical Quarterly* 66 (Winter 1998): 26–47.

———. "Strategies, Conditions, and Meanings of Early Japanese Labor in Salt Lake City, Utah, 1890–1920." Master's thesis, Brigham Young University, 2002.

Call, Lowell E. "Latter-day Saint Servicemen in the Philippine Islands." Master's thesis, Brigham Young University, 1955.

Campbell, Eugene E. *Establishing Zion: The Mormon Church in the American West, 1847–1869*. Salt Lake City: Signature Books, 1988.

Cannon, Donald Q. "Joseph Smith in Salem (D&C 111)." In *Studies in Scripture, Vol. 1: The Doctrine and Covenants*, edited by Kent P. Jackson and Robert L. Millet, 432–36. Salt Lake City: Deseret Book, 1989.

Cannon, George Q. *The Latter-day Prophet: History of Joseph Smith, Written for Young People*. Salt Lake City: Juvenile Instructor Office, 1900.

Cannon, Hugh J. *David O. McKay around the World: An Apostolic Mission*. Provo, Utah: Spring Creek, 2005.

Carpenter, Joel A., and Wilbert R. Shenk, eds. *Earthen Vessels: American Evangelicals and Foreign Missions, 1880–1980*. Grand Rapids, Mich.: William B. Eerdmans, 1990.

Carter, Kate B., comp. *Our Pioneer Heritage*. 20 vols. Salt Lake City: Daughters of Utah Pioneers, 1958–77.

Caruthers (Taylor), Sandra T. "Anodyne for Expansion: Meiji Japan, the Mormons, and Charles LeGendre." *Pacific Historical Review* 38 (May 1969): 129–139.

———. "Charles LeGendre, American Diplomacy, and Expansionism in Meiji Japan." Ph.D. diss., University of Colorado, 1966.

Cary, Otis. *A History of Christianity in Japan: Roman Catholic, Greek Orthodox, and Protestant Missions*. 2 vols. New York: Fleming H. Revell, 1909.

Choi, Dong Sull. "A History of The Church of Jesus Christ of Latter-day Saints in Korea, 1950–1985." Ph.D. diss., Brigham Young University, 1990.

Christian Education in Japan: A Study. New York: International Missionary Council, 1932.

Clark, James R., comp. *Messages of the First Presidency*. 6 vols. Salt Lake City: Bookcraft, 1965.

Clement, Russell T., and Sheng-Luen Tsai. "'East Wind to Hawaii: Contributions and History of Chinese and Japanese Mormons in Hawaii." In *Voyages of Faith: Explorations in Mormon Pacific History*, edited by Grant Underwood, 89–106. Provo, Utah: Brigham Young University Press, 2000.

Conley, Don C. "The Pioneer Chinese of Utah." Master's thesis, Brigham Young University, 1976.

Conkling, J. Christopher. "Members without a Church: Japanese Mormons in Japan from

1924 to 1948." *BYU Studies* 15 (Winter 1975): 191–214.

Cooper, Michael. *They Came to Japan: An Anthology of European Reports on Japan, 1543–1640*. London: Thames and Hudson, 1965.

Cooper, Rex. "The Promises Made to the Fathers: A Diacritical Analysis of Mormon Covenant Organization with Reference to Puritan Federal Theology." Ph.D. diss., University of Chicago, 1985.

Corcoran, Brian D. "'My Father's Business': Thomas Taylor and Mormon Frontier Economic Enterprise." *Dialogue* 28 (Spring 1995): 105–41.

Costa, Ruy O., ed. *One Faith, Many Cultures: Inculturation, Indigenization, and Contextualization*. Maryknoll, NY: Orbis Books, 1988.

Cowan, Richard O. *The Church in the Twentieth Century*. Salt Lake City: Bookcraft, 1985.

———. *Every Man Shall Hear the Gospel in His Own Language: A History of the Missionary Training Center and Its Predecessors*. Provo, Utah: Missionary Training Center, 1984.

Daly, Marlene Y. "Cutler-San: A Mormon Missionary's Experience in Japan, 1912–1915." Closure Project, Brigham Young University, 1998.

Danforth, Samuel. *A brief recognition of New-Englands errand into the wilderness*. Cambridge, Mass.: printed by Samuel Green and Marmaduke Johnson, 1671.

Daniels, Roger. *Asian America: Chinese and Japanese in the United States since 1850*. Seattle: University of Washington Press, 1988.

Davidann, Jon T. *A World of Crisis and Progress: The American YMCA in Japan, 1890–1930*. Bethlehem, Pa.: Lehigh University Press, 1998.

Davis, David Brion. "The New England Origins of Mormonism." *The New England Quarterly* 26 (June 1953): 147–68.

Dawson, David G. "Funding Mission in the Early Twentieth Century." *International Bulletin of Missionary Research* 24 (October 2000): 155–58.

D'Costa, Gavin. *Theology and Religious Pluralism: The Challenge of Other Religions*. New York: Basil Blackwell, 1986.

Dean, Bruce J. M. "Chinese Christianity since 1849: Implications for The Church of Jesus Christ of Latter-day Saints." Master's thesis, Brigham Young University, 1981.

Deseret Morning News 2004 Church Almanac. Salt Lake City: Deseret News, 2003.

Deseret Morning News 2006 Church Almanac. Salt Lake City: Deseret News, 2005.

Douglas, Norman. "The Sons of Lehi and the Seed of Cain: Racial Myths in Mormon Scripture and their Relevance to the Pacific Islands." *The Journal of Religious History* 8 (June 1974): 90–104.

———. "'Unto the Islands of the Sea': The Erratic Beginnings of Mormon Missions in Polynesia, 1844–1900." In *Vision and Reality in Pacific Religion*, edited by Phyllis Herda, Michael Reilly, and David Hilliard, 249–51. New Zealand: Macmillan Brown Centre for Pacific Studies, University of Canterbury, 2005.

Drummond, Richard H. *A History of Christianity in Japan*. Grand Rapids, Mich.: William B. Eerdmans, 1971.

Durfee, Richard E. "Modernity and Conversion: Mormonism in 20th Century Japan." Master's thesis, Arizona State University, 1988.

Dwight, Henry Otis, H. Allen Tupper, and Edwin Munsell Bliss. *The Encyclopedia of Mis-*

sions, 2d ed. New York: Funk and Wagnalls, 1904.

East-India Marine Society of Salem. *By-laws and regulations of the East India Marine Society, Massachusetts: An association of masters and commanders of vessels, and of such persons as may be hereafter described, who have been, or are, engaged in the East India trade from the town of Salem*. Salem, Mass.: Thomas C. Cushing, 1800.

Eck, Dianna L. *Encountering God: A Spiritual Journey from Bozeman to Banaras*. Boston: Beacon Press, 1993.

Edwards, Wendy J. Deichmann. "Forging an Ideology for American Missions: Josiah Strong and Manifest Destiny." In Shenk, *North American Foreign Mission*, 163–91.

Eidelberg, Joseph. *The Biblical Hebrew Origin of the Japanese People*. Jerusalem: Gefen Publishing House, 2005.

Ellsworth, S. George. "A History of Mormon Missions in the United States and Canada, 1830–1860." Ph.D. diss., University of California at Berkeley, 1951.

Ellwood, Robert S. *Alternative Altars: Unconventional and Eastern Spirituality in America*. Chicago: University of Chicago Press, 1979.

Embry, Jessie L. "Without Purse or Scrip." *Dialogue: A Journal of Mormon Thought* 29 (Fall 1996): 77–93.

The Essential Parley P. Pratt. Salt Lake City: Signature Books, 1990.

Fairbank, John K. ed. *The Missionary Enterprise in China and America*. Cambridge, Mass.: Harvard University Press, 1974.

Fallows, James M. "The World beyond Salt Lake City: Mormons in Japan May Lose the Battle for Converts—But They Are Helping to Win the War for American Competitiveness." *U.S. News and World Report* 104 (2 May 1988): 67.

Field, James A., Jr. "Near East Notes and Far East Queries." In Fairbank, *The Missionary Enterprise in China and America*, 23–55.

Fields, Rick. *How the Swans Came to the Lake: A Narrative History of Buddhism in America*. Boston: Shambhala, 1986.

Finamore, Daniel. "Displaying the Sea and Defining America: Early Exhibitions at the Salem East India Marine Society." *Journal for Maritime Research* (May 2002).

Fishburn, Janet F. "The Social Gospel as Missionary Ideology." In Shenk, *North American Foreign Mission*, 218–42.

Flake, Chad J. *A Mormon Bibliography, 1830–1930: Books, Pamphlets, Periodicals, and Broadsides Relating to the First Century of Mormonism*. 2nd ed., rev. and enl. Provo, Utah: Religious Studies Center, Brigham Young University, 2004.

Flake, Kathleen. *The Politics of American Religious Identity: The Seating of Senator Reed Smoot, Mormon Apostle*. Chapel Hill: University of North Carolina Press, 2004.

Forman, Charles W. "A History of Foreign Mission Theory in America." In *American Missions in Bicentennial Perspective*, edited by R. Pierce Beaver and Catherine Albanese, 69–140. South Pasadena, Calif.: William Carey Library, 1977.

Fujita, Neil S. *Japan's Encounter with Christianity: The Catholic Mission in Pre-Modern Japan*. New York: Paulist Press, 1991.

Garr, Arnold K., Donald Q. Cannon, and Richard O. Cowan, eds. *Encyclopedia of Latter-*

day Saint History. Salt Lake City: Deseret Book, 2000.

Gessel, Van C. "'Strange characters and expressions': Three Japanese Translations of the Book of Mormon." *Journal of Book of Mormon Studies* 14, no. 1 (2005): 32–47.

Gibbons, Francis M. *Lorenzo Snow: Spiritual Giant, Prophet of God*. Salt Lake City: Deseret Book, 1982.

Gibson, Arrell Morgan. *Yankees in Paradise: The Pacific Basin Frontier*. Albuquerque: University of New Mexico Press, 1993.

Givens, Terryl. *By the Hand of Mormon: The American Scripture that Launched a New World Religion*. New York: Oxford University Press, 2002.

Gorski, John F. "Christology, Inculturation, and Their Missiological Implications: A Latin American Perspective." *International Bulletin of Missionary Research* 28 (April 2004): 60–63.

Griffis, William Elliot. *Hepburn of Japan*. Philadelphia: Westminster Press, 1913.

Griffiths, Nicholas, and Fernando Cervantes, eds. *Spiritual Encounters: Interactions between Christianity and Native Religions in Colonial America*. Lincoln: University of Nebraska Press, 1999.

Grimshaw, Patricia. *Paths of Duty: American Missionary Wives in 19th Century Hawaii*. Honolulu: University of Hawaii Press, 1989.

Grover, Cynthia. "Peter Bulkeley's Covenant of Grace and the Failure of the Puritan Errand to New England: A Mormon Perspective." University Scholar Project, Brigham Young University, 1992.

Grow, Matthew J. "A Providential Means of Agitating Mormonism: Parley P. Pratt and the San Francisco Press in the 1850s." *Journal of Mormon History* 29 (Fall 2003): 158–85.

Gunson, Neil. *Messengers of Grace: Evangelical Missionaries in the South Seas, 1797–1860*. New York: Oxford University Press, 1978.

Hall, David D., ed. *Lived Religion in America: Toward a History of Practice*. Princeton, N.J.: Princeton University Press, 1997.

Hallen, Cynthia Leah. "LDS Language Teaching and Learning: Highlights from 1830 to 1982." Master's thesis, Brigham Young University, 1982.

Handy, Robert T. *We Witness Together: A History of Cooperative Home Missions*. New York: Friendship Press, 1957.

Hansen, Klaus J. *Mormonism and the American Experience*. Chicago: University of Chicago Press, 1981.

Hardy, Arthur Sherburne. *Life and Letters of Joseph Hardy Neesima*. Boston and New York: Houghton, Mifflin and Company, 1891.

Harrington, Ann M. *Japan's Hidden Christians*. Chicago: Loyola University Press, 1993.

Harrison, Peter. *"Religion" and the Religions in the English Enlightenment*. Cambridge: Cambridge University Press, 1990.

Hartley, William G. "Adventures of a Young British Seaman, 1852–1862." *New Era* 10 (March 1980): 38–47.

Hastings, Thomas John. "Japan's Protestant Schools and Churches in Light of Early Mission Theory and History." In Mullins, *Handbook of Christianity in Japan*, 101–23.

Hill, Patricia R. "The Missionary Experience." In *Encyclopedia of the American Religious*

Experience: Studies of Traditions and Movements, edited by Peter Williams and Charles Lippy, 1683–96. New York: Scribner, 1988.

Hing, Bill Ong. *Making and Remaking Asian America through Immigration Policy, 1850–1990.* Stanford, Calif.: Stanford University Press, 1993.

Higashibaba Ikuo. *Christianity in Early Modern Japan: Kirishitan Belief and Practice.* Leiden: Brill, 2001.

Higginson, Thomas Wentworth. "The Sympathy of Religions." In Barrows, *The World's Parliament of Religions*, 1:780–84.

Hirschman, Charles. "Population and Society: Historical Trends and Future Prospects." In *The Sage Handbook of Sociology*, edited by Craig Calhoun, Chris Rojek, and Bryan S. Turner, 381–402. London: Sage Publications, 2005.

Hisashi Tsurutani. *American-Bound: The Japanese and the Opening of the American West.* Tokyo: Japan Times, 1989.

Hoare, J. E. *Japan's Treaty Ports and Foreign Settlements: The Uninvited Guests, 1858–1899.* Folkestone, England: Japan Library, 1994.

Hocking, William Ernest, et al. *Re-Thinking Missions: A Layman's Inquiry after One Hundred Years.* New York: Harper and Brothers, 1932.

Hogg, W. Richie. "The Role of American Protestantism in World Mission." In *American Missions in Bicentennial Perspective*, edited by R. Pierce Beaver, 354–402. South Pasadena, Calif.: William Carey Library, 1977.

Howes, John F. "Japanese Christians and American Missionaries." In *Changing Japanese Attitudes towards Modernization*, edited by Marius B. Jansen, 337–68. Princeton: Princeton University Press, 1965.

Hughes, William E. "A Profile of the Missionaries of The Church of Jesus Christ of Latter-day Saints, 1849–1900." Master's thesis, Brigham Young University, 1986.

Hunter, Jane. *The Gospel of Gentility: American Women Missionaries in Turn-of-the-Century China.* New Haven: Yale University Press, 1984.

Hutchison, William R., ed. *Between the Times: The Travail of the Protestant Establishment in America, 1900–1960.* Cambridge: Cambridge University Press, 1989.

———. *Errand to the World: American Protestant Thought and Foreign Missions.* Chicago: University of Chicago Press, 1987.

Hymns of The Church of Jesus Christ of Latter-day Saints. Salt Lake City: The Church of Jesus Christ of Latter-day Saints, 1985.

Iglehart, Charles W. *A Century of Protestant Christianity in Japan.* Rutland, Vt.: Charles E. Tuttle, 1959.

Irving, Gordon. *Numerical Strength and Geographical Distribution of the LDS Missionary Force, 1830–1974.* Salt Lake City: Historical Department of The Church of Jesus Christ of Latter-day Saints, 1975.

Isaacs, Harold R. *Scratches on Our Minds: American Views of China and India.* Armonk, N.Y.: M. E. Sharpe, 1980.

Iwaasa, David B. "The Mormons and Their Japanese Neighbours." *Alberta History* 53 (Winter 2005): 7–22.

Jackson, Carl T. *The Oriental Religions and American Thought: Nineteenth-Century Explo-*

rations. Westport, Conn.: Greenwood Press, 1981.

Jansen, Marius B. *The Making of Modern Japan.* Cambridge, Mass.: Belknap Press of Harvard University Press, 2000.

Jensen, Jay E. "The Effect of the Initial Mission Field Training on Missionary Proselyting Skills." Ph.D. diss., Brigham Young University, 1988.

——. "Proselyting Techniques of Mormon Missionaries." Master's thesis, Brigham Young University, 1974.

Jensen, Richard L. "Without Purse or Scrip? Financing Latter-day Saint Missionary Work in Europe in the Nineteenth Century." *Journal of Mormon History* 12 (1985): 3–14.

Jenson, Andrew. *Latter-day Saint Biographical Encyclopedia: A Compilation of Biographical Sketches of Prominent Men and Women in The Church of Jesus Christ of Latter-day Saints.* 4 vols. Salt Lake City: Andrew Jenson History, 1901–1936.

Jones, Garth N. "Spreading the Gospel in Indonesia: Organizational Obstacles and Opportunities." *Dialogue* 15 (Winter 1982): 79–90.

Kang, C. H., and Ethel R. Nelson. *The Discovery of Genesis: How the Truths of Genesis were Found Hidden in the Chinese Language.* St. Louis, Mo.: Concordia Publishing House, 1979.

Katanuma, Seiji. "The Church in Japan." *BYU Studies* 14 (Autumn 1973): 16–28.

Kessler, Lawrence D. "'Hands across the Sea': Foreign Missions and Home Support." In *United States Attitudes and Policies Toward China: The Impact of American Missionaries,* edited by Patricia Neils, 78–96. Armonk, N.Y.: M. E. Sharpe, 1990.

Kling, David W. "The New Divinity and the Origins of the American Board of Commissioners for Foreign Missions." In Shenk, *North American Foreign Mission,* 11–38.

Kume, Kunitake, comp. *The Iwakura Embassy, 1871–1873: A True Account of the Ambassador Extraordinary and Plenipotentiary's Journal of Observation through the United States of America and Europe.* Translated by Martin Collcutt. Princeton, N.J.: Princeton University Press, 2002.

Kunz, Calvin S. "A History of Female Missionary Activity in The Church of Jesus Christ of Latter-day Saints, 1830–1898." Master's thesis, Brigham Young University, 1976.

Lansing, Michael. "Race, Space, and Chinese Life in Late-Nineteenth-Century Salt Lake City." *Utah Historical Quarterly* 72 (Summer 2004): 219–38.

Latourette, Kenneth Scott. *A History of the Expansion of Christianity.* Vol. 6: *The Great Century: North America and Asia, A.D. 1800–A.D. 1914.* Grand Rapids, Mich.: Zondervan Publishing House, 1970.

Lawrence, Bruce B. *New Faiths, Old Fears: Muslims and Other Asian Immigrants in American Religious Life.* New York: Columbia University Press, 2002.

Lee, Chung-Myun. "Korean." In Yang, *Asian Americans in Utah: A Living History,* 145–77.

Lewis, Robert E. *The Educational Conquest of the Far East.* New York: Revell, 1903.

Libby, Justin H. "Senators King and Thomas and the Coming War with Japan." *Utah Historical Quarterly* 42 (Fall 1974): 370–80.

Liestman, Daniel. "'To Win Redeemed Souls From Heathen Darkness': Protestant Response to the Chinese of the Pacific Northwest in the Late Nineteenth Century." *Western Historical Quarterly* 24 (May 1993): 179–201.

———. "Utah's Chinatowns: The Development and Decline of Extinct Ethnic Enclaves." In *Chinese on the American Frontier*, edited by Arif Kirlik, 269–89. New York: Rowman and Littlefield Publishers, 2001.

Livingston, Craig. "Eyes on 'The Whole European World': Mormon Observers of the 1848 Revolutions." *Journal of Mormon History* 32 (Fall 2005): 78–112.

Ludlow, Daniel H., ed. *Encyclopedia of Mormonism*. 4 vols. New York: Macmillan, 1992.

Ludow, Victor L. *Principles and Practices of the Restored Gospel*. Salt Lake City: Deseret Book, 1992.

Luzbetak, Louis J. "Two Centuries of Cultural Adaptation in American Church Action: Praise, Censure, or Challenge?" In *American Missions in Bicentennial Perspective*, edited by R. Pierce Beaver and Catherine Albanese, 332–53. South Pasadena, Calif.: William Carey Library, 1977.

Lyman, Edward Leo. "From the City of Angeles to the City of Saints: The Struggle to Build a Railroad from Los Angeles to Salt Lake City." *California History* 70 (Spring 1991): 76–93.

Madsen, Carol Cornwall. "Mormon Missionary Wives in Nineteenth Century Polynesia." *Journal of Mormon History* 13 (1986/87): 61–85.

Madsen, Gordon A. "Heber J. Grant in Japan: A Personal Account." Paper presented at "A Centennial Celebration: The History of The Church of Jesus Christ of Latter-day Saints in Japan 1901–2001," Brigham Young University, Provo, Utah, October 2001.

Maffly-Kipp, Laurie F. "Assembling Bodies and Souls: Missionary Practices on the Pacific Frontier." In *Practicing Protestants: Histories of Christian Life in America, 1630–1965*, edited by Laurie F. Maffly-Kipp, Leigh E. Schmidt, and Mark Valeri. Baltimore: Johns Hopkins University Press, 2006.

———. "Eastward Ho! American Religion from the Perspective of the Pacific Rim," in *Retelling U.S. Religious History*, edited by Thomas A. Tweed, 127–48. Berkeley: University of California Press, 1997.

———. "Looking West: Mormonism and the Pacific World." *Journal of Mormon History*. 26 (Spring 2000): 41–63.

———. *Religion and Society in Frontier California*. New Haven, Conn.: Yale University Press, 1994.

Maffly-Kipp, Laurie F., and Reid L. Neilson, eds. *Proclamation to the People: Nineteenth-Century Mormonism and the Pacific Basin Frontier*. Salt Lake City: University of Utah Press, 2008.

Malone, Michael P. *James J. Hill: Empire Builder of the Northwest*. Norman: University of Oklahoma Press, 1996.

Martin, Albro. *James J. Hill and the Opening of the Northwest*. New York: Oxford University Press, 1976.

Mauss, Armand L. *All Abraham's Children: Changing Mormon Conceptions of Race and Lineage*. Urbana: University of Illinois Press, 2003.

———. *The Angel and the Beehive: The Mormon Struggle with Assimilation*. Urbana: University of Illinois Press, 1994.

———. "In Search of Ephraim: Traditional Mormon Conceptions of Lineage and Race."

Journal of Mormon History 25 (Spring 1999): 131–73.

McClellan, Robert. *The Heathen Chinee: A Study of American Attitudes Toward China, 1890–1905.* Columbus: Ohio State University Press, 1971.

McConkie, Bruce R. *Mormon Doctrine.* Salt Lake City: Bookcraft, 1966.

Mehr, Kahlile B. "The 1903 Dedication of Russia for Missionary Work." *Journal of Mormon History* 13 (1986/87): 110–23.

Miller, Perry. *Errand into the Wilderness.* Cambridge, Mass.: The Belknap Press of Harvard University Press, 1956.

Millet, Robert L. *A Different Jesus? The Christ of the Latter-day Saints.* Grand Rapids, Mich.: William B. Eerdmans, 2005.

Miyazaki Kentarō. "The Kakure Kirishitan Tradition." In Mullins, *Handbook of Christianity in Japan,* 19–34.

———. "Roman Catholic Mission in Pre-Modern Japan." In Mullins, *Handbook of Christianity in Japan,* 1–7.

Monson, Farrell R. "History of the South African Mission of The Church of Jesus Christ of Latter-day Saints, 1853–1970." Master's thesis, Brigham Young University, 1971.

Moore, R. Laurence. *Religious Outsiders and the Making of Americans.* New York: Oxford University Press, 1986.

Morris, Ivan. *The Nobility of Failure: Tragic Heroes in the History of Japan.* New York: Holt, Rinehart and Winston, 1975.

Moss, James R., et al., eds. *The International Church.* Provo, Utah: Brigham Young University Publications, 1982.

Mulder, William, and A. Russell Mortensen, eds. *Among the Mormons: Historical Accounts by Contemporary Observers.* New York: Alfred A. Knopf, 1958.

Mullins, Mark R., ed. *Handbook of Christianity in Japan.* Leiden: Brill, 2003.

———. "The Transplantation of Religion in Comparative Sociological Perspective." *Japanese Religion* 16 (1990), 43–62.

Murphy, Thomas W. "Reinventing Mormonism: Guatemala as Harbinger of the Future?" *Dialogue* 29 (Spring 1996): 177–92.

Neilson, Reid L. "Alma O. Taylor's Fact-Finding Mission to China." *BYU Studies* 40, no. 1 (2001): 177–203.

———. "Danes Teaching Danes: Missionaries from Zion in the LDS Scandinavian Mission, 1850–99: A Demographic Analysis." Paper presented at the annual meeting of the Mormon History Association, Copenhagen, Denmark, May 2000.

———. "Introduction: Laboring in the Old Country." In *Legacy of Sacrifice: Missionaries to Scandinavia, 1872–1894,* edited by Susan Easton Black, Shauna C. Anderson, and Ruth Ellen Maness, xiii–xix. Provo, Utah: Religious Studies Center at Brigham Young University, 2007.

———. *The Japanese Missionary Journals of Elder Alma O. Taylor, 1901–10.* Provo, Utah: BYU Studies Press and The Joseph Fielding Smith Institute for Latter-day Saint History, 2001.

———. "Mormonism and the Japanese: A Guide to the Sources." In Neilson and Gessel, *Taking the Gospel to the Japanese,* 435–44.

———. "A Priceless Pearl: Alma O. Taylor's Mission to Japan." *Ensign* 32 (June 2002):

56–59.

Neilson, Reid L., and Van C. Gessel, eds. *Taking the Gospel to the Japanese, 1901–2001.* Provo, Utah: Brigham Young University Press, 2006.

Nelson, Terry G. "A History of The Church of Jesus Christ of Latter-day Saints in Japan from 1948 to 1980." Master's thesis, Brigham Young University, 1986.

Newton, Marjorie. *Southern Cross Saints: The Mormons in Australia.* Laie, Hawaii: Institute for Polynesian Studies, Brigham Young University-Hawaii, 1991.

Nichols, Murray L. "History of the Japan Mission of The Church of Jesus Christ of Latter-day Saints, 1901–1924." Master's thesis, Brigham Young University, 1957.

Numano, Jiro. "How International Is the Church in Japan?" *Dialogue: A Journal of Mormon Thought* 13 (Spring 1980): 85–91.

———. "The Japanese Translation of the Book of Mormon: A Study in the Theory and Practice of Translation." Master's Thesis, Brigham Young University, 1976.

———. "Mormonism in Modern Japan." *Dialogue: A Journal of Mormon Thought* 29 (Spring 1996): 223–35.

O'Brien, David J., and Stephen S. Fujita. *The Japanese American Experience.* Bloomington: Indiana University Press, 1991.

Okihiro, Gary Y. *Margins and Mainstreams: Asians in American History and Culture.* Seattle: University of Washington Press, 1994.

Our Heritage: A Brief History of The Church of Jesus Christ of Latter-day Saints. Salt Lake City: The Church of Jesus Christ of Latter-day Saints, 1996.

Palmer, A. Delbert, and Mark L. Grover. "Hoping to Establish a Presence: Parley P. Pratt's 1851 Mission to Chile." *BYU Studies* 38, no. 4 (1999): 115–38.

Palmer, Spencer J. *The Church Encounters Asia.* Salt Lake City: Deseret Book, 1970.

———. *The Expanding Church.* Salt Lake City: Deseret Book, 1978.

———. *The Korean Saints: Personal Stories of Trial and Triumph, 1950–1980.* Provo, Utah: Religious Education, Brigham Young University, 1995.

———. *Religions of the World: A Latter-day Saint View.* Provo, Utah: Brigham Young University, 1988.

Papanikolas, Helen Z. *The Peoples of Utah.* Salt Lake City: Utah State Historical Society, 1976.

Papanikolas, Helen Z., and Alice Kasai. "Japanese Life in Utah." In Papanikolas, *The Peoples of Utah*, 333–39.

Patch, Robert C. "An Historical Overview of the Missionary Activities of The Church of Jesus Christ of Latter-day Saints in Continental Asia." Master's thesis, Brigham Young University, 1949.

Paulsen, David L. "The Redemption of the Dead: A Latter-day Saint Perspective on the Fate of the Unevangelized." In *Salvation in Christ: Comparative Christian Views*, edited by Roger R. Keller and Robert L. Millet, 263–97. Provo, Utah: Religious Studies Center, Brigham Young University, 2005.

Payne, Boyd, ed. "Rudger Clawson's Report on LDS Church Finances at the Turn of the Twentieth Century." *Dialogue: A Journal of Mormon Thought* 31 (Winter 1998): 165–79.

Perlich, Pamela S. *Utah Minorities: The Story Told by 150 Years of Census Data*. Salt Lake City: Bureau of Economic and Business Research, David S. Eccles School of Business, University of Utah, 2002.

Peterson, Levi S. "Thinking Globally: Explorations into a Truly International, Multi-Cultural Church." *Dialogue* 38 (Winter 2005): 1–2.

Pfragner, Julius. *The Motion Picture: From Magic Lantern to Sound Film*. Great Britain: Bailey Brothers and Swinfen Limited, 1974.

Phillips, Clifton J. *Protestant America and the Pagan World: The First Half Century of the American Board of Commissioners for Foreign Missions, 1810–1860*. Cambridge, Mass.: Harvard University Press, 1969.

Poelman, Ronald E. "The Gospel and the Church." *Ensign* 14 (November 1984): 64–65.

Powell, Allan Kent, ed. *Utah History Encyclopedia*. Salt Lake City: University of Utah Press, 1994.

Powles, Cyril H. "Foreign Missionaries and Japanese Culture in the Late Nineteenth Century: Four Patterns of Approach." *North East Asia Journal of Theology* (1969): 14–28.

Price, Rex Thomas, Jr. "The Mormon Missionary of the Nineteenth Century." Ph.D. diss., University of Wisconsin–Madison, 1991.

Prince, Gregory A. *Power from on High: The Development of Mormon Priesthood*. Salt Lake City: Signature Books, 1995.

Proper, David R. "Joseph Smith and Salem." *Essex Institute Historical Collections* 100 (April 1964): 88–97.

Pyle, Kenneth B. *The Making of Modern Japan*. Lexington, Mass.: D. C. Heath and Company, 1996.

Rabe, Valentin H. "Evangelical Logistics: Mission Support and Resources to 1920." In Fairbank, *The Missionary Enterprise in China and America*, 56–90.

Race, Alan. *Christians and Religious Pluralism: Patterns in the Christian Theology of Religions*. London: SCM Press, 1983.

Reilly, Thomas H. *The Taiping Heavenly Kingdom: Rebellion and the Blasphemy of Empire*. Seattle: University of Washington Press, 2004.

Riess, Jana K. "Heathen in our Fair Land: Anti-Polygamy and Protestant Women's Missions to Utah, 1869–1910." Ph.D. diss., Columbia University, 2000.

Robert, Dana L. *American Women in Mission: A Social History of Their Thought and Practice*. Macon, Ga.: Mercer University Press, 1996.

———. "The First Globalization: The Internationalization of the Protestant Missionary Movement between the World Wars." *International Bulletin of Missionary Research* 26 (April 2002): 50–66.

———. "From Missions to Missions to Beyond Missions: The Historiography of American Protestant Foreign Missions since World War II." In *New Directions in American Religious History*, edited by Harry S. Stout and D. G. Hart, 362–93. New York: Oxford University Press, 1997.

Roberts, B. H. *A Comprehensive History of The Church of Jesus Christ of Latter-day Saints, Century One*. 6 vols. Provo, Utah: Corporation of the President, The Church of Jesus Christ of Latter-day Saints, 1965.

Rogala, Joseph, comp. *A Collector's Guide to Books on Japan in English*. Surrey, England: Japan Library, 2001.

Rogers, Richard Lee. "'A Bright and New Constellation': Millennial Narratives and the Origins of American Foreign Missions." In Shenk, *North American Foreign Mission*, 39–60.

Schineller, Peter. *A Handbook on Inculturation*. New York: Paulist Press, 1990.

Schlesinger, Arthur, Jr. "The Missionary Enterprise and Imperialism." In Fairbank, *The Missionary Enterprise in China and America*, 336–73.

Schmidt, W. *The Origin and Growth of Religion: Facts and Theories*. London: Methuen and Company, 1930.

Schneider, Bernardin. "Bible Translations." In Mullins, *Handbook of Christianity*, 205–25.

Seager, Richard Hughes, ed. *The Dawn of Religious Pluralism: Voices from the World's Parliament of Religions, 1893*. La Salle, Ill.: Open Court, 1993.

———. *The World's Parliament of Religions: The East/West Encounter, Chicago, 1893*. Bloomington: Indiana University Press, 1995.

Seferovich, Heather M. "Statistical Profile of Southern States Missionaries, 1867–1898." *Thetean* 25 (1996): 47–67.

Shaffer, Donald R. "A Forgotten Missionary: Hiram Clark, Mormon Itinerant British Emigration Organizer, and First President of the L.D.S. Hawaiian Mission, 1795–1853." Master's thesis, California State University at Fullerton, 1990.

———. "Hiram Clark and the First LDS Hawaiian Mission: A Reappraisal." *Journal of Mormon History* 17 (1991): 94–109.

Shapiro, Sidney, ed. *Jews in Old China: Studies by Chinese Scholars*. New York: Hippo-crene Books, 1984.

Sharpe, Eric J. *Comparative Religion: A History*. New York: Charles Scribner's Sons, 1975.

Shenk, Wilbert R., ed. *North American Foreign Mission, 1810–1914: Theology, Theory, and Policy*. Grand Rapids, Mich.: William B. Eerdmans, 2004.

Shepherd, Gary, and Gordon Shepherd. *A Kingdom Transformed: Themes in the Develop-ment of Mormonism*. Salt Lake City: University of Utah Press, 1984.

———. *Mormon Passage: A Missionary Chronicle*. Urbana: University of Illinois Press, 1998.

Shipps, Jan. "'Is Mormonism Christian?' Reflections on a Complicated Question." *BYU Studies* 33, no. 3 (1993): 438–65.

———. *Mormonism: The Story of a New Religious Tradition*. Urbana: University of Illinois Press, 1985.

———. *Sojourner in the Promised Land: Forty Years among the Mormons*. Urbana: University of Illinois Press, 2000.

Shuckford, Samuel. *The Sacred and the Profane History of the World Connected*. London: Pr. for J. and R. Tonson, 1743.

Smith, Dwight L. "The Engineer and the Canyon." *Utah Historical Quarterly* 28 (July 1960): 263–74.

———. "Robert B. Stanton's Plan for the Far Southwest." *Arizona and the West* 4 (Winter 1962): 369–72.

Smith, Elmer R. "The 'Japanese' in Utah." *Utah Humanities Review* 2 (June 1948):

129–44.

———. "The 'Japanese' in Utah: Part II." *Utah Humanities Review* 2 (July 1948): 208–30.

Smith, Joseph Fielding. *Answers to Gospel Questions*. 4 vols. Salt Lake City: Deseret Book, 1963.

Smith, Sarah Cox. "Translator or Translated? The Portrayal of The Church of Jesus Christ of Latter-day Saints in Print in Meiji Japan." In Neilson and Gessel, *Taking the Gospel to the Japanese, 1901–2001*, 127–45.

Snodgrass, Judith. *Presenting Japanese Buddhism to the West: Orientalism, Occidentalism, and the Columbian Exposition*. Chapel Hill: University of North Carolina Press, 2003.

Sonne, Conway B. *Knight of the Kingdom: The Story of Richard Ballantyne*. Salt Lake City: Deseret Book, 1949.

Spence, Jonathan D. *The Search for Modern China*. 2d ed. New York: W. W. Norton, 1999.

———. *The Taiping Vision of a Christian China, 1836–1864*. Waco, Tex.: Baylor University Press, 1998.

Stark, Rodney. "The Basis of Mormon Success: A Theoretical Application." In *Mormons and Mormonism: An Introduction to an American World Religion*, edited by Eric A. Eliason, 207–42. Urbana: University of Illinois Press, 2001.

———. "Why Religious Movements Succeed or Fail: A Revised General Model." *Journal of Contemporary Religion* 11 (1996): 133–46.

Stark, Rodney, and Roger Finke. *Acts of Faith: Explaining the Human Side of Religion*. Berkeley: University of California Press, 2000.

Stout, Wayne. *Hosea Stout: Utah's Pioneer Statesman*. Salt Lake City: n.p., 1953.

Stuy, Brian H. ed. *Collected Discourses Delivered by Wilford Woodruff, His Two Counselors, the Twelve Apostles, and Others*. 5 vols. Burbank, Calif.: B. H. S. Publishing, 1987–1992.

Takagi, Shinji. "The Eagle and the Scattered Flock: Church Beginnings in Occupied Japan, 1945–48." *Journal of Mormon History* 28 (Fall 2002): 104–38.

———. "Mormons in the Press: Reactions to the 1901 Opening of the Japan Mission." *BYU Studies* 40, no. 1 (2001): 141–75.

———. "Riding on the Eagle's Wings: The Japanese Mission under American Occupation, 1948–52." *Journal of Mormon History* 29 (Spring 2003): 200–32.

———. "Tomizo and Tokujiro: The First Japanese Mormons." *BYU Studies* 39, no. 2 (2000): 73–106.

Takaki, Ronald T. *Strangers from a Different Shore: A History of Asian Americans*. Rev. ed. Boston: Little, Brown, and Company, 1998.

Tanner, John S. "On Sacrifice and Success." *BYU Magazine* (Fall 2003): 3–4.

Tate, E. Mowbray. *Transpacific Steam: The Story of Steam Navigation from the Pacific Coast of North America to the Far East and the Antipodes, 1867–1941*. New York: Cornwall Books, 1986.

Taylor, Sandra C. "Leaving the Concentration Camps: Japanese American Resettlement in Utah and the Intermountain West." *Pacific Historical Review* 60 (May 1991): 169–94.

Thomas, Winburn T. *Protestant Beginnings in Japan: The First Three Decades, 1859–1889*.

Rutland, Vt.: Charles E. Tuttle, 1959.

Thomson, Sandra Caruthers. "Meiji Japan through Missionary Eyes: The American Protestant Experience." *Journal of Religious History* 7 (1973): 248–59.

Tweed, Thomas A. *The American Encounter with Buddhism, 1844–1912: Victorian Culture and the Limits of Dissent*. Chapel Hill: University of North Carolina Press, 2000.

———. "Introduction: Hannah Adams's Survey of the Religious Landscape." In Adams, *A Dictionary of All Religions and Religious Denominations*.

———, ed. *Retelling U.S. Religious History*. Berkeley: University of California Press, 1997.

Tweed, Thomas A., and Stephen Prothero, eds. *Asian Religions in America: A Documentary History*. New York: Oxford University Press, 1999.

Underwood, Grant. *The Millenarian World of Early Mormonism*. Urbana: University of Illinois Press, 1993.

Van Sant, John E. *Pacific Pioneers: Japanese Journeys to America and Hawaii, 1850–80*. Urbana: University of Illinois Press, 2000.

Venugopal, Junias V. "Prolegomena to a Historical Perspective: The Use of Education as a Mission Strategy in Asia." In *Asian Church and God's Mission*, edited by Wonsuk Ma and Julie C. Ma, 233–56. Manila, Philippines: OMF Literature, 2003.

Vogel, Dan, ed. *Early Mormon Documents: Volume One*. Salt Lake City: Signature Books, 1996.

Wacker, Grant. "A Plural World: The Protestant Awakening to World Religions." In Hutchison, *Between the Times: The Travail of the Protestant Establishment in America, 1900–1960*, 253–77.

———. "Second Thoughts on the Great Commission: Liberal Protestants and Foreign Missions, 1890–1940." In Carpenter and Shenk, *Earthen Vessels: American Evangelicals and Foreign Missions*, 281–300.

Walker, Ronald W. "Strangers in a Strange Land: Heber J. Grant and the Opening of the Japanese Mission." *Journal of Mormon History* 13 (1986/87): 20–43.

Walls, Andrew F. "The American Dimension in the History of the Missionary Movement." In *Many Are Chosen: Divine Election and Western Nationalism*, edited by William Hutchinson and Hartmut Lehman, 1–25. Minneapolis, Minn.: Fortress Press, 1984.

Walz, Eric. "Japanese Immigrants and the Mormons." Paper presented at "A Centennial Celebration: The History of The Church of Jesus Christ of Latter-day Saints in Japan 1901–2001." Brigham Young University, Provo, Utah, October 2001.

Welter, Barbara. "'She Hath Done What She Could': Protestant Women's Missionary Careers in Nineteenth-Century America." *American Quarterly* 30 (Winter 1978): 624–38.

Whittaker, David J. "The Bone in the Throat: Orson Pratt and the Public Announcement of Plural Marriage." *Western Historical Quarterly* 18 (July 1987): 293–314.

———. "Early Mormon Pamphleteering." Ph.D. diss., Brigham Young University, 1982.

———. "Mormon Missiology: An Introduction and Guide to the Sources." In *Disciple as Witness: Essays on Latter-day Saint History and Doctrine in Honor of Richard Lloyd Anderson*, edited by Stephen D. Ricks, Donald W. Parry, and Andrew H. Hedges,

459–538. Provo, Utah: Foundation for Ancient Research and Mormon Studies, Brigham Young University, 2000.

———. "Parley P. Pratt and the Pacific Mission: Mormon Publishing in 'that very questionable part of the civilized world.'" In *Mormons, Scripture, and the Ancient World: Studies in Honor of John L. Sorenson*, edited by Davis Bitton and John L. Sorenson, 51–84. Provo, Utah: Foundation for Ancient Research and Mormon Studies, 1998.

———. "Richard Ballantyne and the Defense of Mormonism in India in the 1850s." In *Supporting Saints: Life Stories of Ninteteenth-Century Mormons*, edited by Donald Q. Cannon and David J. Whittaker, 175–212. Provo, Utah: Religious Studies Center, Brigham Young University, 1985.

Wierenga, Richard S. "The Financial Support of Foreign Missions." In *Lengthened Cords: A Book about World Missions in Honor of Henry J. Evenhouse*, edited by Roger S. Greenway, 343–46. Grand Rapids, Mich.: Baker Book House, 1975.

Wilkinson, William C. "The Attitude of Christianity to Other Religions." In Barrows, *The World's Parliament of Religions*.

Williams, George Hunston. "The Attitude of Liberals in New England toward Non-Christian Religions, 1784–1885." *Crane Review* 9 (Winter 1967): 59–89.

Wills, Anne Blue. "Mapping Presbyterian Missionary in *The Church at Home and Abroad*, 1890–1898." In *The Foreign Missionary Enterprise at Home: Explorations in North American Cultural History*, edited by Daniel H. Bays and Grant Wacker, 95–105. Tuscaloosa: University of Alabama Press, 2003.

Wilson, Robert A., and Bill Hosokawa. *East to America: A History of the Japanese in the United States*. New York: William Morrow, 1980.

Woo, Wesley Stephen. "Protestant Work among the Chinese in the San Francisco Bay Area, 1850–1920 (California)." Ph.D. diss., Graduate Theological Union, 1984.

Xi, Feng. "A History of Mormon-Chinese Relations: 1849–1993." Ph.D. diss., Brigham Young University, 1994.

Xi, Lian. *The Conversion of Missionaries: Liberalism in American Protestant Missions in China, 1907–1932*. University Park: Pennsylvania State University Press, 1997.

Xu, Shi. "The Images of the Chinese in the Rocky Mountain Region: 1855–1882." Ph.D. diss., Brigham Young University, 1996.

Yamamori, Tetsunao. *Church Growth in Japan: A Study in the Development of Eight Denominations, 1859–1939*. South Pasadena, Calif.: William Carey Library, 1974.

Yang, John H., comp. *Asian Americans in Utah: A Living History*. Salt Lake City: State of Utah Office of Asian Affairs, Asian American Advisory Council, 1999.

Yohn, Susan M. *A Contest of Faiths: Missionary Women and Pluralism in the American Southwest*. Ithaca: Cornell University Press, 1995.

Index

A "t" following a page number indicates a table.

Harris, Townsend, 64
Harris Treaty, 64
Hashimoto, Yozo, 31
Hawaiian Mission, 54, 149
Hedges, Sanford W., 107, 115, 176n131, 177n8; experiences in Japan, 91, 97–98; tract writing by, 103
Hepburn, James C., 87, 88, 101
Higginson, Thomas Wentworth, 7
Hill, Patricia R., 38
Hong Kong. *See* China and Chinese: mission work in
Hopkins, Samuel, 39
human deployment: of Mormon missionaries, 32, 51, 52, 67, 70, 118, 129–32, 168n28; of Protestant missionaries, 50–51, 52
humanitarian work. *See* social welfare activities
Hutchison, William R., 62, 166n65
Hyde, Orson, 78, 79
hymns, Japanese translations, 101, 105–6

immigrants: Chinese, 26, 27, 30–31, 136; Japanese, 26, 27, 29, 31–32, 136, 138
Immigration Act (of 1924), 138
inclusivism, 7–8
inculturation, 36–37
Ishiye, 21
Ivie, Lloyd O., 124, 125, 144–45, 177n9; as mission president, 101, 102, 130, 131–32, 141
Ivie, Nora B., 177n9
Ivins, H. Grant, 99, 124, 147, 177n10
Iwakura Mission, 22
Iwano Hōmei, 106

Jansen, Marius B., 137
Japan and Japanese: attitudes toward Mormons, 76–77, 91, 97, 128, 136–37, 139; Christian literature in, 87–88, 100–107; Christianity in, 50, 62–63, 64–66, 85, 86, 116; immigrants to America, 26, 27, 29, 31–32, 136, 138; Mormon attitudes toward, 21, 24, 32, 33, 68–69, 89, 139; Mormon missionaries in, 75–76, 83–84, 89–118, 121–22, 138–39; nationalism and national seclusion, 20, 63, 64, 136, 137–38; Protestant missionaries in, 50, 62–63, 65, 84–88, 116–18; relations with the U.S., 20, 64, 122, 136, 137, 138; scriptural lineages of, 68–69, 72, 79, 80, 81, 144–45, 181n101
Japanese Americans. *See* Japan and Japanese: immigrants to America
Japanese–Central Pacific Mission, 149
Japan Mission: apostolic dedication of, 77, 78–80; closing of, ix, 142–44; closing of, external reasons for, 133–39; closing of, internal reasons for, ix, 120–22, 132, 140–42; closing of, as prophetic counsel, 122, 133, 140, 142; in comparison to Protestant missions, 51–52, 57–58, 84, 107, 113, 116–19; delays in establishment of, 22, 24, 66; departure for,

74–75; establishment of, 25, 34, 68, 70–71; general excitement over, 62, 71; reopening of, 149–50; struggles and failures of, 81–82, 116–19, 121–31; successes of, 95–96, 98, 108–9, 113. *See also* missionaries, Mormon

Jarvis, Erastus L., 68, 105, 107
Jarvis, George, 68
Jensen, Nephi, 104
Juvenile Instructor, 24, 33

kakure Kirishitan, 65
Kanagawa Treaty, 64
Katsunuma, Tomizo, 29
Kawai Suimei, 106
Kelsch, Louis A., 94, 123, 125, 177n5, 177n8; as a missionary, 71, 75–76, 124, 146, 177n7
Kimball, Heber C., 70
Kirishitan, 63, 64, 65
Kofu Conference, 132
Koya Saburō, 23

language acquisition: by Protestant missionaries, 46, 53; by Mormon missionaries, 47–48, 53–54, 72, 73, 126–27
LDS Church. *See* Mormons and Mormonism
Lee, LaFayette C., 130, 177n9
Lee, Pearl M., 95–96, 177n5, 177n9
Lewis, James, 53, 54–55, 56
Liestman, Daniel, 28, 31
Liggins, John, 65
the light and spirit of Christ, theory of, 8, 10–11, 12, 13
literature, Christian. *See under* Christians and Christianity
London Missionary Society, 16
Lund, Anthon H., 83–84

Maffly-Kipp, Laurie F., 25, 57, 106
magic lantern lectures, 96–97, 100
mapping: by Mormons, 8–12, 14–15; by Protestants, 5–8, 10, 25; theory of, 4
Marriott, Moroni S., 95, 96, 128
Mather, Cotton, 62
Mauss, Armand L., 32, 34, 66
Mauss, Vinal G., 132, 135, 138, 140
McClellan, Robert, 25
McCune, Henry F., 21
McKay, David O., 94, 131, 132
McLeod, Nicholas, 68
meeting, theory of, 18, 33